Neither Brain nor Ghost

Neither Brain nor Ghost

A Nondualist Alternative to the Mind–Brain Identity Theory

W. Teed Rockwell

A Bradford Book
The MIT Press
Cambridge, Massachusetts
London, England

First MIT Press paperback edition, 2007

MIT Press books may be purchased at special quantity discounts for business or sales promotional use. For information, please email special_sales@mitpress.mit.edu or write to Special Sales Department, The MIT Press, 55 Hayward St., Cambridge, MA 02142.

This book was set in Stone Sans and Stone Serif by SNP Best-set Typesetter Ltd., Hong Kong and was printed and bound in the United States of America.

Library of Congress Cataloging-in-Publication Data

Rockwell, W. Teed.
Neither brain nor ghost : a nondualist alternative to the mind–brain identity theory / W. Teed Rockwell.
    p.   cm.
"A Bradford book."
Includes bibliographical references and index.
ISBN 978-0-262-18247-8 (hc.: alk. paper)—978-0-262-68167-4 (pb.: alk. paper)
1. Mind–brain identity theory. 2. Mind and body. 3. Pragmatism. I. Title.

B105.M55R63   2005
128'.2—dc22

2004062535

10 9 8 7 6 5 4 3 2

To my mother and father, and to my beloved Diana, whose love and support made this book possible

Contents

Acknowledgments

During the many years between my M.A. and Ph.D. work, my primary contacts with academic life were the annual meetings of the Society for Philosophy and Psychology (SPP). It was there that I discovered the books (mostly MIT Press publications), and met most of the people, who shaped my current philosophical perspective. Many of those people were extremely helpful to this musician who was trying to reenter the world of philosophy, and understand the new world of cognitive science. Ruth Millikan read and gave me feedback on some of my first papers in this area. Her ability to cut to the heart of where a paper needs improvement continues to amaze me, as does the depth and originality of her philosophical vision. Carol Slater, Bob McCauley, David Rosenthal, Owen Flanagan, Pete Mandik, Guven Guzeldere, Bill Bechtel, Adele Abrahamsen, Valerie Hardcastle, and many other SPP participants gave papers and participated in discussions that became the context and foundation for my current philosophical perspective. I remain grateful for their encouragement and stimulating conversation.

When I began my Ph.D. work with the Union Institute, many of the people I met at SPP meetings became members of the email list where I discussed my studies, and some became commentators for the papers that appear on my Cognitive Questions Web site, www.california.com/~mcmf. These include Markate Daly, Jim Garson, John Bickle, U. T. Place, Tim Van Gelder, and Bernard Baars. Robert Kane, Richard Rorty, and Elizabeth Minnich also contributed commentaries. These people also made helpful contributions to the mailing list dialogue that guided these papers. Other contributors to that dialogue included Richard Byrne, Richard Double, Sarah Fisk, Edward Hubbard, Stephen Jones, Jed Harris, Sergio Chaigneau, Mark Churchland, Bo Dahlin, Ronald Lemmen, Peter Lloyd, Rick Norwood,

Sue Pockett, Frank Ryan, Gary Schouberg, Ami Thomasson, and Peter Webster. David Chalmers's extensive replies to my email correspondence eventually convinced me that the zombie problem actually is important.

Paul and Pat Churchland's books and articles woke me from a variety of dogmatic slumbers, and taught me the importance of scientific data for philosophy. Paul's decision to serve as an adjunct on my dissertation committee was the stimulus that made me decide to take the plunge back into graduate school. Jim Garson also served as adjunct, and was always there to help when I needed to refocus. His critical sympathy for my counter-intuitive central thesis inspired numerous objections that shaped my dissertation and continued to shape its transition to publication. My frequent citations to his correspondence are only a small indication of his influence on this book. My dissertation committee also included Union Institute "peers" Bruce Kodish and James Stittsworth, as well as Union Institute faculty members Elizabeth Minnich and Robert Atkins. All of them helped in many ways, especially by providing suggestions for research. Bruce Kodish introduced me to Melzack's pain research, and James Stittsworth provided an extensive neuroscience bibliography. I am especially grateful to Elizabeth Minnich for, among many other things, introducing me to the work of John Dewey. I would also like to thank my illustrator, Richard Marchetti, who repeatedly responded to my inarticulate requests by creating imagery that made my points clearer than I would have thought possible.

Finally, I should thank the numerous researchers and philosophers who are cited in this book. The extent of my debt to them is described to some degree in the book itself, so there is no need to repeat it here. I hope that at least some of them will be intrigued by the pattern I believe is lurking behind their data and ideas, and that this pattern might provide them with further stimulus for theorizing and research.

Introduction

This book contains a proposal to replace the mind–brain identity theory with a pragmatist-inspired alternative, which rejects both dualism and the claim that the brain is the only piece of physical stuff that embodies the mind. I refer to the mind–brain identity theory with the more abusive epithet "Cartesian materialism,"[1] because when Descartes formulated the mind–body distinction, he also emphasized that "The soul feels those things that affect the body . . . only in so far as it is in the brain"[2] (quoted in P. S. Churchland 1986, p. 16). He thus emphasized and defended the brain–body distinction as an essential corollary of the mind–body distinction. Modern physicalists have kept the brain–body distinction even though they have thrown away the mind–body distinction, and are thus left with a philosophy of mind that is still in many ways fundamentally Cartesian: Descartes said the soul was *in* the brain, and identity theorists say the soul *is* the brain. Descartes' basic concept of mind is not really changed, it is simply demoted to being a concept referring to a particular kind of physical thing.

I thought this idea was mine until I discovered the following passage in John Dewey's *Democracy and Education*: "Too often . . . the older dualism of soul and body has been replaced by that of the brain and the rest of the body . . ." (Dewey 1916, p. 336). As I continued to read Dewey, I discovered that his criticism of Cartesian materialism was not an isolated insight, but an essential part of his philosophy of mind. Dewey saw reality as fundamentally an ongoing process, whose parts could not exist independently of the interactions in which they participated. Consequently, he was suspicious of any attempt to create dualist distinctions, whether between mind and body, body and brain, or organism and environment. My claim is that the history of science since his time reveals that his suspicions were fully justified. The numerous implications of the mind–brain identity theory (which, in this context, might also be called the brain–body difference theory) have caused crises and paradoxes in many different fields: neuroscience, artificial intelligence, epistemology, and philosophy of language. I will try to show that we can dissolve these problems by accepting a Deweyan alternative to the mind–brain identity theory. This alternative sees the mind not merely as a network property of interacting cranial neurons, but rather as being equally dependent on the interactions among a brain, a nervous system, a body, and a world.

If there were such a thing as retroactive plagiarism, I would gladly have accused Dewey of it. It was sometimes embarrassing to discover that so many ideas that I thought were mine had been written by him almost a century earlier. In this, at least I have distinguished company. Numerous major contemporary philosophers now refer to themselves as pragmatists. On almost every issue in which the pragmatists disagreed with the positivists, it is now widely assumed that the pragmatists were right, for pretty much the same reasons that the pragmatists originally gave in their own defense. Why then did positivism so completely displace pragmatism in American philosophy departments during the 1950s? Why was there not a single course in pragmatism offered at any of the three schools where I did my philosophical studies? Rorty, who was there when the dethronement of pragmatism took place, offers this explanation.

The enthusiasm for the linguistic turn which changed the character of American philosophy departments was due in large part to exasperation with the interminable debates that went on in the 1920s and 1930s between Dewey and [other philosophers]. . . . A lot of first-rate philosophers, in the 1940s and 1950s, were saying that they could never figure out which side of a given issue Dewey wanted to be on. A consensus had grown up that Dewey's terminology fudged, rather than clarified . . . They wanted something new, something they could get their philosophical teeth into. . . . What showed up . . . represented a temporarily fruitful confusion of a very good idea (that language was a more fruitful topic for philosophical reflection than experience) with a couple of rather bad ones. . . . The narrative I have tried to reconstruct in my books tells how the bad ideas gradually, in the course of the 1950s and 1960s, got filtered out and thus made it possible for pragmatism to get a new lease on life by undergoing linguistification. (Saatkamp 1995, p. 70)

I think this is a very good description of how and why the pragmatists came to be supplanted by philosophers like Carnap and Ayer, who in turn came to be supplanted by Sellars, Quine, and Davidson. One of the best things about this description is that it shows there is an assumption that Rorty himself has still not questioned: that the study of experience should be completely supplanted by the study of language—an assumption expressed by Rorty's favorite quote from Sellars that "All awareness is a linguistic affair." Sellars himself was aware that this viewpoint had serious limitations, although he felt that there was little he could say about those limitations given most of his presuppositions. He acknowledged that any given moment of perceptual experience contained not just a sentence like "lo, a pink ice cube" but also a manner of sensing ("pinkly" or "a-pink-cube-ly") that gave the experience its "feel." This could not be reduced to a mere sentence, and it was a kind of awareness, even though it was not linguistic. Dewey's talk about the primacy of experience was an attempt (very different from Sellars's) to deal with this phenomenon, among other things. But because it appeared that experience, unlike language, could not be studied intersubjectively, it was much more fruitful for analytic philosophers to focus on that awareness, which was a linguistic affair. Until there was some way to talk about experience with the same kind of intersubjective precision that the analytic tradition applied to language, it was unlikely that anyone was going to do anything more than what Sellars did for most of his philosophical life: label the problem, and then go back to talking about language.

During the 1970s and 1980s, however, it became more and more obvious to certain analytic philosophers, especially Paul and Patricia Churchland, that all of these years of linguistic analysis were leaving something crucial out. Linguistic philosophy was a fruitful approach during its time, but it was becoming clear that this approach would not bear fruit forever. So the Churchlands began to conceive of the possibility of a postlinguistic philosophy, which would deal with the nonlinguistic aspects of experience by thinking about the philosophical implications of neuroscience. This was very much in the spirit of Dewey, who believed that philosophy should not be distinct from the sciences or any other human activities, but also very different from the armchair approach to the study of human experience that Rorty attributes to most philosophers of Dewey's time. The Churchlands' goal was to see whether modern neuroscience gave support to the possibility that the mind was not fundamentally a linguistic engine, and that not all thought was expressible in a language of thought. Because they were basing their postlinguistic philosophy on new scientific discoveries, rather than on common sense, it left open the possibility of new answers to the important philosophical questions. Perhaps philosophers' attempts to answer these questions degenerated into paradox only because they were ignorant of certain crucial facts about the human brain. If so, careful philosophical analysis of those facts could be the key to a whole new philosophy of mind.

Unfortunately, the Churchlands and many of their disciples have become so fascinated by the key that they seem to have lost interest in what it might unlock. There is nothing wrong with deciding to abandon philosophy. Neuroscience is a noble profession, and the satisfaction of dealing with relatively hard data is no doubt tempting to those of us who deal mostly with arguments and thought experiments. The Churchlands have also added a perspective to neuroscience that clearly shows their philosophical roots. Thanks in part to their influence, there is more recognition of the need for high-level theorizing in neuroscience, and this is a very good thing. But the Churchlands appear to be claiming something much stronger: not that they have changed professions when they abandoned philosophy of mind, but instead that they have come up with a new discipline to replace it. Like many of the functionalist psychologists they have criticized, the Churchlands seem to be operating on the assumption that their discipline is an autonomous specialty, despite their frequent praise of the principle of coevolution. They appear to believe that this autonomous discipline has replaced philosophy of mind, judging from the fact that the only science they actually study in any depth is neuroscience. If the mind–brain identity theory were true, then perhaps they would be right, and neuroscience could completely supplant philosophy of mind.

Because it is widely assumed that the only alternative to mind–brain identity was dualism, the former has rarely been questioned. But the brain need not be the only physical thing that the mind is identical with. If we define the mind as the brain, this definition must be based on empirical facts, which are in principle falsifiable by future scientific discoveries. Because mind–brain identity is also an empirical assumption, it will be very difficult to see those discoveries as long as scientific experiments are based solely on that assumption. There are now a variety of crises in several fields of research, which I claim arise from unconscious acceptance of mind–brain identity. Dewey was one of the first to question this assumption, but his critiques have a lot more "cash value" (in James's sense) when one considers the problems that have arisen for so many different disciplines as a result of accepting Cartesian materialism. What makes Dewey's insights interesting today is that modern cognitive science has discovered plenty of indicators that these insights are not only true, but significant enough that those who wish to really understand the mind ignore them at their peril.

To fully appreciate this significance, we shall start in chapter 1 by showing how these insights can resolve the dialectic that has arisen in this century between the views of (1) mind as brain and (2) mind as behavior. These positions have reached full maturity under the respective names of eliminative materialism and functionalism. When each sheds its commitment to its own brand of Cartesian materialism, they reveal the possibility of looking surprisingly alike. To some degree Cartesian materialism has already been seriously weakened by the externalist philosophy of language defended by Putnam, Burge, Millikan, and Clark. But I propose that we dispense with Cartesian materialism completely and accept that even subjective conscious experience is embodied by the brain–body–world nexus, and not by the brain alone.

Nevertheless, it is still not that obvious that cognitive science needs to free itself from Cartesian materialism. So in chapter 2 we will start looking for the mind where the Churchlands have told us to look: in the brain, using some of the information neuroscience has made available. We will learn a great deal of surprising things about how we think and feel. Neuroscience has a great deal to teach us about the mind, and there is still much that we can learn by following up its still ambiguous implications. But when we continue to try to understand the mind through neuroscience alone, we will soon discover the need to look for more answers elsewhere. Dennett has already criticized what *he* called Cartesian materialism—the belief that some part of the brain is the seat of the soul, rather than the brain as a whole. We shall see, however, that trying to isolate the brain from the rest of the nervous system is vulnerable to most of the same criticisms. Perhaps then we can escape Cartesian materialism by positing a mind–nervous system identity, rather than a mind–brain identity? No such luck—in chapter 3 we discover that there is plenty of evidence that the mind is hormonal as well as neural. Almost anything that takes place within the skin has some claim to being part of the embodiment of mind. The traditional assumption has been that some things that take place in the body may *cause* experiences, but only brain events actually *embody* the mind. But if a close look at the data makes this assumption less plausible, what other criterion can we use to distinguish between causation and embodiment?

In chapter 4 we make an essential side excursion to study the concept of causality itself. Three different concepts of causality appear to provide support for the view that the mind is the brain: (1) the atomistic "one cause–one effect" view; (2) the view that objects possess "intrinsic causal powers." These are shown to be inadequate for our best science, and riddled with philosophical problems. In chapter 5, we consider the view that (3) the mind–brain relationship is not strong enough to be describable as either an identity or a causal relationship, and thus should be described by the technical term "supervenience." The careful ambiguity of the supervenience relationship makes it the best contender for the mental–physical relationship. But the claim that the mind supervenes on nothing physical except the brain is based on (1) a speculative thought experiment, which may be impossible to perform even in principle and has certainly never been performed in fact, and (2) the assumption that experiences are individual sense data, each of which can supervene on independent brain events.

In chapter 6, I argue that Cartesian materialism and sense-datum theory are inseparable. If sense-datum theory must be discarded (as almost all contemporary philosophers think it should be), then Cartesian materialism goes with it. However, if we adopt Dewey's view of experience, which sees experience as a unified process constituted by our goals and purposes, we can dissolve the philosophical problems raised by Cartesian materialism. The biggest of these problems arises from the basic question of Cartesian materialist epistemology, which is "How does the world get inside the head?" Because the world can never get inside the head, skepticism becomes inescapable. My suggestion to this problem is to reframe the problem of knowledge as being not one of the relationship between the world and the head, but rather between my world and the rest of reality. This expands the supervenience base of mental embodiment into the environment in which we dwell. There would be no scientific or philosophical point in saying that the mind supervenes on the entire causal nexus that makes the mind possible. But "mind," like "brain," is a biological concept, and biological concepts are defined functionally, not just causally. Any causal relation that is functionally essential for the existence of conscious experience is a legitimate candidate for the supervenience base of that experience.

This creates a new problem, or rather makes an old philosophical problem more scientifically significant. In chapter 7, I argue that once we acknowledge that assertions about what embodies mind are genuinely in need of proof, the "hard problem" that arises when we attempt to bridge the explanatory gap between experience and objective reality becomes not only philosophically inscrutable, but scientifically important. If it were a brute fact that the mind was the brain, we could accept this as a philosophically puzzling postulate, and then do competent science of the mind by accepting it on faith. But if it we are forced to answer the question "What embodies the mind?" we must deal with the hard problem in order to tell we're even looking for answers in the right place. The choice of the right place, I claim, will continue to seem stunningly arbitrary as long as we assume that the problem of consciousness is totally self-contained. To escape the clearly unsolvable nature of the hard problem as it is currently formulated, we have to consider the presuppositions that make it seem inevitable. Because the problem is how to explain consciousness, we need to rethink not only our concept of consciousness, but also our criteria for what an explanation is. This rethinking reveals a new relationship between subjective experience and objective knowledge, which again makes use of the Deweyan view of experience to dissolve the hard problem.

For Dewey knowledge always exists within a background of experience, which is why any attempt to "solve" the hard problem by completely comprehending experience as knowledge was doomed to failure. In chapter 8, we see that the failure of symbolic AI supports the validity of Dewey's insight. Hubert Dreyfus's critique of symbolic AI showed us that it failed because its goal was a computerized simulation of the Cartesian materialist brain, which tried unsuccessfully to mirror the entire world "inside the head." We also see how Searle's concept of "the background" requires a theory of meaning and mind that makes it impossible for language comprehension to be accomplished by a self-contained system that operates entirely inside the head.

In chapter 9, I deal with the philosophical problems that arise when we no longer have Cartesian materialism to account for illusions and errors. However, it turns out that the Cartesian materialist account has serious problems of its own. Recent developments in philosophy of science and epistemology have led many philosophers to conclude that we cannot draw a sharp line between true and false theories. This is a problem as long as we claim that reality exists in the world, and illusions exists only in our heads. If there is a continuum between true and false theories, at what point should we claim that a theory loses its grip on the world, and collapses back into the head? The pragmatist answer to that question is: all theories and experiences emerge from the relationships that constitute the brain–body–world nexus. But some theories and experiences have an erratic and unpredictable relationship with the world, and thus relate to the world in an equivocal and confused manner. Because all of our theories are imperfect, and none is completely useless, we don't have to posit subjective entities called illusions to explain why we make errors. We just have to say that some theories have better relationships with the world than others, and science and other forms of inquiry must help us find the best theories we can.

In chapter 10, I discuss why dynamic systems theory (DST) could be the discipline that gives specific scientific content to a Deweyan philosophy of process and experience. The above Rorty quote suggests that pragmatism had gotten stale because American philosophy had degenerated into a series of debates over what exactly Dewey was saying. If American philosophers had lived Dewey's philosophy rather than merely argued about it, they would have kept things fresh by thinking philosophically about the newest scientific data, rather than merely rehashing the arguments themselves.[3] This would have helped to determine the Jamesian cash value of the different forms of pragmatism by discovering how each one affected research and life. To some degree, this is what cognitive science is doing today with DST, beginning with the discovery of connectionism.

I will conclude this introduction by describing some of the maxims and principles that guided and motivated the writing of this book. Those who want to continue reading about philosophy of mind should go right into the first chapter.

I believe that philosophy should be satisfied with nothing less than new and better answers to the questions it asks: answers that will work better for us than the answers we currently have, that is, answers that if accepted as true will enable us to move more skillfully through the world in which we dwell, and with fewer errors. To nonphilosophers, this position may seem trivially true, and to many contemporary philosophers it will hopefully seem reasonably sensible. But for most of this century, the English-speaking philosophical world would have dismissed this claim as naive and outdated. Because philosophy had tried for so long to come up with *the* answers to its questions, and so many of the world's greatest minds had failed in the attempt, it seemed necessary for philosophy to have a different job description. Better answers were apparently of no interest, only an answer that everyone could agree on would do. So philosophers tried to show why its questions were unanswerable, or what ordinary language thought were the answers, or why these important questions were less important than they appeared because they were really questions about language or logic.

One of the reasons this approach to philosophy seemed so plausible and responsible was that science appeared to be continually finding *the* answer to each of *its* questions. The difference between philosophy and science, which seemed to account for this success, was that science, unlike philosophy, appeared to rest on empirical foundations provided by direct observation. The guiding myth was that if only the Aristotelian opponents of Galileo had been willing to look into the telescope, they would have seen for themselves that the evidence proved them wrong. For (supposedly) when the facts speak for themselves, they never lie. If this theory of knowledge were true, science would have been equally independent from both common sense and metaphysics, as long as it kept its eye on the facts. However, to the degree that modern philosophers have ever agreed about anything, they have agreed that although science is probably tops in epistemic virtue, this cannot be the reason why. The idea that a single observation can provide direct and certain knowledge was dismissed by Sellars as the myth of the given, and by Quine as one of the two dogmas of empiricism.

But what other alternative is left to explain where it is that science begins, and how it develops? Well, if science cannot begin with self-contained, directly given observations, it must develop by refining what is sometimes called common sense. All inquiry must start with the presuppositions shared by the community that conducts it, and that community will naturally think of those shared presuppositions as "common sense" because they are common to that community. However, as science develops, it ends up becoming a subcommunity of its own, whose presuppositions partially overlap, and partially extend beyond, the many other communities that make up society. This is not, however, a situation unique to science, for the idea that there was ever a single consistent set of commonsense principles was an illusion that could be maintained only if one remained in a community (like early twentieth-century Oxford) that was sufficiently small and homongeneous.

Because science is a refinement of everyday thinking, there is no longer any reason to assume that scientific facts can be independent from either philosophical "speculations" or the unstated assumptions of what is often called "common sense." It is thus possible for a highly effective scientific theory to be built upon concepts derived from everyday thinking, which are, from a philosophical perspective, vague and garbled. If these concepts form a useful structure for gathering and organizing data, they become enshrined, garble and all, as scientific truth. It then becomes tempting for philosophers who are materialistically inclined to demand that the presuppositions that have been used for gathering this data be regarded as scientific fact, and therefore not vulnerable to philosophical questioning. It becomes even more tempting to think that the subset of commonsense assumptions that are used by science are somehow more unassailable than the common sense that enables people to perform other human activities.

To some degree this assumption is justified. The insights that scientists share in common are in many ways more sensible than those of the person-on-the-street (if there is such a person). The reason that society pays certain people to do science is that we believe that their expertise makes them more knowledgeable about certain things than the rest of us. However, the process of scientific development does not necessarily clear up philosophical confusions. Just because science has developed a high level of quantitative precision in the measurement and prediction of a certain entity does not necessarily mean that there are no confusions in our understanding of the nature of the entity being measured. Concepts like energy, life, space, mind, and consciousness can be defined precisely enough by scientists to make measurements possible and still cause problems down the road that can only be answered by asking questions like "What is space?" or "What is consciousness?" But often the need to ask such questions can be ignored if the focus is on gathering data, and the project of making the greatest possible sense out of the data is postponed.

This view of philosophy's relationship to science is essentially the same as that of Dewey and James, despite the common misinterpretation that sees pragmatism as being as antimetaphysical as positivism. The pragmatists believed (unlike the positivists) that all knowledge of facts presupposes knowledge of theories,[4] and consequently that it is impossible to have opinions about anything without making implicit commitments to high-level philosophical generalities. They recognized that our philosophical assumptions would be inadequate and fallible, but that did not free us from the need to make those assumptions. According to the pragmatists, there are only two ways of doing philosophy—badly and not-so-badly—and it was essential for our well-being to have the most appropriate philosophical convictions possible. The idea that pragmatism was hostile to philosophical questions sprang partly from the fact that the pragmatists insisted that many philosophical claims made no difference, so they would often ask whether a given philosophical claim had what James called cash value (i.e., a significant application to a specific situation). If it didn't, they would suggest that there was no point in continuing to ask the question. But the pragmatists never claimed that *all* philosophical questions lacked cash value. In fact, they had new and important answers to many of these questions, and many of us believe that their answers were the best that anyone in the history of philosophy has yet come up with. Furthermore, they expected those ideas to contradict much of ordinary experience, because they believed that ordinary experience, like philosophy, was a series of footnotes on Plato and Aristotle. They were philosophical revolutionaries, but they were not anarchists, for they had a detailed alternative to the philosophical tradition they were attacking. This book is an attempt to give certain aspects of that detailed alternative even greater detail (and thus greater cash value, in their sense) by applying some pragmatist insights to a variety of contemporary scientific and philosophical problems. In so doing, I have hopefully changed those insights in ways that their originators would never have thought or even approved of. I have no interest in adding to the elaborately footnoted discussion over what Dewey actually meant, which Rorty sees as the cause of the decline of interest in Dewey.

Ruth Millikan ends the introductory chapter of her *Language, Thought, and Other Biological Categories* with this self-deprecating caveat, which applies to this book far more than to hers.

Like other large scale theories, philosophical theories too do not rest only upon previously secured foundations—upon point by point prior arguments. As in the case of other theories, the general coherence of the whole is often the beginning point.

Details, and also foundations are constructed or perfected later, the value of the theory depending upon whether or not it is in fact possible to accomplish this. My purpose is to argue for a program; the various rough foundations and the details of results that I will sketch, taken distributively though not of course, collectively, are tentative. (Millikan 1984, p. 14)

As a pragmatist, I must acknowledge that the real worth of any philosophical theory will be determined by whether anyone will embrace its claims and start doing things based on its assumptions (in this case, scientific research). Many of my claims will contradict some of the assumptions of the orthodox Cartesian materialism that governs much scientific research, and I can offer no point-by-point arguments to compel people to accept them. But if anyone does make this leap of ontological faith and reject the mind–brain identity theory in favor of a brain–body–world theory of mind, and they start to get outstanding research results, this will be the only evidence I have that anything I have said in this book is in some sense true. I believe that some researchers have already embraced many of these principles, and I hope they find my exegesis of these principles helpful and clarifying. But those of us who do naturalized philosophy need to remind others and ourselves (usually at the end of introductory chapters) that we are only sketching out rough foundations, and all details are tentative.

1 Minds, Brains, and Behavior

It is usually assumed that when we say "the mind is the brain" we are taking a concept from neurophysiology (brain), and saying that it translates to a concept from common sense (mind). In fact, something very much like the opposite is the case. The idea that the brain is the organ of the body that feels and thinks was not something discovered by modern science. It is at least 2,000 years old, for Hippocrates wrote "Men ought to know that from the brain, and the brain alone, arise our pleasures, joys, laughter, and jests, as well as our sorrows, joys, and fears" (quoted in Bailey 1975, p. 10). Plato also believed that reason resided in the brain, although he thought that courage and ambition resided in the heart, and desire resided in the stomach. When Aristotle said the heart was the center of the soul, and that the brain's function was to cool the blood, he was probably contradicting the common wisdom of the time, not stating it. It is thus not surprising that ordinary language is filled with assumptions that the mind is the brain. After all, people do speak of thinking as "using your brain," of stupid people as being "brainless," and so on. Neuroscientists (like everyone else) learned the mind–brain identity at their mothers' knee and brought it with them to the data.

Yet although there is this vague sense that the brain is somehow responsible for mental activities and phenomena, there is no clear understanding in common sense of *how* the brain is so responsible. So when Gilbert Ryle began to explicate a commonsense alternative to dualism in his *The Concept of Mind*, he made almost no reference to the brain at all. Instead he tried to explain the ordinary concept of mind in terms of what ordinary people experience: human behavior, both their own and other people's. He claimed that when we say "Jones is in pain," what we mean is that Jones is either wincing, or jumping up and down and holding his thumb, or doing some other combination of behaviors that we have learned to associate with pain. Ryle claimed that when I say "I am in pain," what I mean is either that I observe myself performing such behaviors, or that I experience a disposition to perform such behaviors, which I must repress. Similarly, statements like "I believe that it will rain this afternoon" supposedly could be replaced in principle by lists of statements about behavior (and disposition to behave) that made no reference to beliefs or other mental entities. Unfortunately, it was simply impossible to describe mental states by substituting descriptions that referred only to behavior. The alleged substitutions turned out to be infinitely long, and/or to have other statements in them that referred to beliefs. Mental entities were simply too tough to yield to Occam's razor, so philosophers had to accept the fact that in some sense there really are such things as thoughts, beliefs, pains, and pleasures. But because no one wanted to return to Cartesian dualism, these had to be some sort of physical things. But what?

The next answer, suggested by D. M. Armstrong, J. J. C. Smart, and U. T. Place was that mental states are really brain states. Being philosophers, however, they were not claiming to have proven this in the laboratory. Their point was somewhat similar to one made by Hilary Putnam several years later (Putnam 1975). Many concepts in ordinary language are considered to be understood if you know which experts to ask for further clarification. If the ancient Greeks ever talked about brain states, they might have meant "those occurrences in the skull that Hippocrates could explain to us if we asked him" and the modern person-on-the-street's understanding of "brain state" is essentially the same, except that we have better-informed experts to fall back on. Thus when the mind–brain identity theorists tried to explicate the meaning of commonsense concepts about mentality, they used carefully ambiguous locutions like "something is going on in me which is like what goes on when I have my eyes open and there is an orange in front of me." Or else they compared references to brain states to phrases like "someone telephoned" in which we later identify who the someone is (Borst 1970, pp. 14, 28). The mind–brain identity theorists believed that it is the job of neuroscientists to identify the "something" we are referring to when we say I am having a sensation of red, or a thought about George Washington. Because discourse about brains appears to be very different from discourse about feelings and thoughts, the mind–body problem came to be seen as a subspecies of the sense–reference problem. If X is both a brain state and a thought, isn't this the same situation as when X is both the morning star and the evening star, or both the mayor of Dublin and the ugliest Irishman?

There are numerous problems with this position, however, and two closely related alternatives arose to circumvent them and to create new problems of their own.

Functionalism

Functionalism pointed out that there are too many different physical ways that mental predicates could be instantiated for them to be reduced to single physical predicates. Nor was this problem limited to the mind–brain relationship. It arose in biology, economics, and almost any science other than physics when one tried to identify its kinds and predicates with purely physical terms. As Fodor points out, a monetary exchange could be instantiated physically by handing over a dollar bill, or by writing a check, or by using a string of wampum, and it would obviously be only an improbable coincidence if any of these actions had anything in common physically (Fodor 1975, ch. 1). And as Putnam (1960) pointed out, the same problem arises when we talk about the physical substrate that instantiates beliefs or pains or fears in humans, dogs, and Martians. Even if it were a matter of empirical fact that there was some physical attribute they all had in common (perhaps they are all made of protein), this would be a trivial coincidence that would probably tell us nothing of importance, and certainly leave out much that was essential. The factor that makes a belief a belief, or a sensation a sensation, is not what it is made of, but the functional role it performs in a biological and cognitive system.

Like any philosophical position that survives for any length of time, functionalism has received a lot of criticism. It has been taken by Ned Block (Block 1978) to be incapable of accounting for subjective experience (although Block has admitted in conversation that he still considers himself to be a functionalist in some sense). Fodor has implied that functionalism provides proof that psychology can be an autonomous science, a position that the Churchlands have, in my view, successfully refuted (especially Churchland 1989, pp. 12–17). Putnam (1988) has renounced his own version of functionalism, because it ignored multiple realizability at the computational level while acknowledging that it existed between the computational and the physical. But none of these criticisms has shaken the fundamental insight of functionalism: that physical kinds cannot be the only kinds in the world, and therefore the language of physics cannot tell the whole story about the way things are. Physics will always have *something* to say about everything we encounter. Even though functionalism denies the existence of type–type identities between the physical and the functional, each token of any functional type is physical, and therefore functionalism is usually considered to be a kind of physicalism. But the fact of multiple realizability guarantees that the physical story cannot be the whole story.

Functionalism poses a more serious threat to the mind–brain identity theory than is usually acknowledged. In many ways, it is a revitalized form of Rylean behaviorism, for it defines the mind in terms of what we do rather than what we are made of. But unlike behaviorism, functionalism grants a genuine ontological independence to mental entities, an independence that apparently frees them not only from behavior, but also from brains. It therefore leaves open at least the possibility that whatever replaces the concept of mind might not be a precisely bordered chunk of biological stuff. If the mind is seen as identical with certain abstract causal roles performed by an organism or its parts, almost any part of the body could be seen as mental when it performed those roles, and some such roles might even be performed by the entire body (the way moves in chess are performed by an entire chess piece). If this were the case, no part of the body would be identical with the mind, just as no single building would be identical with Oxford University.

According to functionalism, the physical characteristics of the brain embody the mind, but they are not essential to the nature of mind. Consequently, many people used functionalism as a way of freeing the study of the mind from the study of the brain. However, at the same time that functionalism was formulated, another philosophical position called eliminative materialism was demanding that brain studies be the sole, or at least the primary, source of information about the mind.

Eliminative Materialism

Eliminative materialism was first formulated by Richard Rorty and Paul Feyerabend (see their articles in Borst 1970 and Rosenthal 1971) and then developed into a manifesto for a research program by Paul Churchland. The eliminative materialists claimed that the problems of the mind–brain identity thesis can be dissolved by simply saying that there will be no one-to-one correspondence in future neuroscience between mental events and physical events. In fact, they claim that future neuroscience may prove that there are no such entities as thoughts or sensations, and never were. The fact that functional states cannot be identified with brain states does not necessarily show that they have an independent reality distinct from brain states. The history of science has shown us that when a scientific reduction takes place, it is often impossible to formulate what were called bridge laws, that is, logical identities between entities in the reduced and reducing domains. But this does not make the entities in the old theory independent, it makes them nonexistent. We did not establish identities between the chemical elements and the alchemical essences. Why should we assume that we can establish identities between mental states and brain states?

The fullest articulation of this position is in *Eliminative Materialism and Propositional Attitudes* (P. M. Churchland 1989, pp. 1–22), where Paul Churchland claims that "mind" and all of those entities that allegedly inhabit mind, such as beliefs, hopes, sensations, thoughts, and so on, are part of a conceptual system he calls *folk psychology*. Churchland also claims that folk psychology does not have any claims to certainty, that Descartes was wrong when he said that direct introspection could produce an infallible awareness of the mind and its contents. Because folk psychology is based on personal introspection, not laboratory research, it could be just plain wrong about many things, just as folk physics was wrong when it claimed that heavy objects fall faster than light ones, and that the earth is flat. We should therefore be willing to look at research on brains as *the* source of new information about our minds, and whenever this research contradicts our commonsense view of ourselves, we should be willing to accept that the brain researchers are right and that common sense is wrong.

Eliminative materialism and functionalism have no official quarrel with each other, although each has been unjustifiably pressed into the service of other causes that have created the illusion of conflict. The essential points that both sides agree on can, I think, be summed up in the following four principles. In fact I don't see how anyone who has faith in the scientific method could doubt these principles. If I were not a pragmatist, I would probably call them "fundamental a priori principles" or "necessary truths." But although I recognize that these presuppositions are doubtable in principle, I accept Peirce's maxim that we must not doubt in our philosophy what we do not doubt in our hearts. Few people in the cognitive science community would question these four claims, and the rest of this book will be written on the assumption that they are true.

(1) Mental properties are not inherent in some particular physical stuff.
This was not always as obvious as it is now. In William James's time, there were scientists who claimed that thought was phosphorus, because they found large amounts of this element in the brain. This was what gave rise to the modern folk idea that fish is brain food. And from James's description (James 1890, vol. 1, p. 101), these scientists appeared to believe that this relationship was a straightforward identity, as if a bottle of phosphorus sitting on a chemist's shelf would be vaguely thinking about something or other. John Searle occasionally appears to be advocating a similar position when he claims that consciousness is a biological, not a functional property, and infers from this that consciousness cannot be any sort of abstract pattern. But as arguments by Lycan (1987) and Millikan (1984) show, biological properties are also functional properties. A heart is a heart because it performs a particular function in the circulatory system, not because it is a particular shape or made out of a particular kind of protein. The shape and chemical composition of any particular heart will determine its ability to perform its function. But that is because those physical characteristics must relate to other physical characteristics of other parts of the system. It is not an intrinsic or necessary characteristic of all hearts that they must be a particular shape or substance.

(2) This therefore means that mentality must be a property of some kind of system. This system must consist of parts,[1] each of which must have certain physical characteristics within the context of that particular system. These physical characteristics are constitutive of consciousness only within the context of that system, however. In and of themselves, no particular physical characteristic is essential to consciousness. This is the fundamental assumption of what is called strong AI: that it is possible in principle to build a conscious creature out of silicon, even though all such creatures we know of are made of protein. Silicon could turn out, for some physical reason, not to be flexible enough to duplicate what organic minds do. But if so, there would be a characteristic of protein that is in principle duplicatable in some other substance, even if it was not duplicatable in fact.

(3) Every physical part of a mental system will possess not only those characteristics that are essential to its function in that system, but also other characteristics that are irrelevant to that function. I will refer to the former set of characteristics as *functional*, and the latter as *epiphenomenal*. Strictly speaking I should probably refer to them as *relatively epiphenomenal*. Some recent philosophical discourse has defined "epiphenomenal" to mean absolutely epiphenomenal, that is, irrelevant to every possible causal system, not just to one particular system. Because I believe this meaning of the term is useless, and probably empty, I will use the term "epiphenomenal" to mean relatively epiphenomenal. This is the way it is often used in scientific discourse (see Dennett 1991, p. 402), where it helps to make distinctions similar to the one I am making here. When any biological research goes beyond describing morphology to developing explanations, it must make a distinction between those characteristics that perform functions (like the connections between axons and dendrites in a brain) and those characteristics that are merely epiphenomenal (like its gray color and lumpy shape). The epiphenomenal characteristics will of course have causal properties in other contexts. It is just that these properties will not be in any way responsible for the emergence of mental processes.

(4) A science of mental processes must concern itself with distinguishing between (1) those characteristics of a thinking–feeling creature that perform functions that help constitute mental processes, and (2) those characteristics that are epiphenomenal with respect to mental processes. We will be able to judge what is functionally essential and what is epiphenomenal with regard to mind only if we know the pattern of systematic structure that actual and possible minds share, regardless of what they are made of physically. Note that I am using the words "pattern" and "structure" here in the broadest possible way, so that to say anything at all about why something has a mind would be to articulate a pattern of some sort. Paradoxically, despite the fact that these assumptions require us to see mental processes as something abstract and distinct from any particular physical characteristics, they are also the only way to make any form of physicalism coherent. If physical matter is not itself mental, and no pattern can be made out of physical matter that can produce mental processes, then mind would be inexplicable. We would then be stuck with some form of dualism, in which mind magically oozes out of organisms like a glowing fluid.

These four principles are the basis of a bare bones functionalism that would be considered trivially true by both functionalists and eliminative materialists. These are the ground rules of the search for that pattern in physical stuff that embodies mind, or is identical with mind, or on which mind supervenes. (We'll deal with the differences between these three descriptions in later chapters.) The disagreements between the functionalists and eliminative materialists arise only because this is a discussion of what future science may look like, and only research can decide between the various possibilities.

The eliminative materialists will admit when pressed that there will probably always be separate sciences of psychology and neuroscience to study the functional and physical characteristics of mind respectively. (Although they sometimes point out that neuroscience *could* eliminate psychology, and that the psychology of the future will probably have even less resemblance to folk psychology than the psychology of the present.) The functionalists will admit that of course one needs to study neuroscience to learn how psychological functions are implemented (although they disagree, with each other and with the eliminative materialists, as to how independent psychology and neuroscience can be). The only real difference between the two camps is who their heroes are, and where they search for scientific facts to bolster their arguments. Eliminative materialists admire the "wet" neurosciences that study actual neurons, and functionalists admire the computer sciences and artificial intelligence. Conflict arises between them when either group presumes that the cognitive science of the future will most resemble their own favorite science of the present. But if things turn out as I believe they will, many of these surface differences will vanish. Future wet cognitive science will have to stop focusing on the cranial region of the nervous system and pay attention to the rest of the organism and the environment. AI will recognize that the multiple realizability of functional categories does not entail the autonomy of an inner language of thought, which means AI will also have to pay more attention to the whole organism and the environment. What we really have here is a conversation masquerading as an argument.

The main thing that keeps both functionalism and eliminative materialism at loggerheads with each other is that each has embraced a slightly different form of Cartesian materialism, neither of which is essential to the basic program they both share.

Some Cartesian Materialist Presuppositions

When Patricia Churchland says "I am a materialist and hence believe that the mind is the brain" (P. S. Churchland 1986, p. ix), she does not treat this assertion as a position to be defended, but as an uncontroversial given that would be accepted by all factions of the materialist camp. But the fact that most of the eliminative materialists do accept this assumption shows that they are not being completely true to their own principles. As long as they claim that the mind is the brain, they are in fact still identity theorists, and I believe that this alleged identity actually shackles us to certain concepts from folk psychology that could seriously hamper future scientific growth. Eliminating the one-to-one correspondence between mental states and brain states was a step in the right direction, but to be truly consistent they should have also called into question the identity of the mind as a whole with the brain as a whole. I will try to show in this book that careful analysis reveals even the current state of neuroscientific knowledge no longer fully supports this identity, although the presuppositions of both philosophers and scientists have made it very difficult to see this.

A perfect example of this kind of confusion is seen in two essays from the anthology *The Mind–Brain Identity Theory* (Borst 1970). In one of these essays, the classic "Is Consciousness a Brain Process?", U. T. Place recognized that the mind–brain identity claim could not be defended on philosophical grounds alone, and should be considered only as a reasonable scientific hypothesis (p. 42). However, in "Sensations and Brain Processes," J. J. C. Smart dismissed this call for caution by saying that "If the issue is between a brain thesis, or a heart thesis, or a liver thesis, or a kidney thesis, than the issue is purely an empirical one, and the verdict is overwhelmingly in favor of the brain." The verdict is in favor of the brain, however, only if we assume that the mind must be identical with one particular giblet in the body, as folk anatomy divides it. (Note that all of the alternatives that Smart lists can be found in any Oxford butcher shop.) However, as Patricia Churchland points out "the available theory specifies not only what counts as an explanation, but also the explananda themselves" (P. S. Churchland 1986, p. 398). In other words (my words, not hers), advanced neuroscience will not just give us more information about what the brain does and how it does it. It could also end up eliminating the whole concept of brain, just as easily as it could eliminate any other concept originally derived from folk psychology.

The functionalists have also made a commitment to their own brand of Cartesian materialism, usually unconsciously. Fodor, however, is quite explicit in this commitment when he claims that psychology must accept what he calls "methodological solipsism" (Fodor 1987). What he means by this is that mental states must be studied as an independent system that takes place entirely within a brain, which can be understood without any reference to the outside world. Paul Churchland almost breaks free of this assumption when he points out that even the most radical eliminative materialist must endorse functionalism "construed broadly as the thesis that the essence of our psychological states resides in the abstract causal roles they play in a complex economy of internal states mediating environmental inputs and behavioral outputs" (1989, p. 23). But the grammatical structure of the definition, as well as the fact that he focuses so heavily on brain data in his own work, reveals a commitment to the assumption that the internal states are the only real subject matter, not the environment and the behavior. The functionalist usually sees the system that is receiving inputs and giving outputs as a self-contained system, rather than a dependent pattern that gets its cognitive and biological significance from the context in which it dwells. This gives rise to a myth that is closely related to what Ryle called the "ghost in the machine."

I call this myth, with a similar deliberate abusiveness, the myth of the "machine in the machine." It is the basis for Fodor's "language of thought" theory of mind, and any other theory of mind that holds that all we need to do to understand the mind is to open Skinner's "black box," without worrying about how its contents relate to the organism, environment, and society in which it functions. One of Ryle's biggest mistakes, for which he has been justly criticized by cognitive philosophy and science, is conflating these two myths. Cognitive science is quite right to claim that the latter is nowhere near as bad a myth as the former. But precisely because it has been accepted for so long, the machine-in-the-machine myth has recently begun to reveal its weaknesses, many of which Ryle accurately foresaw in his original conflated attacks on both myths.

Ryle's Dispositional Psychology

Ryle specifically attacks the machine-in-the-machine myth when he rejects the belief that we can know about minds through "a process of inference analogous to that by which we infer from the seen movements of the railway signals to the unseen manipulations of the levers in the signal box" (Ryle 1949, p. 52). There is obviously nothing ghostly about a signal box. It is every bit as physical as a computer. However, Ryle's rejection of the signal-box analogy makes no distinction between those who believe that minds are brains and those who believe that minds are ghosts. Consequently, much of what he says has no impact on the mind–brain identity theory. Dualists believe that "one person cannot in principle visit another person's mind as he can visit signal boxes" (ibid.), but we can study brains with electrodes, PET scans, and hosts of other technologies that are becoming more sophisticated all of the time. Even if one does not want to describe these methods as "visiting" the brain, we use similar methods to learn about protons and neutrons, even though we will never have knowledge by acquaintance with them. So why should the fact that we can't visit the mind stop us from studying it?

Ryle then says something that could be used as an objection to this reply. We already know a great deal about minds, even though the science of psychology is still in its infancy. So how could we be dependent on some sophisticated theory for this knowledge, the way the physicist is dependent on a sophisticated physical theory? The answer that Paul Churchland gave to this question decades later was based on an insight of Wilfrid Sellars: we know what we know about minds thanks to a *folk-psychological* theory which, like many kinds of folk theories, has respectable predictive power even though it is theoretically confused. Ryle managed to avoid this conclusion by saying that the concepts we think of as being mental are not theoretical, but dispositional, and that it is the nature of our best dispositional theories to be able to predict by something like conceptual inference. To say that someone is in pain simply means that they have the propensity to perform pain behaviors, that is, wince, cry out, and perform a variety of other actions whose exact boundaries are not delineated, but which everyone knows. This is one of the reasons that Fodor and others referred to Ryle's position as *logical* behaviorism. Fodor was able to come up with a convincing argument why logical behaviorism did not exclude the mind–brain identity theory, and why it could not give any sort of answer that could satisfy science.

He pointed out that many questions have both a causal answer and a logical answer. For example, the question "What makes Wheaties the breakfast of champions?" could be answered by saying that they are full of vitamins and protein. But it could also be answered by saying that a nonnegligible number of champions eat them for breakfast (Fodor 1975, p. 7). Similarly, when we say "Jones is in pain," we mean he's behaving like he's in pain, and our concept doesn't have to be significantly more informative than that to be effective in ordinary discourse. But Fodor points out that although this is fine for common sense, it would never do for scientists to give explanations of this sort. It would be like the police saying that they have recently discovered that the robbery was the work of thieves. This would not be an acceptable answer from a policeman, even if it was fleshed out with further conceptual analysis like: "The tell-tale signs are there: the stolen property, the loss of the moneyed substances, it all points to thieves."[2] Or a more famous example, it would be like saying that opium puts people to sleep because it has dormative powers. Science sets itself the goal of giving a causal story of why Jones is in pain, and for that, Fodor claims, we must look inside the brain.

A Rylean Alternative to Functionalist Cartesian Materialism

Here is where I part company with Fodor, and to some degree rejoin Ryle. For there is no necessary connection between a causal story of mind and the mind–brain identity theory. The basic dogma of Cartesian materialism is that only neural activity in the cranium is functionally essential for the emergence of mind. This implies that all of the behavioral elements that take place in the world, which Ryle considers to be the essential constituents of mind, are actually epiphenomenal with respect to mind, and consequently a brain in a vat would be conscious even if it never interacted with a body to cause behavior. This might be true, but it is an empirical claim and, as we shall see, one that is perhaps uniquely difficult to prove.

Why should we assume that all human behavior is caused by a machine that lives in our skulls? Many of Ryle's criticisms of this assumption are as valid as ever. Most of what makes a clown's clowning clever takes place in the circus ring, not in the clown's brain. As Andy Clark pointed out again several decades later, when we do math on paper whatever is happening "in our heads" is not sufficient to solve the problem, even though it is necessary (Clark 1997). That is why we need the paper. So why assume that the brain is a closed causal system that creates mind and thought all by itself? Why not say that the mind is dependent on the causal interactions of the brain, the body, and the world?

Ryle was not able to conceive of this possibility, because he wanted to see talk about minds as being reducible to talk about dispositions. Science is no longer willing to accept dispositional "explanations" the way it did in Aristotle's and Molière's time. Science today posits the existence of unseen theoretical entities that are more ontologically fundamental than the variety of dispositions that each one explains. These entities are not unseen because they are very small, a fact that is blurred by the frequent use of atoms as the paradigmatic scientific entities. They are unseen because they are abstractions that enable us to make sense out of higher-level generalities. Theoretical entities are not inside the perceptible entities whose behavior they explain, they are above and beyond them. Gravity is not just the disposition possessed by apples that makes them fall. It has rules of its own that explain the behaviors of apples, planets, and acrobats in ways that are impossible to reduce to discourse about any one of the items that it affects. The mind–brain identity seems inevitable when we see scientific entities as being like atoms. The fundamental assumption of atomism is that we understand things by breaking them down into parts. When we ask the question "What part of the body is the mind?" the best answer to that question may be "the brain." But that is the wrong question if the mind is not part of the body, but rather a pattern that emerges when a living body interacts with a world. In that case a mind would not be any sort of organ. It would be what Dewey called a system of tensions, and what is now called a dynamic system by philosophers like

Tim Van Gelder. We needed gravitational and magnetic fields to go beyond Aristotelian physics to modern physics. Perhaps the thing that is holding psychology back is that it is not yet thinking in terms of "behavioral fields."

Dormative powers are completely ontologically dependent upon sleep and so cannot provide an explanation that meets modern scientific standards. Ryle tried to expand the concept of disposition by saying that "some dispositional words are highly generic or determinable, while others are highly specific or determinate" (Ryle 1949, p. 118). The specific and determinate dispositions are referred to with expressions like "Wheaties-eater" or "cigarette smoker." To say that a Wheaties-eater eats Wheaties is clearly a tautology. But to say that a doctor performs surgery, or that a solicitor drafts wills, is to name only one of the many ways that a doctor can be a doctor or a solicitor can be a solicitor. Ryle, however, is completely silent on how we know which activities of a generic disposition belong to a particular genus, and which don't. Why is it that we know that surgery and writing prescriptions are forms of doctoring, and that tap dancing and water skiing are not? Why is it that if we see a doctor using a brand new surgical technique, we will probably know that he is doctoring even though we have never seen that technique before? The obvious answer, which Ryle occasionally comes close to acknowledging,[3] is that we have a concept of doctor that is more than the sum of the discrete dispositions in which it manifests. Similarly, because we cannot make sense out of human behavior without a theory that posits mental entities that are more than the sum of the individual human actions, we must operate on the assumption that minds are ontologically distinct from those actions.

Ryle's failure to reduce mind to purely dispositional terms shows that even folk psychology is not satisfied with a purely dispositional explication of mind. Infants do learn a folk-Aristotelian dispositional psychology in the (western European) nursery, as Peirce claimed, but they learn a great deal else as well. They learn a causal theory about the mind, which enables them to predict human behavior based on a theory that posits the existence of mental entities like beliefs and desires. Ryle was wrong to think that this causal theory could be reduced without remainder to a list of dispositions. But I believe he was right that this causal theory is not about brains any more than it is about ghosts, despite a few expressions that have trickled down into folk psychology from Hippocratean neuroscience. Any theory of mind must be a theory about human beings interacting with each other and with their environment. Ryle was also wrong to think that a commonsense theory of mind could be completely independent of neuroscience. Sellars's scientific realism was intended largely as a critique of ordinary language philosophers like Ryle, to remind them that common sense never has this kind of independence. It is always being changed by new scientific discoveries. But Ryle was right to object to the idea that science will ever be able to replace folk psychology with a theory that talks *only* about brains. There is no question that brains are an essential part of the puzzle, but there is also no reason to assume that they are the entire puzzle. If every brain that ever existed did nothing but what brains do in vats (release neurotransmitters, shift blood flow, etc.), then no one would ever have thought that brains had anything to do with minds at all.

In fact, if we take Ryle's famous Oxford University example seriously, we might very well decide that locating the mind in any single organ was a category mistake. Even if we performed rigorous quantitative tests that proved that the administration building controls and directs all of the activity in the other buildings, and that all of the really important classes are given there, this would not prove that Oxford university was identical with the administration building, because buildings and universities are members of different categories. If Oxford decided to rent out a local theater to hold especially large classes, that theater would be part of what was identical with Oxford while the classes were being held there. It would not be identical with Oxford when the town drama society held amateur theatricals there. Similarly, the brain (or the retina or the spinal chord) would be identical with the mind when it performed mental functions, and identical with the body when it performed physical functions (if these two are separable from each other at all). It would be a mistake to argue over whether the theater was part of the drama society or part of the university. It would be a similar mistake to claim that any one part of the body was the mind if the entire body was participating in mental functioning in varying degrees and ways.

When Armstrong put forth his version of the mind–brain identity theory, he paid homage to the Rylean position he was criticizing by saying it was an essential step in a dialectical process.

. . . classical philosophy tend to think of the mind as an inner arena of some sort. This we may call the Thesis. Behaviorism moved to the opposite extreme: mind was seen as outward behavior. This is the Antithesis. My proposed Synthesis is that the mind is properly conceived as an inner principle, but a principle that is identified in terms of the outward behavior it is bringing about . . . if we have . . . general scientific grounds for thinking that man is nothing but a physical mechanism, we can go on to argue that the mental states are in fact nothing but physical states of the central nervous system (Borst 1970, p. 75).

There is a tension in this paragraph that captures the essential error of the mind–brain identity theory; an error that was compounded by the practices of the eliminative materialists who followed the identity theorists. For if mental states are identified by the outward behavior they produce, it seems inevitable that they will be ontologically constituted by that outward behavior as well. Thus we cannot make the claim that mental states are nothing but brain states and keep the synthesis described by Armstrong above. On the contrary, this claim produces a return to the thesis, not a synthesis of the thesis and antithesis. The thesis does change: it becomes Cartesian materialism rather than Cartesian dualism. But it does not incorporate the antithesis and thus resolve the conflict, it continues to "think of the mind as an inner arena of some sort." And this Cartesian materialism justifies the view of mind as an inner arena with a non sequitur, for it does not necessarily follow from the claim that people are physical mechanisms that mental states are in fact nothing but physical states of the central nervous system. On the contrary if we accept the synthesis described by Armstrong above, the inner principle and the outward behavior together constitute the mind.

This conclusion is especially unavoidable with those aspects of mind that are closely associated with language. Externalist philosophers of language, such as Putnam and Burge, have argued that meaning cannot be in the head, because language has an intentional relationship to the world of the speaker (i.e., it is "about" the world). If the word "Paris" means what it means because it has a relationship to Paris, surely our thoughts about Paris must have a similar relationship to Paris. And if so, how can our thoughts be nothing but neurological processes confined to a cranium?

Many contemporary philosophers are claiming that they cannot. Jerry Fodor tried to have it both ways by saying our thoughts consisted partly of a narrow content that supervened only on our brains (Fodor 1981) but later rejected this idea (Fodor 1994). Ruth Millikan has created a detailed critique of what she calls "meaning rationalism" (the belief that meanings exist only in the head), and in her 1993 she makes the point that "I no more carry my complete cognitive systems around with me as I walk from place to place than I carry the U.S. currency system about with me when I walk with a dime in my pocket" (p. 170). Hubert Dreyfus has introduced a whole generation of scientists and analytic philosophers to Heidegger's idea that an essential characteristic of mind is "Being-in-the-world," and consequently that no self is strictly distinct from the world in which it dwells. Andy Clark makes a similar claim in his book *Being There: Putting Brain, Body, and World Together Again.*

But even though these and many other thinkers are willing to locate verbalizable conceptual thought partly in the world, they are usually not willing to make the same step for feelings, sensations, and conscious experience. Clark gives detailed arguments for showing that language and other forms of cognitive activities could not be seen as self-contained languages of thought within the skull. But in a section entitled "Where does the mind stop and the rest of the world begin?" he deliberately refuses to apply the implications of his argument to subjective experience: "I assuredly do not seek to claim that individual consciousness extends outside the head . . . conscious contents supervene on individual brains. . . . Thoughts, considered only as snapshots of our conscious mental activity, are fully explained, I am willing to say, by the current state of the brain" (Clark 1997, pp. 215–17).

In Clark and Chalmers 1998, Clark gets a bit bolder and merely concedes that "some mental states, such as experiences, *may* be determined internally" (italics added). What I am claiming here is that Clark and the other externalist philosophers of mind have not been bold enough. I am not merely repeating the slogan in Putnam 1975 that "Meaning ain't in the head." I am also saying that "Consciousness ain't in the head." Most of the strongest objections against externalism can be best dealt with by completely rejecting the distinction between intentional mental processes and so-called raw feels. All experience is, I claim, completely and irreducibily intentional, and thus gets its meaning from relationships that the living self maintains with the outside world.

I do not mean by this that all experience is really linguistic. This misinterpretation of Sellars has many contemporary defenders, most prominently Dennett and Rorty. (Fodor is not included in this company only because he refuses to say anything at all about consciousness.) But I am not one of them. I believe that although language and experience are both intentional, they relate to their intentional objects in importantly different ways. To my knowledge, Dewey was the first philosopher to recognize and describe these differences. He showed why an intentional theory of experience would be safe from both the incoherent concept of "raw feel," and the dangerously oversimplified view that language is all there is to mind. What we have learned since his time, both philosophically and scientifically, has made his intentionalist view of experience more relevant than ever.

Is this perhaps only a philosopher's quibble? It is not immediately obvious that a laboratory neuroscientist needs to worry about this question at all. After all, the idea that the mind is the brain is not really that far off. Doesn't modern neuroscience confirm Hippocrates' claim that most of the important mental processing occurs in the skull, even if we have to acknowledge, if pressed, that perhaps someday we may discover that not all of it does? So what's the big deal? Do the confusions in the mind–brain identity theory really lead to any important philosophical or scientific confusions? Not perhaps in the short run, but in the long run, such confusions can lead to crisis and sometimes scientific revolutions.

There is no denying that the mind–brain identity theory works, in a rough and ready sort of way, just as folk psychology works in a rough and ready sort of way. But it may very well be that most mental functions have been found in the skull only because that is where people have been looking for them. As Kuhn has taught us, the paradigm always sets the rules for the puzzles that normal scientists must try to solve. If one of the rules is "Don't run experiments that test for mental functions anywhere but in the brain," the fact that almost no cognitive action has been found anywhere else doesn't really prove that much. Perhaps if laboratory researchers began recognizing that the mind is not simply the same thing as the brain, they might look elsewhere for mental functions, and they might find them. It *could* be a matter of contingent fact that all mental functions are performed exclusively by a single organ or system of organs. But we will never find evidence proving or disproving this claim if we assume it to be true before we begin.

Unless experiments are performed that are expressly designed to falsify the claim that the mind is the brain, we cannot say that this claim has been scientifically established, no matter how natural it may seem to us.

Nor, for that matter, can my suggestion that the mind is distributed elsewhere be any more than a suggestion until experiments are performed that are designed to falsify it. My only claim is that a noncranial mind is a genuine empirical possibility, and not an empty logical possibility of the sort that interests no one but philosophers. The assumption that the mind is the brain will probably always be a useful working hypothesis for certain forms of research. But my hunch is that it may someday be seen to resemble Newtonian physics when compared to Einsteinian physics. In other words, there may be certain kinds of data that can only be accounted for by a whole new theory. If such a theory does become necessary, we will have to concede that the mind–brain identity theory is false in scientifically significant ways: that, strictly speaking, there can be no mind without a brain–body–world nexus. The hope is that serious attention to this possibility will either confirm or refute it. In the next two chapters, I will look at some scientific data that do seem to be pointing in that direction, despite most scientists' lack of interest in the fact. In later chapters, I will claim that many of the most stubborn philosophical paradoxes arise from the unconscious (and arguably unjustified) assumption that science has proven that the mind exists only in the head.

2 Beyond the Cranium

Descartes's attempts to explain how disembodied thought managed to affect the brain, and from there the rest of the body, have been justifiably discredited. But his ideas about the relationship between brain and body are very similar to those held by most modern materialist philosophers. For Descartes, the body was seen as basically an elaborate piece of clockwork, no more alive than any other machine. Its many reflex functions, such as eye blinks, were performed without the intervention of the mind at all. The brain, however, had a special significance for Descartes, for it was the mainspring for the clockwork of the body. It provided the emotional and sensuous impulses that motivated people to do things. He thus agreed with modern materialistic philosophers in saying that sensations and raw feels were brain states, not mind states. The only activity that was purely disembodied was thinking, not feeling (Cottingham et al. 1649, p. 335). Feelings were able to affect the rest of the body through "the spirits contained in the cavities of the brain making their way to nerves" (ibid., p. 342).

For Descartes, the rest of the nerves were, in Patricia Churchland's paraphrase, "essentially message cables to and from the brain" (P. S. Churchland 1986, p. 16) that established communication between the brain and the body. Patricia Churchland cites Descartes's distinction between brain and message cables with approval, perhaps as a way of charitably balancing her numerous critiques of Cartesian dualism. Nevertheless, the data she presents in *Neurophilosophy* indicate that modern neuroscience no longer supports this model. She would have described the implications of her own position more accurately if she had said " I am a materialist, and hence believe that the mind is the nervous system." In the introductory data presented in *Neurophilosophy*, the first chapter is called "The Science of Nervous Systems," and nowhere is there any indication that the part of the nervous system located in the skull is significantly distinct in any way from the rest. Indeed the words "brain" and "nervous system" are used in a way that implies that they are somehow the same and yet somehow different. Consider these sentences:

In trying to understand the functional principles governing the human *nervous system*, we must remind ourselves that our *brain* has evolved from earlier kinds of brains. (Ibid., p. 15)

... relevant also is the cultural evolution of the science of *nervous systems*. *Brains* are extremely complex and delicate. . . . (Ibid., all italics mine)

Are we talking about brains here or about nervous systems? What is the point of using two different terms to describe what is apparently the same thing? This confusion is not unique to Churchland by any means. The books I have read on neuroscience usually have the word "brain" in the title, and almost never use the word at all after that. There is a lot of talk about the hippocampus, the cerebral cortex, the cerebellum, and the spinal chord, and about the various functions that these regions appear to be responsible for. But rarely is there any indication that those neural structures located in the skull have any significant kinship that marks them off from the rest of the nervous system. There is a special set of membranes called the blood–brain barrier, which separates the neurons in the skull from the rest of the nervous and circulatory systems. This barrier protects the brain from certain kinds of disease and makes it vulnerable to others. There is also a much higher ratio of connectivity in the neurons in the skull than there is in the rest of the nervous system, but this is a difference in degree, not in kind. Neither of these factors is enough to support the claim that the brain, and the brain alone, has the right to be called the mind.

But even though most neuroscientists have been at least somewhat aware that the brain is not that distinct from the rest of the nervous system, the Cartesian distinction between brain and message cables became the basis for the first mechanical models of mind. The inventors of the digital computer were aware that the nervous system was highly decentralized, but they found it fruitful to model this Cartesian distinction by creating a centralized "CPU," which performed cognitive functions by focusing on the information that was presented to it one piece at a time, in much the same way that the Cartesian brain received information from its message cables. This sequential, centralized model, despite its biological inaccuracy, made the computer revolution possible, and obviously captures some important truths about cognition. But as more data came in about how the nervous system operates, a whole discipline of neurally inspired computations arose, called variously parallel distributed processing, or connectionism or neural networks. Most of the scientists in this field do not constrain themselves to copying networks that exist (or even could exist) biologically. Nevertheless, the term "neurocomputational" is often used to describe the models they create, for the basic principles that those models share with biological nervous systems tell us a great deal about the nature of our minds. Much of what it tells us reveals the differences between us and those computers that are modeled after Cartesian theories of the brain.

The effectiveness of the classical computer metaphor made it seem natural to assume that the brain is the CPU of the nervous system: a sort of mechanical philosopher–king that rules the body from its throne in the skull. But neural networks, both natural and artificial, use a system that operates more like a democracy, with each neuron "voting" by adding or subtracting its synaptic weight in a neural network. It is thus not surprising how much new evidence reveals that the neural networks spread throughout the rest of the body are not structurally that different from the ones in the cranium, and perform many functions that could be described as mental or cognitive.

An important functional distinction in neural networks is that between *receptor neurons* and *interneurons*. Receptor neurons are those that respond directly to signals from the outside world, such as light rays or sound vibrations. Interneurons are those that interact with the receptor neurons and with each other in various functional patterns. A receptor neuron's purpose is to produce a series of electrical pulses that are somehow isomorphic with the signal that is striking it. Receptor neurons are thus best describable by the electronics term *transducer*. (A transducer is any electronic or mechanical device that transfers a signal from one medium to another. A microphone is a transducer that transforms a sound vibration into an electrical signal. A loudspeaker operates in the other direction and transforms an electrical signal into sound.)

A transducer can be a very sophisticated device, as any audiophile can tell you, and there are many complex scientific laws (such as Shannon's

laws of information transfer) that an engineer must take into consideration if she is to design a transducer that does its job with maximum effectiveness. But no matter how sophisticated a transducer is, it does nothing
that could be described as "understanding" the signal it receives, it merely
mirrors or mimics the signal. It does not interrelate any signal to signals
it has received in the past, or might receive in the future. It merely records
the signal as accurately as possible, without trying to change it. A neural
network can be described as cognitive only because the interneurons take
the raw signal from the transducing receptor neurons and establish a
relationship between it and past and/or future signals. A transducer, in
contrast, must always deliver the same response for the same stimulus,
and different responses for different stimuli. A tape recorder playing two
recordings of two different people saying the letter "A" must preserve the
differences in the two voices, or the transducer in the tape heads is not
doing its job. In contrast, the output of an appropriately trained neural
network will give the *same* output for two different recordings of the
spoken letter "A," and thus signals to the rest of the system that those
two different recordings have something in common. It is this ability to
filter out differences and recognize similarities that makes the interneurons
in a connectionist system cognitive.

If all the neurons in the sense organs were receptor neurons that functioned as transducers, and all of the interneurons were in the skull cavity,
the brain could be seen as the sole seat of cognitive activity, and the
neurons that connected the receptor neurons to the brain would be the
message cables that Patricia Churchland attributed to Descartes's theory of
the nervous system. In fact, most of the neurons in the sense organs are
not receptor neurons. In the retina the only receptor neurons are the rods
and the cones, which produce an electrical charge in proportion to the
intensity and frequency of the light that strikes them. The rest of the
neurons in the retina (the bipolar, horizontal, and amacrine cells) connect
groups of rods and cones into networks that interpret their combined
signals and send the result to a ganglion cell. Each ganglion cell then sends
its signal to the cranial neurons for further interpretation.

The signal sent by the ganglion cell is a long way from being a "raw
feel," however. Each ganglion cell is responsible for interpreting a single
receptive field (typically about 1 mm in diameter), in a very specific way
(Dowling 1987, p. 33). One kind of ganglion, called contrast-sensitive
units, is divided into two subcategories, called on-center cells and off-

center cells. An on-center cell produces a positive, excitatory signal when the center of its receptive field is stimulated by light, and a negative, inhibitory signal when the periphery is stimulated. The receptive field of the off-center cells responds as the mirror image of the on-center cell. Another kind of ganglion responds positively to spots of light moving through its receptive field in one particular direction, and either negatively or not at all to the same spot of light moving in the opposite direction. These direction-sensitive cells respond equally well to a dark spot moving across an illuminated field and a bright spot moving across a dark field. It is very tempting to say that the networks connected to these ganglia actually possess an abstract concept of motion, because they can detect a similarity between two signals that would be unrelated if they were responded to as mere "sense data." Also, ganglia compare information with each other in certain ways, producing an effect called the *silent inhibitory surround*. When a spot is presented to a receptive field immediately adjacent to that of a given ganglion, it will depress the response of that cell to any stimulus within its field. This probably helps to clarify the awareness of borders and edges (Dowling 1987, p. 37). The inhibitory surround effect also occurs in the sense of touch, where it is largely mediated by connections in the spinal cord (Dr. Glen Rein, Stanford University, personal communication. See also the research by Ronald Melzack described below).

Many of the researchers in this field use cognitive terms to describe these other forms of signal processing that occur in the sense organs. Barlow (1953) refers to the on-off cells in frog retinas as "fly-detectors," and Letvin et al. (1965) classified cells according to the operations they appeared to be carrying out: boundary detectors, dark convex boundary detectors, dimming detectors, and changing contrast detectors. Although the description of the particular functions is necessarily somewhat speculative, it seems that some sort of cognitive description is unavoidable. If this kind of activity were performed by a machine, it would be called information processing, not transduction. If it were discovered to be occurring in the brain, materialist philosophers and scientists would have unhesitatingly called it thinking. If this sort of neural activity is called thinking when it occurs in the brain, there seems to be no reason to call it anything else if it occurs at another location in the nervous system.

It stretches the ordinary concept of thinking to use the word in this way, but modern cognitive theory has already made this stretch when talking about brain activity. Cognitive science sees high-level thinking as created by the cooperative interaction of a network of relatively simple homunculi. When the neural networks in the cranium are analyzed down to the homuncular level, the tasks those homunculi are performing are no more abstract or complex than those performed by the retina and have the same basic functional structure. As both cranial and peripheral networks are connected within the same nervous system and perform the same sorts of tasks, there seems to be no reason to continue to think of the latter as mere message cables.

Many apparently effective arguments for the mind–brain identity theory arise from assuming that any alternative must locate the mind in some place *other* than the brain. There is certainly plenty of evidence that if there must be a single location in the body for consciousness, then the brain is the most likely candidate. A person with a damaged body can still think and feel, after all, and one with a damaged brain often cannot. Perhaps the most dramatic example of this is the existence of phantom limb pain. The fact that the sensation of a missing limb endures when the limb is gone seems to indicate that the sensation existed only in the brain, and not in the limb itself. But given our current state of knowledge about pain, it would not be wise to assume that the most obvious interpretation is the only possible one.

According to Ronald Melzack, one of the most prominent figures in pain research, most amputees experience phantom limbs, and even people with paralyzed limbs experience phantoms that respond to their will in ways that their real limbs can't. Some phantom limbs even have something like wills of their own, sticking out at odd angles from the body and making the patient feel that they must go through doors sideways. Nor can phantoms be explained by saying they are caused by memories, for they are also experienced by some patients who were born without limbs. (See Melzack 1992.) So if people without limbs can have the sensations of having limbs, it seems that the obvious explanation is that our sensations are embodied by the brain activity that receives messages from the limb, and not by the neural activity in the limb itself.

It is true that the sensations of a limb would have to disappear upon amputation if the sensation existed *only* in the limb. But if the embodiments of the sensation were distributed throughout the nervous system, we would expect the loss of the limb neurons to produce not a disappearance, but only a distortion or degeneration of the awareness of the limb.

This is almost certainly what happens. Melzack reports that shooting pain, burning sensations, and cramping are commonly felt in phantom limbs. He says this is probably because the brain is sending signals out to limbs that aren't receiving them, which results in abnormal patterns in neural signaling. One of the characteristics of a neural network is that its functions are distributed throughout the network. This means that the loss of any given neuron never causes a complete breakdown, but only a slight degeneration, which increases gradually as more and more neurons are lost. There are, of course, more neurons in the cranium than anywhere else, so we are most likely to make the qualitative leap to cognitive damage if we traumatize its contents. But because there are millions of neurons outside the cranium as well, which are apparently also helping to constitute consciousness, it appears that this fact indicates a difference only in degree and not in kind.

Melzack is currently advocating a theory that posits the existence of what he calls the neuromatrix, which, in the following quote, sounds like the most orthodox form of Cartesian materialism imaginable: "[A]ll the qualities we normally feel from the body, including pain, are also felt in the absence of inputs from the body; from this we may conclude that the origins of the patterns that underlie the qualities of experience lie in neural networks in the brain; stimuli may trigger the patterns but do not produce them" (Melzack 1993).

Things look different, however, when one considers the recent history of pain research. Melzack's first work was actually a frontal attack on Cartesian materialism, which he rejects when he describes it as the belief that "injury activates specific pain receptors and fibers which, in turn, project pain impulses through a spinal pain pathway to a pain center in the brain" (ibid.). His first important contribution was called the gate control theory of pain, which did for pain what the research I quoted earlier did for visual perceptions: attacked the view that the noncranial regions of the nervous system were mere message cables that transmitted pain impulses without processing them. Melzack showed that there was cognitive processing, and not just transduction, in the dorsal horn of the spinal cord, produced by separate excitatory and inhibitory fibers. Melzack specifically says that his theory received tremendous resistance because it contradicted the presuppositions that neuroscience inherited from Descartes. However, because all attempts to cure pain by removing a specific "pain center" had been unsuccessful, there was a strong need for an alternative approach. Because the gate control theory eventually was accepted, almost all pain research since then has focused on the spinal chord.

Some of the most dramatic experiments on the spinal processing of pain are described by James Grau in an article anthologized in Bekoff, Allen, and Burghardt 2002. Rats who are exposed to a mildly painful stimulus will show less response to another stimulus that comes immediately after it. In ordinary folk-psychological terms, we would say that the rat was distracted by the first stimulus and thus didn't pay as much attention to the second stimulus, but behavioral psychologists don't like to talk that way. Grau, however, was aware that these behaviorist limitations on theorizing make it impossible to make sense out of most behavior, and so he was willing to use some technical terminology from cognitive psychology to make a similar, but more precise, claim. He theorized that the first stimulus remains in the animal's short-term memory (STM), and that this memory produces signals from the brain that effect the response in the spinal chord. Mary Meagher, however, discovered that this decrease in response (called antinociception) still occurred in rats even after she had cut the connection between the rat's spinal chord and its brain. Grau and many other psychologists found Meagher's results quite surprising, and decided that they could no longer take for granted the assumption that cognitive processing took place entirely in the brain. So they proceeded to do experiments that revealed that spinalized rats could make far more "cognitive judgments" than anyone would have ever assumed. Because a great deal had been discovered about what rats are capable of learning through Pavlovian conditioning, Grau was able to test for these abilities by running the same experiments on intact and spinalized rats, and comparing their performances.

Surprisingly, although the responses of the spinalized rats were often slower, the rats were able to develop many of the same conditioned reflexes, even though their spinal chords were incapable of communicating with their brains. These include forms of learning such as overshadowing (the rat learns when exposed to two different stimuli to respond only to the more prominent one), instrumental conditioning (in this case, the rat learns that it needs to keep its foot out of salt water to avoid an electric shock), and cognition of no control (the rat learns that there is nothing it can do to avoid the shock, and so gives up trying). The folk psychological explanations in the preceding parentheses all would presuppose that the rat is representing the stimulus in some way in order to make a judgment about what to do, and the usual assumption is that this representing process takes place in the rat's brain. The spinalized rats, however, were able to respond appropriately to this conditioning even though the limbs doing the responding were severed from the brain. If there was any representing going on, it appeared to be taking place in the spinal chord.

Melzack's neuromatrix theory is largely an attempt to deal with problems in pain research that arose from too many years of focus on the spinal cord. It should be seen not as a return to a centralized brain theory, but as an expansion beyond the idea that pain is a product of a self-contained spinal module. He sees the neuromatrix as being distributed throughout the nervous system, which would account for why the previous attempts to find "pain centers" were unsuccessful. Given that so much recent work has been on the spinal cord (largely because people have followed in his footsteps), it is appropriate for him to urge that pain research start looking at the brain again. But the only thing that Melzack is really advocating now is that spinal cord activity cannot explain everything about pain. He is surely right that at least some of the rest of the story will be found by looking in the cranium, because that is where most of the nervous system is. One of his strongest arguments against the message-cable view of perception was his evidence that "The spinal gating mechanism is influenced by nerve impulses that descend from the brain" (Melzack 1993). This means that the brain is contributing to the perceptual process, not just responding to it. The main point of Melzack's theory is that the neuromatrix must be distributed throughout the nervous system, and that the brain doesn't sit passively there and simply record what the message cables send to it. (As I will discuss in the next chapter, there is even some evidence that embodiments of feeling could be distributed *beyond* the nervous system.)

As long as we are asking what part of the nervous system embodies consciousness, the least inaccurate answer may be "the brain," but the distributed nature of neurocomputations may make this the wrong question. There are two slightly different ways of stating the relationship between the brain and conscious experience that are often used by neuroscientists who study pain. Both of them are unassailably supported by scientific evidence, but neither is actually strong enough to be an endorsement of Cartesian materialism.

(1) No Brain, No Pain.   This implies only that the brain is necessary for conscious experience. Mind–brain identity requires that the brain be both necessary and sufficient for conscious experience.

(2) The Pain in the Sprain Is Mainly in the Brain.[1]   This is also fully compatible with the distributed view of consciousness defended in this book. Cartesian materialism must make the stronger claim that

(3) The Pain in the Sprain Is Entirely in the Brain.   This means that for every experience or thought that we have, every shift in qualitative nuance or cognitive deliberation, there must be something in the brain that is not only co-occurrent with it, but also robust and detailed enough to be entirely responsible for it. Even if there is some kind of neuromatrix in the brain that acts as a template for bodily experience, the mind would not be identical with the brain if the details of that experience emerged from interactions between the brain and the rest of the nervous system.

Suppose we were able to prove that certain aspects of sensory experience would not emerge unless there were specific interactions between the brain and the rest of the body? Would this leave us with a somewhat narrower, retrenched mind–brain identity theory? Could we then say that thoughts existed in the brain but that sensations existed in the noncranial neurons? This may seem like a real possibility, but it has some serious problems. For one thing, I think that what we have learned about cognitive activity in the rest of the nervous system requires us to question the entire distinction between thoughts and sensations. If the retina and the skin are "thinking," is there anything left of the nervous system that could be said to be "just feeling"?[2] In the retina, for example, only the rods and cones are doing anything that might be called pure sensing, and even they are not providing anything like the "sensa" or "sense data" of traditional epistemologies. As Paul Churchland remarks,

No cognitive activity takes place save as the input vectors [i.e., the signals from the rods and cones] pass through that speculative configuration of synaptic connections, that theory. Theory ladeness thus emerges . . . as that which makes processing activity genuinely cognitive on the first place . . . there can be no question of grounding all epistemic decisions in some neutral observation framework. (1990, p. 355)

All the other neurons in the sense organs "sense" by performing computations of the same fundamental structure as those in the so-called brain.[3]

This is why Churchland concludes "there is just as much room for conceptual variation and conceptual exploration at the perceptual level as there is at any other level of knowledge" (ibid.). If perceptual and conceptual knowledge are thus not distinguishable from each other in any significant way, it would not be possible to separate them spatially by putting one in the brain and the other in the sense organs.

I do not mean to imply that the mainstream neuroscientific community is in agreement that the mind is the nervous system, and that philosophers have been ignoring this fact. The data I have been citing are widely accepted and highly regarded; the concept of a decentralized brain is an essential assumption of Rumelhart and McClelland 1986 (perhaps the most influential text ever written on neurally inspired computation), and the fact that the retina is described in the subtitle of Dowling 1987 as "an approachable part of the brain" shows that the orthodox view no longer sees the retina as a mere message cable. But the philosophical implications of these facts have been only dimly noticed, because neuroscientists are more interested in gathering data than in pondering its implications. Also, because philosophers have assumed that the brain–body distinction has been proven by neuroscience, rather than presupposed, they have gotten themselves entangled in a variety of pseudoproblems.

Natika Newton (1986) criticizes Paul Churchland (P. M. Churchland 1989, pp. 47–66) by claiming that perceiving a sensation of foot pain as a brain state would require us "to stop experiencing pain as something in our foot, and instead experience it as something in our head" (Newton 1986, p. 100). She is thus assuming that all future neuroscience would necessarily assume that the brain is conscious and the rest of the body is not. (Given his choice of words, perhaps Churchland was assuming the same thing.) All her example really indicates, however, is that there are problems with the mind–brain identity theory that future research will have to solve. To assume that the mind exists in the entire nervous system and not just in the head creates no such problems. Because the nervous system interconnects throughout the body, the supposedly necessary shift in consciousness to the head would, under such an assumption, be almost as misleading and confused as thinking a pain in the foot actually occurred in the liver. If future neuroscience does decide that the mind is most accurately identified with the entire nervous system, common sense would be correct in assuming that the pain is, to some degree, actually located in the foot.

In Daniel Dennett's delightful story, "Where Am I?", the confusion that arises from the Cartesian materialism inherent in the mind–brain identity theory is elegantly visualized. Dennett imagines that his brain is transplanted into a glass vat and attached to radio receptors that hook up back to the rest of his body, including his sense organs. He then says to himself, "Here I am sitting on a folding chair staring through a plate glass window at my brain . . . But wait, shouldn't I have thought 'Here I am, suspended in a bubbling fluid, being stared at with my own eyes?'" (Dennett 1982, p. 219). Dennett claims (it is hard to tell with how much seriousness) that even though he feels as though he is residing in his body, science tells us that he must actually be residing in the brain in the vat. Nevertheless, experientially he appears to himself to still be in his body. He tries to bring his perceptual consciousness in line with the scientific facts (in a manner similar to that described in Churchland 1979, pp. 25–36). Like Natika Newton, Dennett at first assumes that this must necessarily mean to experience himself as simply being inside his brain. However, a few paragraphs of dialectic prompts him to say that this could not be the whole story. He eventually concludes that the answer to the question "Where am I?" is "both places" (Dennett 1982, p. 223). He thus sees his situation as rather like that of the scarecrow in *The Wizard of Oz*, who was able to say, after being dismembered by the winged monkeys, "That's me all over." However, this answer is not at all satisfactory if we assume that his mind exists only in his brain and that the rest of his body is an unconscious machine. I am sure Dennett does not claim that after having his hair cut that he is both sitting in the barber's chair and lying in little fragments in the trash can. Why are the two cases so different? Perhaps because the millions of neurons that remain in his body have as much right to be called his mind as do the ones in the vat as long as they are all appropriately joined together. He *feels* as though he were in his body because the neurons in his body are essential constituents of the part of his mind that *feels*. There are, in other words, sensory neurons located outside the skull, and sensations are unquestionably mental entities. As long as the neurons in both places are linked into the same network, there is no reason to think that either location has any more or less right to claim that it is "the person."

Dennett came very close to decentralizing the nervous system in this manner when he wrote *Consciousness Explained* several years later. He introduces (and ridicules) his own version of Cartesian materialism, which he defines as the idea that there is one particular part of the brain where consciousness takes place. But he does not follow his own arguments to their logical conclusion. I agree with Dennett that consciousness is a "network property," that is, it does not reside in any single neuron or organ, but rather is a property that arises when neurons are arranged in a particular kind of "nervous system." This is why there is no single place in the nervous system where it all comes together, just as there is no single place on a tennis court where the tennis game takes place. But if this is true, why should we insist, as Dennett does, that "the brain is Headquarters, the place where the ultimate observer is" and that "to deny that the head is Headquarters would be madness" (Dennett 1991, p. 106). It is obviously false to claim that some other part of the body is Headquarters, and that the brain therefore is not. But the distributed processing model of the brain that gives rise to Dennett's multiple drafts theory of consciousness seems to imply that it was a mistake to assume that *anywhere* was Headquarters. Why does there have to be a headquarters at all if there is no "central meaner" to occupy it?

If the head really is Headquarters, then Dennett's answer to the question "Where am I?" could no longer be "both places." Instead we would be stuck with yet another Cartesian image, with the self residing in the brain and the rest of the nervous system as message cables that carry information (whose ultimate destination is the stage of a Cartesian theater that now occupies the entire cranium). The facts I have mentioned earlier seem to imply, however, that there are good reasons for applying the multiple drafts theory to the entire nervous system. If we did this, there would be no need for the information to be delivered anywhere. A pain in the foot would not be caused by an unconscious signal that travels up the leg and into the brain. Instead, the pain would be revealed to be a network property that arises out of the relationships between the nerves in the foot, the spinal cord, and the various neuronal ensembles in the cranium. If this were the case, the pain would not be only in the foot, but it would also not be only in the head as most scientists since Hippocrates have assumed. It would instead be in both places, as Dennett claimed in "Where Am I?" (or more accurately, it would occur in one large single place spread throughout the body).

This theory of distributed location for body sensations would also completely reframe the problem of explaining the anomalies encountered in

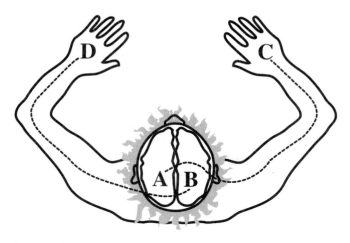

Figure 2.1
The traditional Cartesian materialist view. The "light of consciousness" dwells only in the brain. Until a signal enters the brain, the self cannot be aware of it.

the experiments of Benjamin Libet (discussed in Dennett 1991, pp. 153–166). Let us consider one of these experiments by referring to figure 2.1, which shows the commonsense (i.e., Cartesian materialist) view of the relationship between the brain and the rest of the nervous system. A stimulus in the hand (point C or D) is supposedly a nonconscious event, which sends a signal that does not create a conscious experience until it triggers a signal in the sensory cortex, which contains those neural events that allegedly fall within the "light of consciousness." Point A, on the left side of the cortex, creates the sensation of right-hand stimulation, and point B on the right-hand side creates the sensation of left-hand stimulation. Libet discovered, however, that if one stimulated the left cortex directly at point A and then stimulated the left hand at point D, the subject did *not* experience "first right hand (cortically induced), then left hand." Instead they were experienced in the opposite order from the occurrence of the stimuli, that is, first left hand, then right. Some people, including neuroscientist Sir John Eccles, claimed that these results proved that subjective experience must exist in a separate nonphysical realm in which time could be reversed. Others claimed that there must be something wrong with Libet's data, because its implications were so outrageous. Dennett, however, came up with an ingenious solution that accepted the data as possible without requiring dualism.

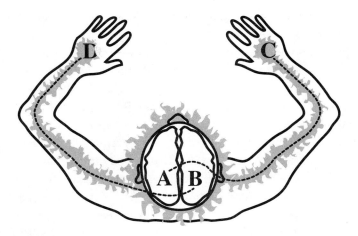

Figure 2.2
If the "light of consciousness" emerges from activity that is distributed throughout the nervous system, the signal does not have to travel to the brain for the self to be aware of it.

Dennett's basic point is that there is not a one-to-one correspondence between the points in the *subjective* time line that gives order to our experience of successive events, and those in the *objective* time line of the neural states that constitute those experiences. This correlation has to be reasonably close most of the time to enable us to survive in the objective world, but it is not an absolute necessary connection. Consequently, it is not surprising that there can be mix-ups under unusual laboratory conditions. This is why when Libet stimulates the somatosensory cortex of a subject and then stimulates the nerve endings in the hands, the subject can sometimes reverse the order in subjective time, and experience the stimulation in the hand first.

Suppose, however, that figure 2.2 is a more accurate representation of the embodiment of conscious experience. Suppose, in other words, that "the light of consciousness" was embodied by the entire nervous system and not just by the part of the nervous system that occupies the skull. If that were the case, all of the questions underlying this debate would have to be completely rephrased. Events C and D would not have to travel anywhere to become conscious, any more than events A and B would. Consciousness would emerge as a result of events taking place at points A, B,

C, and D, but the travel metaphor would no longer be appropriate. It might not even be necessary for there to be a distinct event A or B for every subjective experience caused by stimulus C or D. Suppose, for example, that a hot stimulus to point C in the hand causes exactly the same brain state A as a cold stimulus to the hand (or, more plausibly, that the difference between the two brain states was functionally trivial). If this were the case, we would have to say that the unique qualitative difference between cold sensations and hot sensations was embodied by neural events C, the neural event in the arm. Brain event A would still partly embody the sensations of hot and cold, but it would not be "the difference that makes the difference." If no one ever conceives of the possibility that the brain is not a separate organ distinct from the rest of the nervous system, there would be quarrels that are analogous to the ones that now occur over the Libet data. The "materialists" would assert on faith that there must be a brain event that no one has discovered yet, and the "mystics" would claim that there is some sort of psychic power that carries the information from the arm neurons to the brain neurons. But if the self is embodied by the entire nervous system, rather than just by the brain alone, there would be no need for a distinct brain event to account for the qualitative differences between the sensations of hot and cold. There would be no need to convey the information in the arm's neural event to "the seat of the soul," because it would already be there.

Could it be that the word "brain" does not denote a natural kind within the context of neuroscience; that it is really only a category, like "gems" or "dirt," that is useful only for what Locke called the vulgar discourse of the marketplace? Throughout this book, I will try to use substitute locutions like "cranial neurons" to help demonstrate my belief that the word "brain" appears to have no essential use in neuroscience. When I am critiquing the views of those who still accept the mind–brain identity, I will of course have to use the word "brain" in quoting them. Sometimes I will even use it myself to make my critiques a bit smoother stylistically, but it could be easily replaced in any of those contexts by phrases less than a sentence long. As far as I can see, the only people who would need to keep using the term "brain" would be doctors studying the functions of the blood–brain barrier. This is why I will use the word "brain" as little as possible throughout this book.

3 Beyond the Neuronal Mind

Although the mind–nervous system identity is a more accurate description of the available facts than the mind–brain identity, it is still not a position that we should treat as a necessary truth. What we have learned about the decentralization of cognitive activity could have even broader implications than we have ever imagined, and we must be willing to consider those possibilities seriously. There is already some interesting data and arguments indicating that certain mental functions are performed by parts of the body other than the nervous system, and any serious philosophy of mind must be willing to deal with the possibility that there could be more.

The James–Cannon Debate

Dewey was not the only pragmatist philosopher to question certain aspects of the mind–brain identity theory. In James 1884, William James used examples from nature and human experience to argue for many of the same points made in chapter 1 of this book.

As surely as the Hermit Crab's abdomen presupposes the existence of empty whelk shells somewhere to be found, so surely do the hound's olfactories imply the existence, on the one hand, of deer's and foxes' feet, and on the other the tendency to follow up their tracks. The neural machinery is but a hyphen between determinate arrangements of matter outside the body and determinate impulses to inhibition or discharge within its organs. (James 1884, p. 190)

Ultimately James accepts that the brain is totally responsible for cognition, perception, and volition. But he argues that some emotions are at least partly embodied elsewhere. His most widely quoted illustration was his claim that we do not run from a bear because we are frightened, rather we are frightened because we are running from a bear. He claimed that unless there is a neural feedback loop that flows from the brain to the muscles and viscera and then back again, no emotions would be felt: "Without the bodily states following on the perception, the latter would be purely cognitive in form, pale, colorless destitute of emotional warmth" (ibid.). He cites a variety of sources in defense of this claim: psychological research, phenomenological thought experiments, interviews with actors who testified that performing the bodily actions associated with an emotion almost always produced the emotion itself. But, not surprisingly, this rejection of Cartesian materialism was frequently challenged, most notably by a neuroscientist named Walter Cannon.

Cannon (1929) appears to offer exactly what I was asking for at the end of chapter 1 of this book: experiments and data designed to falsify a claim that the mind extends beyond the brain (pp. 348–375). He did experiments in which the sensory inputs from the visceral and circulatory systems of a cat were surgically severed, and discovered that, when provoked, the cat still performed many of the behaviors that would ordinarily be associated with strong emotions of fear and anger. For those who might object that we cannot infer from mere behavior that the cat actually felt these emotions, he discovered clinical testimony from a patient who had lost all sensation from the neck down but said that he nevertheless still felt all the standard emotions as intensely as ever. Cannon also gave neurological evidence that there was simply not enough sensitivity in the viscera to account for the variety of human emotions, because very different emotions had essentially the same effect on the human viscera. Perhaps most important, he discovered evidence that there was a particular part of the brain—the thalamus—whose presence was essential for the experience of emotional affect, and whose absence seemed to be always correlated with the loss of emotional affect.

Cannon's critique, however, is not completely decisive for two reasons. First of all, it is often aimed at aspects of James's position that are a consequence of his partial commitment to Cartesian materialism. For example, Cannon argues that visceral changes are too slow to be a source of emotional feeling, because "there must be added the time required for the nerve impulses to pass from the brain to the periphery and back again" (p. 355). This is only a necessity if we assume (as James apparently did) that the self is dwelling inside the brain, and therefore something happening in the viscera cannot be felt unless some signal is returned to the brain. If consciousness is an emergent property of the brain–body, there is no need for information to be carried back to the brain for the self to be aware of something. Any appropriate physiological event in principle could embody a mental event no matter where it took place. There would be no need to create an extra copy of that event in the brain. (This is essentially the same point made at the end of chapter 2 of this book.)

More important, however, is that although certain data discovered between James 1990 and Cannon 1929 may have supported a kind of Cartesian materialism, new data is constantly coming in, and much of it puts Cartesian materialism into question. The title of Joseph LeDoux's 1996 book, *The Emotional Brain*, seems to endorse Cartesian materialism and speaks favorably of Cannon's critique of James. LeDoux's own research supports the amygdala, rather than the thalamus, for the title of emotional brain center. But he also cites research showing that the feedback of adrenaline from the blood stream to the hippocampal system apparently helps to form explicit memories (p. 207). This goes beyond what James himself was willing to claim for noncranial mental functions. Memory is not just emotional, it is unambiguously cognitive. There is also a substantial amount of data from other sources showing that sensations and perceptions, not just emotions, are in some sense embodied by physiological processes that are orthogonal to the nervous system. In other words, there might very well be something to the idea that J. J. C. Smart dismissed as unthinkable: that other organs, including the kidneys, have some claim to being partial embodiments of the mind. Some of this research is controversial and perhaps deservedly so. But it also seems highly likely that some resistance arises not because of the quality of the work itself, but because of the widely held misapprehension that Cartesian materialism is a scientifically proven fact.

New Data on the Relationship between the Body and Emotions/Sensations

Neurosurgeon and research scientist Richard Bergland has done extensive research on the pituitary, and believes that the brain is fundamentally a gland that secretes hormones, rather than an electroneural system. His commitment to this idea stems from the fact that he has performed numerous unsuccessful operations in which he cut out neurons (in one case over half of a patient's spinal chord) in an attempt to eliminate chronic pain. He claims that modern neuroscience has created an unnatural dualism by saying "molecules shape the body, but electricity shapes the mind" (1985, p. 80). His research has revealed that the pituitary gland is not merely a transducer that turns hormonal information into electrical information. Instead chemical information flows both to and from the brain and the pituitary, and from the pituitary out to the body by purely chemical means. (There are no nerves in the pituitary gland, but many blood vessels [ibid., p. 86].) He claims that experiments involving the body's secretions of various endorphins show that at least one kind of pain is created in the body by the brain releasing hormones through the pituitary gland, without the use of any electrical information transfer (ibid., pp. 102–104). This would explain why a person could still feel pain even after most of her spinal chord had been removed.

In 1985, neurochemists F. O. Schmitt and Candace Pert discovered what they called a parasynaptic system, which operates independently of any neural networks by using chemicals they call information substances (IS). These ISs communicate without synaptic firing by being released into the extra cellular fluid (ECF), through which they float until they reach a receptor molecule they are compatible with. Thus, even though there is no neural network connecting these two different organs, the specificity of the receptors makes it possible for them to exchange information chemically. There is, for example, a neuropeptide called angiotensin, for which there are receptors in both the limbic system (a neural structure located in the skull) and the kidneys. There is evidence that by releasing and receiving angiotensin, the limbic system and the kidneys create a balance between thirst and the body's need for water (Pert 1987, p. 83). Activity in the limbic system has also been found to correlate with a variety of other emotional states, and it contains very high concentrations of neuropeptide receptors. Many of these neuropeptides include substances that, when they are secreted by the endocrine glands, are called hormones. Insulin, for example, traditionally considered to be a secretion of the pancreas, is also made and stored in the limbic system, as are its receptors. The fact that the endocrine glands and the limbic system share what is in effect a common chemical alphabet makes it highly plausible that they communicate with each other chemically, without having to rely on synaptic connections.

There are also several other locations throughout the body, which Pert calls nodal points, with very high concentrations of these informational substances and their receptors. It seems likely that the limbic system may have a much closer functional relationship with these nodal points then with the other various neural structures in the skull that make up what we call the brain. All of this has led Pert to conclude the following: "In the beginning of my work, I matter of factly presumed that emotions were in the head or the brain. Now I would say they are really in the body as well. They are expressed in the body and are part of the body. I can no longer make a distinction between the brain and the body" (1987, p. 84).

In her 1997 book, *Molecules of Emotion*, Pert was able to give more evidence for this claim, summarizing new discoveries about chemical information transfer that overturned many presuppositions about the relationship between the nervous system and the rest of the body. Until recently, it was widely assumed that the cerebral spinal fluid that occupied so much space in the cranium had no function that related to consciousness or cognition. (Bergland claimed in his 1985 book that there was no real understanding of why it was there at all.) The fact that there were dozens of different neurotransmitters in the nervous system was also considered to be a fact that was purely biological (and thus cognitively epiphenomenal). Consequently, there were few attempts in AI to model the differences between the various neurotransmitters. Connectionist researchers built artificial neural networks that ignored the fact that the signals in real brains changed from chemical to electrical to chemical.

Now, however, there is considerable evidence that the primary function of the cerebral spinal fluid is to carry chemicals in and out of the brain in ways that make communication possible with the rest of the body. The reason that there are so many different neurotransmitters (which she prefers to call neuropeptides) is to make specific communications possible among a variety of different cells and organs. When one organ or system of organs sends out a certain chemical (called a ligand), the cells of other organs have chemicals (called receptors) that bind specifically to that chemical being sent out. This enables the receptors to pick up signals from the ligand-emitting organs that are meant specifically for them, just as a radio receiver will only pick up the signals it is tuned for. The connection between the kidneys and the limbic system is one example of this kind of communication, but since the previously cited Pert article was published several others have been discovered. The vasoactive intestinal peptide (VIP) can be found in the frontal cortex of the brain, the thymus gland, the gut, the lungs, some immune cells, and parts of the autonomic nervous system (Pert 1997, p. 208). Pert speculates that because the frontal cortex is the part of the brain associated with long-range planning, the chemical connection between the gut and the frontal cortex could partially account for the cognitive efficacy of "gut feelings." The nucleus of Barrington in the hindbrain uses the neuropeptide CRF to control both colonic distension and sexual arousal. Neuropeptide receptors on the mobile cells of the immune system have been found to be indistinguishable from those in the brain (ibid., p. 79). Pert quotes neurochemist Miles Herkenham as saying that less than 2 percent of neuronal communication occurs at the synapse (ibid., p. 139). We cannot, however, see most of this communication if we study just the nervous system, which by definition only includes synaptic connections. To account for the patterns constituted by these chemical exchanges we have to think in terms of a single unified system that includes the nervous system, the endocrine system and the immune system (i.e., the spleen, bone marrow, and lymph nodes).

From this perspective, it becomes possible to give concrete physiological detail to William James's proposition that emotions exist in the body, not in the brain. James saw emotions as analyzable into a constellation of particular physical feelings (James 1890, pp. 443–449). Apparently the release of a particular neuropeptide can produce a particular set of sensations in certain organs and muscles due to the existence of receptors in their cells, and that specific neuropeptide is released when certain emotions are felt. Norepinephrine, for example, is released from the locus coeruleus in the hindbrain, and when that region of the brain is electrically stimulated it produces strong sensations of pleasure in rats and humans (ibid., p. 138). If every cell in the body contains different amounts of different kinds of receptors for each ligand, and a different ligand (or combination of ligands) is released for each emotion, it would be reasonable to say that this chemical exchange of information embodied that emotion. This would mean that emotions as a class of mental phenomena would actually exist in the body, not in the brain. To say that one felt a certain emotion would mean not that one was in a certain brain state, but that the cells distributed throughout one's body had received the particular dosage of ligands that was responsible for that emotion. This would have concrete practical implications if it were true. It could mean, for example, that the best way of treating emotional disturbance would not be to send ideas up to the brain by talking to the patient. Rather one might have to do some kind of work directly on the body, as do the therapies of Wilhelm Reich and Alexander Lowen. Massage, for example, could stimulate the tissues in such a way as to cause the release of the neuropeptides whose excess binding to the cells was causing emotional trauma. (Whether these therapies, or any others, are actually doing the right sort of work that actually gets results is, of course, another very empirical question.) Nor can we assume that we can neatly divide thought and emotions, putting one in the brain and the other in the body. Damasio (1994) gives plenty of evidence that the loss of emotional sensitivity that results from damage in the prefrontal cortex produces serious cognitive impairment, and the prefrontal cortex's importance for emotions probably stems largely from the connections that exist between it and the body via neuropeptide receptors and ligands.

What would the mind be identical with if the body was filled with cognitive activity occurring in several different systems simultaneously? The most dramatic result of such a discovery would be the transmutation of many of the most fundamental concepts that underlie both science and common sense. Thought, cognition, and consciousness have traditionally been assumed to be synonymous, or at least coextensive. The assumption that we are conscious because we think dates back even before Descartes to Aristotle's definition of man as a rational animal, and the development of computers has strengthened our assumption that all thinking is in some sense cognitive or computational. But there is no reason to assume that these ideas will remain inseparable forever. We might end up concluding that there is a distinctive kind of functional noncognitive activity that is consciousness (see Jackendoff 1987). There may also be activities our bodies perform that resemble what we call cognition in a computer that have nothing to do with consciousness, which might prompt us to conclude that the large amount of cognitive activity in the brain no longer grants it the right to be seen as identical with the mind. The immune system, with its sophisticated ability to recognize, remember, and classify different kinds of viruses and molecules, could be seen as performing functions that use chemicals cognitively. And Searle (1990) has pointed out that even the stomach could be seen as a cognitive system, given its ability to make sophisticated distinctions between what should be digested and what should be excreted (a point that Searle, with his usual stunted genius, uses as an excuse to retreat to common sense rather than to provide a basis for a new theory). Is the mind identical with consciousness or with cognition, given that the two might be separate? The data may force us to ask these questions, and the presuppositions that science has adapted from common sense could hinder our ability to answer them.

To say, however, that we can separate the inner processes of an organism into those that constitute consciousness and those that are only biological is to assume that we have a definable distinction between *consciousness* and *life*, and this is far from obvious.[1] It makes sense to assume, given what scientific research has discovered, that sea slugs probably are not conscious in the sense that we are conscious. This is part of what we mean by consciousness, and any definition that claimed otherwise would bear so little relationship to our current understanding of the concept that we would really be defining something else. But this does not require positing that we became conscious because we evolved one organ or system of organs that embodies consciousness, and that bestraddles several other organic systems that are "only" alive and not conscious at all. It could be that we became conscious by acquiring more sophisticated versions of many different faculties that sea slugs also have, and that the transition to consciousness through evolutionary history was gradual and decentralized. As Dennett puts it, "Since selves and minds and even consciousness itself are biological products (not elements to be found in the periodic table of chemistry), we should expect that the transitions between them and the phenomena that are not them should be gradual, contentious, gerrymandered" (1991, p. 421).

Is Causation Different from Embodiment?

One way of rescuing the mind–nervous system identity might be to say that these various hormonal activities may *cause* mental states, but they do not *embody* mental states. If we want to explain the condition of the unfortunate woman who lost her spinal chord but could still feel pain, we need not claim that the hormones floating in her system *are* the pain. We need only say that they floated through her extra cellular fluid until they made causal contact with her pituitary and then her pituitary caused some neural activity (which *is* the pain). Similarly, for Pert's data we can say that the angiotension in the kidneys caused a change in the limbic neurons, and the resulting neural activity *is* the pain. In any attempted counterexample, we can easily draw a distinction between the nonneural activity that causes mental states, and the neural activity that embodies them. The mind–nervous system identity thus appears to be completely safe from any critique of this sort.

This unassailability should be viewed with deep suspicion, however, because in this case it is produced only by dogmatic and arbitrary proclamation. I cannot imagine any way that this distinction could ever be confirmed or refuted, because everything we know about the nervous system is gathered by establishing causal relationships between neural states and mental states. Some argue that the mind–brain identity theory is not supported by all of these causal correlations, because, in the words of Shaffer, "For one property to be reducible to another, they must be different; something cannot be reducible to itself" (Borst 1970, p. 120). This was one of the reasons that many philosophers of mind describe the relationship between mind and brain with the technical term *supervenience* (which will be discussed at greater length in chapter 5). But even if we gloss over this problem, we still have another serious dilemma once we acknowledge that there are significant correlations between mental states and nonneural physical states. We know that damaging Broca's area causes aphasia, so we assume that this part of the brain partly embodies our ability to speak. If we learn that angiotension traveling from the kidneys to the limbic system causes thirst, why assume that only half of that process embodies the thirst, and the other half "merely" caused it? In fact why not use this same argument to save the mind–brain identity: we could say that the rest of the nervous system causes mental activity, but only the cranial neurons embody it. But why stop there? Why not say that most of the brain only causes mental activity, but that there is a small part of the brain that actually embodies consciousness, such as the cortex or the pineal gland? Do we really want to return to this kind of dogmatic Cartesian materialism on the basis of such arbitrary foundations? For that matter, as Rob Wilson (2001) rightly points out, we could use the same kind of reasoning to say that a single neuron could embody almost any mental state that it helped to cause. How can we choose any of these alternatives over the others except to claim that one of them (somehow) satisfies our "intuitions"?

One could try to dispose of this problem with a reductio ad absurdum. If we abandon the mind–brain identity theory, what would stop us from saying such counterintuitive things as "Because the tree I am observing outside my window is causally connected to my psychological state, my mind is partially instantiated by that tree"? But there are far more arguments for biting such a bullet than one might first suppose. Such a conclusion would not be resisted by Berkeley, Kant, the psychological tradition stemming from Soviet activity theory, or the philosophical traditions of Hinduism and Buddhism. And J. J. Gibson, a controversial but still respected psychologist, had a theory of perception that required the moving of mental embodiment not only outside the nervous system, but completely outside the skin.

If J. J. Gibson's theory of perception is correct, our visual experience is embodied not only by the nervous system, but also by the patterns of light of the perceiver's environment. Gibson attacked the idea that "Perception is supposed to be based on sensation" (Gibson 1955). He figured that because there was so much information in the array of light in our environment, there was no reason that every bit of that information had to have an analog as a sensation in the brain. He claimed that if there is no such analog, we could think of the perception as "direct," because the sensation wasn't getting between the stimulus and the perceiver. Consequently, Gibson claimed that as far as perceiving the outside world was concerned, we could "dispense entirely with the concept of sensation" (ibid.). He did qualify this bold claim by admitting that the concept of sensation could be useful for studying certain phenomena such as visual afterimages. But he considered these phenomena to be "a psychological curiosity" (ibid.) not a fundamental component of those perceptual processes that make us aware of the world.

Because Gibson discovered so much information about the environment in the light itself, he thought this proved something like the radical anti-mentalism that Skinner and Ryle advocated. To some degree it does, if we see mentalism as being necessarily brain centered. But few of Gibson's contemporary admirers agree that locating the embodiment of perceptual experience partly outside the brain requires us to assume that neurological activity is irrelevant to perception (see Millikan unpublished; and Kelso 1995, p. 188). A more sensible interpretation of Gibson's position was paraphrased from one of his lectures by U. T. Place. Place saw Gibson's theory as a rejection of "the Gestalt theory of isomorphism insofar as it implies that in order for perception to be veridical, an accurate reproduction of the stimulus environment must be constructed in the cortex from the input arriving at the cortex from the retina" (Place and Gibson 1999). Perhaps this is not an accurate summation of Gestalt theory, but it is a perfect description of what I call Cartesian materialism. Because Gibson did not object to this paraphrase in his correspondence with Place, Gibson is apparently rejecting Cartesian materialism, saying instead that the brain does not need to make a reproduction of a stimulus in order for us to be aware of it. *But if the brain does not record certain features of a perception that the mind is nevertheless aware of, this must mean that the mind is not identical with the brain.*

Let us consider a thought experiment analogous to the one at the end of chapter 2. Suppose some neuroscientists of the future are studying the brain activity that occurs when a laboratory subject has two distinctly different phenomenal experiences, such as seeing two slightly different shades of green. The shades have been identified as being spectrally different from each other and the subject correctly identifies each of them when they are presented to her. However, a thorough brain scan reveals that there are no differences in brain activity that can account for her ability to make the distinction. Does this mean that she must have made the distinction by means of some psychic power? Only if we assume that embodiment stops at the skin. But if the differences are captured in the light array, which is every bit as physical as the brain, and we accept that the light array partly embodies the sensations, then no psychic powers are necessary.

Many of the tensions in Gibson's theorizing could be resolved if he saw the mind as a field of activity, some but not all being neurological, that radiates out from the organism into its environment. This is an effective alternative to the assumption that the mind is a machine (or ghost) controlling the body from inside the skull, without the radical antimentalism that creates so much resistance to Gibson's theories. It would also save him from a kind of phenomenalism that sometimes seems to be implied by his talk of the visual field. Sometimes Gibson is willing to see only the light in the perceptual field as embodying perception. But whenever he is criticized for this by U. T. Place, he is very quick to say that the perceptual field is not separable from the world, and that it is the world, not just the light, that is responsible for our perceptions. It is, however, extremely difficult to distinguish between this kind of causal responsibility and full-blooded embodiment, for reasons we will discuss in chapter 4.

In the next few chapters I will show how we can draw a principled line between causation and embodiment, even though it may not always be a sharp one. To do this, however, I need to take what may appear to be a lengthy digression from philosophy of mind into the metaphysics of causality, and then into epistemology. But although this digression may seem to be off the point at first, I believe that it is the only thing that can save us from going around in circles within the confines of a single so-called "specialty."

Specialization of subject matter, although often a good strategy for scientists, is usually a terrible strategy for philosophers. The thing that gives a philosophical inquiry focus, and saves the philosopher from the epistemic sin of dilettantism, is not concentration on a *subject matter*, but concentration on a *problem*. Philosophical dead-ends almost always arise when philosophers try to resolve a paradox on its own terms, rather than question the presuppositions that make the paradox seem unavoidable. Assuming that philosophy of consciousness is a self-contained subject will probably ensure that its problems generate journal articles until everyone gets tired of getting nowhere and starts thinking about something else. But if we start asking ourselves what other philosophical assumptions give rise to the key problems of philosophy of mind, we may be able to come up with a different ontology or epistemology or metaphysics that could help dissolve them. Questioning philosophical presuppositions with a specific problem in mind (i.e., what sort of metaphysics would give us a coherent philosophy of mind) is very different from simply doing metaphysics. Focusing on the assumptions that create problems for philosophy of mind reveals one particular kind of cash value for these assumptions, and this gives us a concrete reason for preferring one metaphysics over another.

Currently the most talked about problem of mind is the problem of consciousness, which David Chalmers calls *the hard problem*, and which gives rise to what is called *the zombie problem*. Some sort of confusion is certainly the cause of paradoxes like the zombie problem, but we need to keep an open mind as to where the confusion begins. Many philosophers feel that the zombie problem is nothing but talk, and talk that rests on obviously confused presuppositions. There is some justice to this claim, for many of the arguments that describe the zombie problem are based on unjustified presuppositions. There are, however, other unjustified presuppositions that have not been questioned by either side of this debate, that make the problem seem both less real and less important than it actually is.

The most crucial of these is that there is a clear-cut line between what causes conscious experience and what embodies it, and that the line can be drawn at the borders of the brain. Note that this distinction between causation and embodiment is significantly different from the distinction between functional and epiphenomenal discussed in chapter 1. All functional properties are causal, and it is the study of those causal properties that perform mental functions that is the subject matter of psychology and other cognitive sciences. But not all causal properties are functional. The fact that a brain or a person could cause a horse to trip if either were placed in the middle of a racetrack has no functional significance for scientific research, even though it is a genuine causal property. Even among causal properties that are functional, not all of them are considered deserving of the honorific of "embodiment." This much of the common wisdom I accept, to some degree. But I also maintain that to say a mind must be embodied only by the brain of an organism is a hangover from a justly discredited epistemology that builds its foundation on atomism and sense-datum theory. Those who join me in rejecting these two closely related dogmas will find themselves having to bite a variety of other bullets if they wish to remain consistent.

Perhaps the toughest of these bullets is that the zombie problem becomes not only real, but scientifically important. It then become necessary to formulate an epistemology that explains why the zombie problem seems so inescapable. Briefly, my explanation goes like this: If no theories seem to be capable of accounting for conscious experience, this probably means that there is something inherent in our assumptions about theories that divorces theories from conscious experience. To consider the possibility of an explanation for consciousness, without also calling into question our conception of an explanation, is going to go nowhere if our concept of explanation is designed to exclude conscious experience. That is why the hard problem will always remain not just hard, but impossible.

But in an attempt to assure my reader that the next few chapters will be on track, I have gotten ahead of my story. If it is not yet obvious why the hard problem cannot be solved by the most popular skeptical dismissals, it might not be obvious why my explanation is even necessary. So let us begin in the next chapter with a reanalysis of the concept of causality, and see where it takes us.

4 Causation and Embodiment

John Stuart Mill made two very important criticisms of the commonsense idea of causality. These criticisms seem so justified that, once one hears them, it seems incredible that anyone has ever believed otherwise. But these aspects that Mill was criticizing are so deeply ingrained that almost no one, including Mill himself, has ever completely escaped them.

Mill's Criticism of Atomistic Causality

The first commonsense mistake about causality is the idea that a single cause produces a single effect all by itself. Mill was not willing to completely let go of this possibility for he said that such a thing happens "seldom, if ever" (Mill 1851, bk. 3, ch. 5, sec. 3, p. 214). But his arguments seem to make the idea of a single cause being responsible for an effect to be almost inconceivable. He acknowledged that people often make a distinction between a *cause*, which supposedly takes an active role in bringing the event about, and the *conditions*, which supposedly take a somehow humbler role in the whole process. But Mill argued that this distinction was spurious: "The real cause is the whole of these antecedents; and we have, philosophically speaking, no right to give the name of cause to one of them exclusively of the others" (ibid.).

Mill gives numerous examples to illustrate the arbitrariness of the distinction between cause and conditions, and anyone can, with a little reflection, come up with several more. When the chairman of a legislative assembly casts the final vote that passes a law, we sometimes say that this is what caused the law to pass. But his vote had no more or less effect than that of any other legislator. If someone takes poison, we say it was the poison that caused his death, even though the fact that this person had a certain kind of digestive system was equally responsible for his death. But if Faust and Mephistopheles both drank the same poison, and Faust died but Mephistopheles did not, we would say that Faust's having a body with a digestive system was what killed him. These and numerous other examples prompted Mill to reach the following conclusion: "Nothing can better show the absence of any scientific ground for the distinction between cause of a phenomenon and its conditions, than the capricious manner in which we select from among the conditions that which we choose to denominate the cause" (ibid., p. 215).

I think this claim is a bit stronger than it needs to be, for we need not think of a distinction as being capricious merely because it is not intrinsic. The distinction is a pragmatic one, which means that, although it will shift depending upon our goals and projects, it doesn't shift completely capriciously. To emphasize this fact, I would like to rename Mill's distinction. What Mill refers to as the popular or vulgar idea of a cause[1] I will call a *pragmatic cause*. What Mill calls the conditions I will refer to as the *compleat cause*.[2] When we use the word "cause" in ordinary language, we essentially always mean pragmatic cause. Mill is quite right to point out the hopelessness of ever making a hard and fast distinction between the pragmatic cause and the rest of the causal nexus, which is the compleat cause. There are, however, a few rough rules that usually govern the pragmatic usage of the word "cause." Two that spring to mind are the following. We usually use the term "cause" to refer to:

(1) The causal factor that changed most recently. We say that the match caused the explosion. But of course we admit when pressed that the striking of the match by itself didn't cause the explosion. The presence of the oxygen also caused the explosion, as did the presence of the gunpowder, the desire for a united Ireland, and so forth. But presumably, the oxygen, the gunpowder, and the desire for a united Ireland were in existence for some time prior to the explosion. The match was the most recently introduced factor, and therefore it is referred to as *the* cause. Emphasizing this aspect of causality makes it appear that we can distinguish clearly between *states* and *events*, and say that only events can be causes. This is what makes the presence of things like the gunpowder and the oxygen seem to be not really causes, and enable us to speak of the match as the cause. Mill gives several detailed examples showing why this distinction will not stand up to careful scrutiny, and his arguments are, I believe, completely sound. Without the oxygen, the explosion would not have happened, so we cannot place the entire causal burden on the match. But because we rarely subject this distinction to this kind of scrutiny, it remains an important one pragmatically. The main reason that the state–event distinction is important is that it helps us to zero in on:

(2) Which factor we have most chance of controlling. In many cases, this factor will be the one most vulnerable to change, which usually means we ourselves have some possibility of making it change.[3] When it was discovered that mosquitoes (biting people) caused malaria, the fact that malaria could exist only if people had a certain kind of circulatory system was irrelevant, because there was no known way of changing people's circulatory system. There were, however, ways of getting rid of mosquitoes, so once their part in the coming to existence of malaria was discovered, the cry went out that we now knew what caused malaria.

We can thus see that although the way we choose to distinguish the pragmatic cause from the rest of the compleat cause will shift dramatically, this shifting is not unprincipled. It is based on what we are trying to understand, and/or trying to control. When we say that the explosion was caused by the striking of the match, that may be very useful in certain contexts, such as a physics class. But if we are trying to understand why an explosion occurred in Belfast, no one would be satisfied if a political commentator appeared on the BBC and told everyone that it occurred because someone lit a match. What interests us in that context are the political causes of the action, not the physical ones. On the other hand, if the IRA had been without explosives for several weeks, and then recently acquired some gunpowder, it would make sense to say that the explosion was caused by (the acquisition of) the gunpowder. If the explosion had been detonated on the moon, it might have been that the astronaut's carefully timed release of oxygen near a heating element could have been the pragmatic cause of the explosion, and so on. Only one part of the entire network of conditions that is "compleat-ly" responsible for the event is singled out as the pragmatic cause, and which part is chosen for this honor is completely dependent on the projects and priorities of the person and/or community observing and/or interacting with it.

One such project is neuroscience. For those who do neuroscience, it is highly effective to assume that brain events are "the" cause of mental events. There is overwhelming empirical evidence that whenever a mental event occurs, something happens in the brain. Conversely, when something happens to the brain, it frequently[4] has an effect on the mental events of the person who possesses that brain. The omnipresence of these reciprocal causal connections has prompted the natural assumption that the mind is the brain. But that assumption works only if we assume that the pragmatic cause is the same as the compleat cause. Because of these numerous causal connections, neuroscience has become the science that studies what happens in the brain when we think and feel. Because common sense assumes that the pragmatic cause is the compleat cause, it also assumes that the effectiveness of the neurological designation of brain events as "the cause" of mental events must prove that the mind is identical to, or is embodied by, the brain. But we cannot assume that only those physical events that occur in the brain have the right to these honorific titles of "identity" and "embodiment," merely because singling brain events out from the entire causal nexus is the fundamental strategy for doing neuroscience.

The goal of neuroscience is to discover the brain events that participate in the causal nexus responsible for mental events. Because there are many crucial things happening in the brain every time we feel or think, neuroscience naturally assumes that brain activity is the sole cause of mentality. There is no denying that this is a very useful assumption for doing neuroscience. But this does not prove it is a metaphysical fact that the mind is the brain, and that therefore all other forms of inquiry should accept this assumption as true. Psychology studies the relationship between behavior and mentality. Artificial intelligence studies aspects of thought that could be realized in a variety of different physical substrates. Linguistics studies language, which necessarily has an intentional relationship with things outside the brain. (For a thought or a sentence to be about Paris, it has to have some sort of relationship with Paris, not just with neurons in a skull.) The fact that all of these disciplines are now recognized as contributing to our understanding of the mind indicates that we can no longer understand the mind by merely understanding the brain. All of these sciences have recently been using information about the brain to varying degrees. But they use it by relating brain activity to behavior, language, and so forth. They do not study the brain's "intrinsic causal powers" (a concept I will critique more thoroughly later on in this chapter). These sciences study brain activity as one small part of a nexus of relations between brain, body, and world.

There was a time when many eliminativist philosophers and scientists thought that neuroscience could simply replace psychology and the other sciences of the mind. But now even Pat Churchland believes that the various disciplines of cognitive science will coevolve, rather than be eliminated by or reduced to neuroscience (Churchland 1986, p. 362). However, there seems to be relatively little awareness of an important implication of this fact. For if we cannot understand the mind without referring to extraneurological factors like behavior and reference, why are we still so sure that the mind is identical to the brain? Wouldn't it be more appropriate to assume that the mind emerges from *all* of the various causal factors in the brain, body, and world that produce mental events?

The Lure of Atomistic Causality

There are many assumptions within the British empiricist tradition that imply that the pragmatic cause is usually the same as the compleat cause, and these assumptions are often taken for granted by many practicing scientists. If our knowledge consisted of aggregates of what Hume called simple ideas, a single factor, describable by a single sentence, could be entirely responsible for an events taking place. These two sentences from Wittgenstein's *Tractatus* probably state this atomistic metaphysics most explicitly.

1.2 The world divides into facts.
1.21 Anyone can be the case or not be the case, and everything else remains the same.

Wittgenstein himself, like Hume before him, concluded that this view of reality implies that causal explanations are actually illusory (*Tractatus*, par. 6.371) But the common sense accepted by most practicing scientists glosses over the mystery of this connection. For those who accept the assumption that such connections are knowable, it seems plausible that a single fact about a single event produces a causal relationship with another single event, and that this connection could be completely independent from any other fact in the universe. If it turned out that, in some cases, two or more events were necessary to cause a certain kind of effect, it would also be plausible that, in most cases, it would be an easy matter to enumerate those facts as well. Mill himself came from this empiricist tradition, and was never able to completely free himself from it, despite his numerous arguments against the distinction between causes and conditions. In fact, once he starts talking in some detail about scientific method, he inexplicably begins to assume that the goal of science is to discover the single cause that is totally responsible for each effect.

We have thus far treated plurality of causes as only a possible supposition which, until removed, renders our inductions uncertain, and have only considered by what means, where the plurality does not really exist, we may be enabled to disprove it. (Mill 1851, bk. 3, ch. 5, p. 288)

Needless to say, the expression "thus far" does not refer to the section fifty pages earlier, quoted above. At that point, he was arguing that *every* effect is dependent on a plurality of causes, and that there is no meaningful way of asserting that one of those causes is *the* cause. Now he is speaking of a "plurality of causes as only a possible supposition," which it is the goal of science to disprove. He admits later on in this passage that under certain circumstances an event can have two or more causes. But this is a far cry from the vast network of causal conditions described earlier. Even effects with only two or three causes are here described as merely anomalies, for Mill adds that "When an effect is really producible by two or more causes, the process for detecting them is in no way different from that by which we discover single causes" (ibid.). Here Mill seems to be saying that in a few annoying cases, an event can have "two or more causes," but the norm is that each event has only a single cause. How can we reconcile this view of causality with Mill's denial (only fifty pages earlier) of the distinction between causes and the vast network of conditions they depend upon?

This kind of double vision about causality is not unique to Mill by any means. It has, in fact, become so much a part of our philosophical consensus that it is taught in countless logic and critical thinking classes. The most widely used logic text in American colleges, Hurley's *A Concise Introduction to Logic*, contains a chapter that paraphrases Mill's theory of causality for the benefit of undergraduate Logic and Critical Thinking students. In this chapter, Hurley does speak briefly about the necessity for background conditions of any cause. But he then gives several examples of individual causes that are supposedly completely responsible for their effects—and none of them works. He says, for example, that "When we say that taking a swim on a hot summer day will cause us to cool off, we mean that the dip itself *will* do the job" (Hurley 2000, p. 505). But it will not do the job unless a literally infinite number of background conditions remain in place. It will not cool me off if I have a skin condition that is aggravated by exposure to water, or if there is a forest fire surrounding the pool, or if the earth falls out of its orbit and careens into the sun.

There is an understandable reason why Mill, Hurley, and almost everyone else feels a strong commitment to the idea that a single cause is sufficient to produce an effect. It seems that this assumption is essential for science to be possible at all. Leibniz referred to this assumption as the Principle of Sufficient Reason. It may seem that denying this principle is tantamount to saying that the universe is completely incomprehensible, even in principle. This is why Mill naturally assumed that his "Methods of Agreement and Difference" (ibid., bk. 3, ch. 8) imply that the goal of scientific inquiry is to isolate the single cause of any given effect.[5] The Method of Difference works like this: consider two groups of mice from the same litter raised in identical conditions, except that one group is painted with extract of tobacco. Because the only difference between the experimental and control groups is the extract of tobacco, doesn't the fact that the experimental group gets cancer prove that the tobacco is *the* cause of the cancer? The Method of Agreement also seems to imply single discrete cause–effect relations. To use Hurley's example: suppose twelve people eat at the same restaurant, five of them get sick, and all five of those people (and none of the others) ate the fish. Doesn't this prove that eating the fish was *the* cause of their sickness?

What evidence like this actually proves is something a bit more cautious, and fully in harmony with Mill's original claim that causes cannot be separated from their context of conditions. As Nagel rightly puts it, "Both theoretical and experimental science proceed on the assumption that everything is not relevant to everything else, and occurrences in one part of the world are not dependent upon what happens everywhere else" (Nagel 1961, p. 323). In other words, what science must assume is that every event has a nexus of responsibility that caused it to occur, and that an event outside of that nexus did not cause the event to occur. We can (and must) salvage a weaker version of Leibniz's principle by stating it in the negative: Even though there is never one cause for something, there is also never anything that happens for no reason whatsoever. It is perhaps the fundamental assumption of all human inquiry that we will find a pragmatic cause for anything we encounter. Uncovering one such cause is the first step toward the unattainable goal of completely revealing the compleat causal network that is responsible for that event's taking place.

If we were going to list all the events and circumstances that "compleat-ly" caused a particular explosion in Ireland, the list would probably be so long that we could never finish writing it, and it would include elements that no one ever would or could know about. But the fact that someone ate three mouthfuls of rice in Singapore two weeks earlier would probably not be on that list, and neither would millions of other facts too numerous to mention. Even though certain interpretations of chaos theory might even include things as surprising as those three mouthfuls of rice in the causal nexus of an Irish explosion, there would still probably be some border where the nexus of responsibility would stop.[6] In a completely deterministic universe, the border would be sharp and precise. In a probabilistic universe, the border would be as blurry as that universe was probabilistic. How wide those borders extend, and how blurry they are, is an empirical question in each case, although fully answering such questions is almost certainly beyond our capabilities.

But—and here is the punchline—the causal nexus that is responsible for the experiences of a conscious being is *not* contained entirely within the brain of that being. Because a heck of a lot of stuff that participates in the causation of consciousness happens in the brain, brain activity seems to be the most likely candidate for the title of *the* cause of consciousness. And so it would be—if there were such a title. But the idea that there is a single winner in the race for this title is a presupposition of atomism that is no longer tenable. The concept of the single pragmatic cause is merely a heuristic device that helps us in attaining control of the world. But for that reason it is dependent on what goal we have set for ourselves; what we want the control for. That distinction has nothing to do with what brings consciousness into being, for everything in the causal nexus of a conscious state is responsible for that conscious state coming into being.

But, you may protest, surely we don't want to say that the mind is identical with the entire causal network that brought it into being? Don't we want to make a distinction between what causes a mental state and what embodies it? Even if we do not accept atomistic causality, don't we have to say that the brain possesses certain *intrinsic causal powers* that enable it to embody mental states, and not just cause them? Otherwise, how can we avoid claiming that a person is embodied by things like the big bang, or the assassin's bullet that failed to kill her parents? In chapter 6 I will present my alternative answer to that question. But first let's take a closer look at the many problems with the assumption that the brain can possess intrinsic causal powers.

Mill's Criticism (and the Modern Defense) of Intrinsic Causal Powers

Although the prevalence of this kind of atomism is one of the strongest reasons that Cartesian materialism remains so popular, it is not the only possible defense for it. One could acknowledge that causality always includes a network of causes but claim that the borders of that network are the brain. This view of causality holds that certain systems possess what are sometimes called *intrinsic causal powers*. If we accept this view of causality, it seems plausible that the brain is a system with the intrinsic causal power of producing mental states. In his *Psychosemantics*, Fodor claims that it is impossible to do psychology scientifically unless we assume that "causal powers . . . in the psychological case . . . supervene on local neural structure. We abandon this principle at our peril; mind/brain supervenience(/identity) is our only plausible account of how mental states could have the causal powers that they do have" (Fodor 1987, p. 44). Fodor claims that these kinds of assumptions are inherent in the very concept of science itself; that science must operate by classifying things into natural kinds, each of which possesses intrinsic causal powers.

The concept of intrinsic causal powers does appear to make sense if one focuses exclusively on certain examples: knives really do seem to possess sharpness, and gunpowder does seem to be intrinsically explosive. It thus seems natural to assume that there is a clear distinction between intrinsic causal powers, which somehow inhere or are predicable to the objects described by natural kind terms, and the extrinsic causes that push the buttons that release those powers. This concept enables us to see causal powers as attributes of objects, and to see the universe as a network of objects interacting with each other. According to this view, when an object encounters other objects, they will both release each other's intrinsic causal powers, rather like the way bump cars at an amusement park will ring the bells in their bumpers when they collide. This distinction is also what makes the distinction between cause and effect work. When object A activates one of its causal powers, it has the effect of releasing the causal powers of B, which in turn have an effect on A or C or whatever and so on with each effect becoming a cause for the next effect in the chain.

This distinction works pretty well in many of the sciences and in common sense. It may, in fact, be a distinction that is wired into our cognitive processes. But that does not mean that we should do as Colin McGinn did, and elevate it to a metaphysical principle.[7] There is no reason to assume that, just because this distinction is often useful to us, it therefore reflects something intrinsic about the world independent of all of our concerns and projects. A nexus of causes is just a nexus of causes, and all of them are equally responsible for the events occurring regardless of which ones we think of as being internal or external. The explosion is every bit as dependent upon the oxygen as it is on the match, despite our tendency to take the oxygen for granted. Causal properties are fundamentally relations, not monadic predicates, and sometimes the simplification that enables us to refer to them as intrinsic powers is not going to be useful. We say that an object has a certain causal power because there are so many different situations in which it will produce a certain effect. Knives are considered to be intrinsically sharp because they can participate in butter-cutting events, paper-cutting events, wood-cutting events, and so forth. But exactly how many such situations do there have to be before we should ascribe the causal power to the object rather than to the situation as a networked whole? There is no reason we should assume that there is always (or ever) a single metaphysically correct answer to that question.

Mill was fully aware of both the wide acceptance and the limitations of the concept of intrinsic causal powers. He pointed out that we usually divide a causal relationship into a cause, which is assumed to be the *agent*, and an effect, which is assumed to be the *patient*. Even with the most ordinary physical causes, "we might say that the stone moves towards the earth by the properties of the matter composing it" or that the cause is "the weight or gravitation of the stone" (1851, p. 219). Mill, however, did not accept this distinction:

Even those attributes of an object which might seem with greatest propriety to be called states of the object itself, its sensible qualities, its color, its hardness, shape, and the like, are in reality phenomena of causation. . . . What we call states of objects are always sequences into which the objects enter. . . . This capacity is not a real thing existing in the objects; it is but a name for our conviction that they will act in a particular manner when certain new circumstances arise. (Ibid., pp. 219, 221)

It seems to me that Mill is clearly right about this, and several contemporary philosophers have raised objections to Fodor's concept of intrinsic causal powers that are very similar to Mill's objections. Burge (1986), Wilson (1995), and Baker (1995) argued against Fodor's claims in *Psychosemantics* by offering examples of actual laws, in both psychology and other sciences, that used properties that are relational rather than intrinsic. When one is uncovering causal connections in scientific research, some of them end up not being attributable to any particular object. Most of chapter 2 in Wilson 1995 consists of examples of scientific causal laws that are irreducibly relational. Wilson's argument against Fodor is relatively cautious. He does not claim that there are no intrinsic causal powers. He only wants to argue that at least some causal properties are relational properties, rather than intrinsic properties of objects. I think, however, that even if science must frequently refer to objects with causal powers, this requires us to assume only that *any given scientific specialty* must refer to intrinsic causal powers. When we use the terminology of a different specialty, we usually redefine the object in one science as a system of relations in another. A chemist, for example, may refer to the intrinsic causal properties of sulfur or magnesium. But a particle physicist will see those intrinsic chemical properties as being relations between subatomic particles.

In other words, the borderline between objects and relations will shift depending on what one is talking about. The only way that one can actually *explain* an object's "intrinsic" causal powers (rather than merely describe or refer to them) is to analyze the object into its parts, and then talk about the relations between the parts. To say that certain properties are intrinsic is simply to say that for the moment we are going to refrain from analyzing them. Because discourse has to start somewhere, every science will have to talk about entities with intrinsic causal powers, and such talk will describe the relations between those entities. (As Wilson points out, sometimes those relations will be seen as having causal properties of their own.) But this doesn't eliminate the possibility (or the necessity) of another scientific specialty redescribing these "fundamental" entities by analyzing them into relations among other "fundamental" entities.

Nor is downward analysis the only way to shift the definition of what is intrinsic. To see an object as possessing intrinsic causal powers is to see it as an autonomous closed system of relations that interacts with other autonomous systems. Unfortunately, this idea contains an inherent contradiction, because once an "autonomous" system interacts with another "autonomous" system, the two systems are no longer genuinely autonomous. Instead they become parts of a larger system that could be seen as a unified whole with "intrinsic" causal powers of its own. Because there are many different ways that parts can be assembled into wholes, or wholes analyzed into parts, each science designates different entities as possessing so-called intrinsic causal powers.

In a materialist ontology, the one science that has the strongest claim to an understanding of intrinsic causal powers is physics. It was once widely assumed that an orthodox materialist had to believe that the only real properties were intrinsic causal properties of fundamental physical particles. But two great materialist philosophers, Ernst Nagel and Bertrand Russell, eventually reached conclusions that implied that intrinsic causal powers are not necessary for physical science. These conclusions were not aimed specifically at the idea of causal powers, but rather at the concept of causality itself. They argued that causality was a commonsense concept that had to be radically revised, and sometimes even dispensed with, for us to be truly scientific. But the revisions they proposed left no room for the concept of intrinsic causal powers. For there to be such powers, there must be some sense in which the cause has power over its effect and is distinct from it. Supposedly, the cause resides in the object, and the effect is the impact that the cause has on the outside world. But if the cause and the effect are equally dependent on each other, we have a causal network, rather than a community of autonomous objects with intrinsic causal powers. This view of causality as a functionally interdependent network was essentially the view that Nagel and Russell ended up defending.

One of Ernst Nagel's greatest virtues as a philosopher of science was that he valued empirical accuracy over consistency. He saw his job as describing how scientists actually thought about science. If he found inconsistencies, he didn't feel it was his place to tell scientists how to do their job. Consequently, he was comfortable with the fact that scientists appear to have many different views of causality that could not be reduced to a single principle. Among those views, however, was one that essentially dissolved the distinction between a cause and its effect, and prompted Nagel to say that "A scientific explanation is often regarded as satisfactory even though the laws cited in the premise are not 'causal' in the ordinary sense" (Nagel 1961, p. 78). He described this relationship as "functional dependence (in the mathematical sense of 'function')" between two or more variable magnitudes associated with stated properties or processes" (ibid., p. 77). The Boyle–Charles law for ideal gases, for example, states the relationship that exists between the pressure, volume, and temperature of a gas. But it does not say anything about a temporal sequence that must occur for these factors to interact with each other, as a cause would precede its effect. Nor is any one of these factors seen as exerting power over the others; they are all equally interdependent. Dynamical laws, such as Galileo's law for freely falling bodies, "are not causal . . . for . . . the state of the system at a given time is determined as completely by a later state as by an earlier one" (ibid.). This view of scientific law as describing only functional dependence eliminates the concept of power altogether from scientific law, and describes everything in terms of relational, rather than intrinsic, properties.

Bertrand Russell claimed that causality was unnecessary, not just for some, but for all scientific laws. He described causality as "a relic of a bygone age, surviving, like the monarchy, only because it is erroneously supposed to do no harm" (Russell 1913, p. 1). He believed that "it is not in any sameness of causes and effects that the constancy of laws consists, but in sameness of relations" (ibid., p. 14), and that scientific laws "make no difference between past and future: the future 'determines' the past in exactly the same sense in which the past 'determines' the future" (ibid., p. 15). This view clearly leaves out any possibility of a cause having intrinsic powers that can compel the occurrence of an effect.

Fodor is probably correct when he claims that psychology and neuroscience assume that brains have the intrinsic causal power to produce mental states. But if physics doesn't need to refer to causal powers, it seems unlikely that this assumption is necessary. In fact, it may be an indication that these sciences have not freed themselves from the naïve Aristotlean assumptions of common sense to the same degree that physics has. If we assume, as Aristotle did, that biological science is only supposed to catalog dispositional properties, then it is true in some sense that the brain has the power to cause mental states. But it is also true in the same sense that opium has the power to cause sleep, and no one considers that to be a sufficient scientific explanation any more. It seems likely that the cognitive science of the future will dispense with this kind of talk about causal powers altogether, just as Nagel and Russell claim that physics has. This is especially likely if the next paradigm for cognitive science grows out of the dynamic systems theory that I describe in the last chapter of this book.

5 The Myth of the Autonomous Mind–Brain

Neuroscience does provide evidence that whatever else is present during a mental event, there must at least be *something* significant going on in a brain. This fact does seem to produce support for an argument that goes like this. "When I have an experience of a tree, both the tree and my brain states cause it. But if you replace the tree with a pink ice cube I will still have an experience. On the other hand, if you remove my brain and replace it with a pink ice cube, I won't have an experience. So that proves that the brain possesses the intrinsic power to produce mental states." Remember, however, that in chapter 2 I said that Cartesian materialism claims that for every experience or thought that we have, every shift in qualitative nuance or cognitive deliberation, there must be something in the brain *that is not only co-occurrent with it, but also robust and detailed enough to be entirely responsible for it.*

I don't deny the possibility that *some* of our experiences could be caused entirely by our brain, such as the experiences we would have if we were in a sensory deprivation tank. I could argue that even such experiences are still causally dependent on the interactions between the brain and the rest of the body. I could even argue that such experiences are still causally dependent on past interactions with the world. After all, we cannot temporarily shut out our experience of the world and think that this is the same as never having experienced a world. That would be like saying nothing caused a string to vibrate because nobody is plucking it right now.

But the only thing I need to claim is that, even if there are or could be times when the brain is having experiences without receiving stimuli from the outside world, at least some of our experiences would not be recreated even if all of the appropriate neural activity were duplicated. This seems to me to be a genuine scientifically discoverable possibility, which could end up being supported by many different kinds of data. It seems, for example, to be supported by Gibson's ecological theory of perception, which claims that the information that creates visual experiences is in the light, not in the brain (see chapter 3). If something like Gibson's theory of perception turns out to be correct, this would be scientific evidence that Cartesian materialism is false. One of the defining principles of Cartesian materialism is that if it doesn't happen inside the brain, it isn't experienced. And given that this is a possibility, it seems scientifically irresponsible to unquestionably accept that only neural events embody experience, and that all other events are mere causes of experience.

I would like to believe that, if there are any nonphilosophers reading this, at least some of them would think that this is so obvious that no one could believe otherwise. However, the idea that our brains are fully responsible for all of our conscious experiences actually passes for something like a necessary truth among most philosophers. This is usually justified by a thought experiment that is the materialist equivalent of Descartes's suggestion that an "evil genius" could be producing the illusion that an external world exists. In the Cartesian materialist version, a mad scientist is substituted for the evil genius, and Descartes's noncorporeal mind is replaced by a brain in a vat. To many philosophers it is intuitively obvious that if that brain in a vat was going through all of the physical changes that your brain would go through while watching a production of *Hamlet*, wearing a scratchy wool suit and eating popcorn, then the brain in the vat would have exactly the same experiences you would. In the real world, these brain events are caused by the actor playing Hamlet, the light bouncing off the actor and hitting your retina, the contact of the wool with your skin, and so on. In the thought experiment, they are caused either by chance, by miracles, or by an impressive array of bioelectric gizmos. But because the experience would allegedly be the same regardless of which set of causes produced the brain events, the gizmos and/or the external world merely cause the experience. The experience, however, is said to *supervene* on the brain events because they will produce the same experiences regardless of whatever causes them. Supervenience is a technical concept in philosophy that is both significantly similar to and significantly different from the concept of identity. It will be explained in some detail in the next section of this chapter. For the moment, the reader can assume (as Fodor does in the previous quote) that the word means basically the same thing as "identity." In other words, the claim here is that the mind is identical to the brain because a brain in a vat would have the same thoughts and experiences as a molecule-for-molecule identical brain in a human body.

There are three slightly different versions of the brain in a vat, none of which provides any real support for Cartesian materialism when properly clarified.

(1) The brain is sitting in a vat, and being causally triggered by a battery of bioelectric gizmos that are making it have worldlike experiences. This version appears plausible only if we assume that experience consists of the discrete particles of sense-datum theory. If we imagine those devices to be something like videotapes or electrodes, then it is easy to also imagine that we could stimulate a brain to have experiences of green tree-shaped patches. But what Dewey claimed, and what modern neuroscience appears to confirm, is that experience does not consist of discrete moments like frames in a film. Even when perception scientists show individual flash cards to subjects and have them report what each one looks like, the subjects do not experience those flash cards as genuinely discrete sense data. What they experience is being involved in an experiment, which requires them to look at certain things and follow certain instructions, which they find to be either boring or interesting or an important contribution to science. Even if the subject is a devout Humean empiricist and believes that she is experiencing sense data, her beliefs and mood are still there to provide the context for what she takes to be sense data.

If there can be no experience at all without extended interactions with the world that can last for minutes or even hours, then such interactions must be constituted by skillful and flexible responses to a world that has enduring physical laws. What would be required would be a device that responds to us, the way the world responds to us, and that we could learn to respond to skillfully because it created experiences that obeyed all the laws of science and common sense. What this means is that any device capable of creating world-experiences in a brain would have to be *informationally identical* to the world it was simulating in order to completely create those experiences. In other words, these devices would not be a simulation of a world, they would *be* a world, and would also have to throw in a simulation of a body somewhere if they were to complete the picture. This world-simulation system could be different from the so-called real

world in ways the brain could not detect, the way Putnam's XYZ is different from water. But it would still be every bit as ontologically robust, unless
you posited some sort of miracle to make up the difference. So in this case,
as in our own, experience would be an emergent property of a brain, body,
and world. The brain would not be creating those experiences all by itself.
We have merely created functional equivalents for the body and world
with silicon (or whatever); we have not dispensed with them. Dennett
makes a similar point in *Consciousness Explained* (1991, pp. 3–4), but settles
for the more modest claim that even if such a system of gizmos is possible in principle, it is almost certainly impossible in fact. My point is slightly
different: even if building such a system is possible, it would not prove
that the mind is identical to the brain. This is because the experiences
emerge not from the neural activity alone, but from the interaction
between the brain and the devices.

(2) Another version of this thought experiment requires no bioelectric
gizmos. It says that if the brain goes into the exact brain state of a person
having a particular experience through a miracle, the experience would be
the same as if it were caused by a world. In worlds where brains are made
of such wonder tissue, it may be the case that such brains could have experiences exactly like ours even without a world to stimulate them. But until
somebody travels to such a world and conducts the appropriate experiments, there is no way of knowing. It is far from obvious what the appropriate experiments would be, but even if that problem were solved we
would simply have to wait and see. Perhaps a brain in a vat would feel disembodied, even if all of the cranial activity ordinarily caused by embodiment were perfectly duplicated. Perhaps every single bit of the cranial
activity ordinarily produced by the sight of a tree produces only a pale
simulacrum of a tree experience, rather than the robust experience that
happens when a real tree is present. In a world where skulls are filled with
wonder tissue, there's no way of knowing what would happen until the
experiment was run, and no reason to assume that anything discovered in
such a world would be applicable to ours.

(3) James Garson suggested in correspondence that if we waited long
enough, brains could form into molecular duplicates of ours purely by
chance, without violating any physical laws. But the same objection would
still hold even if this is true. When and if this unlikely event happens, we
need to get that brain into a laboratory and make the appropriate tests

(assuming the idea of appropriate tests makes sense, which I don't neces-sarily grant). Only then can we determine whether or not such a brain is conscious. Having just written a book arguing that it wouldn't, my impulse is to say no. Other people, caught up in the throes of Cartesian material-ism, would probably say yes. But I don't see any reason why either set of intuitions would be any more useful in answering that question than in determining the chemical composition of the moons of Jupiter.

However, although one of the main themes of this chapter is that mind–brain identity is far more problematic than is usually assumed, I do not dispute the technical philosophical claim that minds *supervene* on something that is physical. What I am disputing is the claim that the brain is the complete "supervenience base" of the mind. "Supervenience" is a technical term used only by philosophers, with many refinements that are not essential to the points we are considering here. It is, however, a sig-nificantly different concept from either causation or identity, and needs to be explained in some detail to show why it does not necessarily support Cartesian materialism.

Supervenience, Causation, and Embodiment

The concept of supervenience is a scrupulously downsized technical term, with some similarities to both causation and identity, which apparently frees the mind–brain identity theory from a variety of philosophical prob-lems. It is usually communicated not with a specific definition, but with a thought experiment. Suppose that there were two people who were molecule-for-molecule identical with each other. Would not those two people have identical mental states? Most of us would say yes, but notice that this does not require many of the commitments that one ordinarily associates with identity. The two most important differences are the following:

(1) This thought experiment does not require that physical identity be *nec-essary* for mental identity. It requires only that such physical identity be *sufficient* for mental identity. In other words, accepting that this is true still leaves open the possibility that two beings who were physically different could be mentally identical; that is, one could in principle make a silicon duplicate of a protein human that was mentally identical to that protein human.

(2) This thought experiment commits us only to the claim that these two physical *individuals* are mentally identical. It does not commit us to the claim that any mental *properties* are identical to any physical properties. Philosophers usually express this fact by saying that we have token-identity in this case, but not type-identity.

Kim says that the concept of supervenience is a technical term with no significant roots in ordinary language, and that it therefore means pretty much whatever the philosophical community says it means (Kim 1993, p. 133). It was first used in ethics to describe the relationship between moral and natural properties, and Kim suggests that it might be useful in epistemology as a description of the relationship between theories and data (ibid., p. 56). What all of these relationships have in common is that they are dependencies that operate one way, and may or may not operate in another way. Identity is a relationship that implies supervenience, as does causality. But if a relationship is merely supervenient and nothing else, this means that what is supervenient is in some sense more dependent on that which it supervenes. In philosophy of mind, the claim that mental states supervene on brain states means that two physically identical brains have identical mental states, and there are no variations in mental states without some variation in brain states. But with causality and identity, the relationship always works the other way as well, and is specifiable by a specific predicate every time. If there was a mental state that was identical to a physical state, then the two would always go together. If there was a causal relationship between a physical state and a mental state, the two would always go together ceteris paribus. Because philosophical analysis and scientific research show that the relationship between the physical and the mental is more problematic than that, philosophers of mind have retreated to the more cautious supervenience relationship as a way of dealing with those problems while avoiding dualism.

Although I accept that supervenience is the minimum relationship that must exist between the physical and the mental, I do not agree with the current philosophical consensus as to what physical entities the mind supervenes on. I do think that we have good reason to believe that some sort of brain activity is *necessary* for any human mental state (and that Martian or robot mental states would require something that was functionally equivalent to brain activity). But I see no reason to believe that brain activity is *sufficient* to account for every mental state, and sufficiency is what defines supervenience. Both Kim and Fodor argue that mental states must supervene only on the intrinsic properties of brain states, because to spread the supervenience base to relations between the world and the brain would be to believe in something like magic. However, they stack the deck in favor of intrinsic neurological properties by their choice of examples of relational properties. Obviously, mental properties are not going to supervene on things like the brain's distance from the moon, or its being larger than a typewriter (Kim 1993, p. 178), or on properties possessed by the entire universe if a particular coin flip comes up heads instead of tails (Fodor 1987, p. 33). Examples like this obscure the undeniable fact that there are genuinely causal relations between mental states and physical non-brain-states. Our visual mental states, for example are caused not only by brain states, but by light rays, and the objects that bounce off them. And as I pointed out in the previous chapter, our best science often concludes that it is impossible to reduce all such relations to intrinsic powers. The brain dwells in a body, which in turn dwells in a world, and everything that happens to the brain is dependent on the causal relations that bind the brain–body–world together. I am claiming that it is these kinds of causal relations that the mind supervenes on, not just the relationships that exist between the neurons in the skull.

Furthermore, I claim that this is true not just of abstract mental properties, such as thoughts and beliefs. There has recently been a gradual warming up to the possibility that thought and abstractions do not supervene on the brain. Kim gives several examples of abstract properties that would not supervene on the brain or even on the body,[1] such as knowing or remembering a fact about the world, which presupposes that a person has had some direct contact with the world he knows about or remembers. Fodor also has been concerned recently about the fact that concepts make no sense if we ignore what they refer to, and reference cannot supervene entirely on brain states (Fodor 1994). Clark (1997) has also argued that language and conceptual thinking requires some sort of "scaffolding" in the outside world. What I am claiming is that not only thoughts, *but also feelings and sensations*, must be seen as supervening on the entire brain–body–world nexus. We feel what we feel because of the light rays and vibrations that are impinging on our bodies, and because of our personal histories, and none of those exists solely in our brains. These relationships, and others like them, have as much right to the titles of "embodiment" and "supervenience" as do the relationships that exist between brain cells.

Because Kim and Fodor chose such causally impotent examples of relational properties, their criticisms of relational supervenience are, I believe, answered by the points made above. James Garson, however, suggested an example in correspondence, which refers only to genuine causal relations, and thus requires a more detailed response.

Say the temperature of my pot of boiling water is 212 degrees. What molecular state is that state identical to? Answer: the state of the average kinetic energy of the molecules in the pot being a certain amount. So it is the molecular energy that is identified with the temperature. Temperature supervenes on molecular motion.

Now in providing this (interesting and ontologically simplifying) story about identity or realization of temperature, we are totally unimpressed by the answers one could give to the question: "What causes the pot to have the temperature 212 degrees?" the answers to which could be the fire under the pot, or even my desire for spaghetti. The temperature of the pot does not supervene on my desire to eat spaghetti, or even the fire under the pot. These are clearly causes that are not part of the supervenience base. (Pers. comm.)

Garson is obviously right when he says that somehow we feel that the boiling of the water is identical with (supervenes on), the causal properties of the molecular motion, and is not identical with the causal properties of the fire. This naturally leads us to think that questions about the nature of causality are irrelevant to understanding supervenience. Both sets of properties are causal, so causality can't be the difference that makes the difference. Furthermore, when we start speaking of identity, causal language starts to become confusing, because it makes no sense to say that something caused itself. It seems strange to say that the boiling was caused by the molecular motion; what we want to say is that the boiling *is* the molecular motion. This also leads us to think that supervenience and causality have nothing to do with each other.

But we cannot infer from this that we can completely ignore the question "What causes the water to have a temperature of 212 degrees?" when trying to determine the supervenience base for the boiling of the water. We cannot stop with the answer to that question, but that is where we must start. This is unavoidable, because the fire and the molecular motion, like everything else, are both describable and comprehensible only by talking about cause and effect relationships. This is the meaning of C. Lloyd Morgan's claim (which Kim frequently cites) that if something has no causal properties, it doesn't exist. The question that needs to be answered is thus "Which causal properties are part of the supervenience base and which ones aren't?" The answer to that question, as far as I can tell, is essentially indistinguishable from the question "Which causal properties are intrinsic, and which ones are relational?"

Is there any difference between saying that the boiling supervenes on the molecular motion and saying that the molecular motion has the intrinsic causal power to make the water boil? In both descriptions, we are saying that the boiling and the molecular motion are coextensive; they occupy the same space. There is arguably more to the concept of *type*-identity than this, but as far as I can tell the *token*-identity provided by supervenience will not have any other characteristics that will make a difference for our purposes here. When we say that a causal power is intrinsic to a substance, we are also saying it occupies the same space. Isn't the explosiveness of gunpowder present in all of the gunpowder? Otherwise we'd have to say something like "the explosiveness is three degrees to the left of its blackness, and wedged up along side its granularity." What in the world could such statements mean? The answer is, I believe, that we don't have any idea what they could mean. These two concepts cover essentially the same metaphysical territory, and are too muddled for us to make a sharp distinction between them. But this is only a problem if we think that the intrinsicness of a causal property is something that exists in the world independent of our projects and goals. Consequently, my answer to Garson is contained in my previous comments about so-called intrinsic causal powers: the borders of the supervenience base are a function of the goals and purposes of the various sciences. The knife is seen as intrinsically sharp because it participates in many different kinds of cutting-events. The boiling is seen as intrinsic to the molecular motion because the latter occurs regardless of whether the water is heated by gas, or electricity, or for the purpose of making spaghetti. I can see no difference between these two relationships.

There are undeniably many examples where it seems intuitively obvious that certain properties must be seen as intrinsic to a given object, and in those cases we unhesitatingly assert that those properties form the supervenience base of the intrinsic properties of that object. But we should not kid ourselves into thinking that just because a distinction is intuitively compelling, it is therefore absolute. It's natural to assume that if one is a physicalist, one must believe that properties like molecular motion are intrinsic to the physical world. But Russell's and Nagel's arguments against causal powers in physics seriously weaken the distinction between "internal" properties that provide the supervenience base, and the "external" properties, such as the heat of the fire. There is a functional interdependence among the causal factors that result in the boiling-water-event, and it is no doubt convenient to refer to the molecular motion as the one of greatest interest. But that doesn't necessarily imply that the molecular motion is absolutely intrinsic, and all the other factors are absolutely extrinsic. For reasons presented earlier, it seems to me far more plausible that the distinction between intrinsic and relational is context dependent, and will thus vary from science to science.

We would like to think that the internal properties are somehow independent of the external ones; the water would still boil regardless of whether it was heated by gas, electricity, or thermonuclear explosion. But the relationship is not completely independent: the events that generate enough heat to boil water are a relatively closely related family when compared to the range of all possible events. We cannot boil water by using a tornado, a sunset, or a ballet performance.[2] Our concept of boiling is to some degree defined by its relationship to heat sources and vice versa. Furthermore, the entire nexus of causal relations that resulted in boiling water could be divided up into a different set of objects with different causal powers if our interests had a different focus. There is no compelling reason to claim that the boiling water supervenes on anything else but the molecular motion in this particular example. But that does not mean that an assumption of intrinsic independence is a metaphysical fact that can be assumed without question in every single circumstance.

In much the same way, most neurological research can assume that mental events supervene on brain states without serious negative consequences. But that doesn't mean that this assumption won't give rise to paradoxes when it is made a foundation for other areas of inquiry, such as psychology, linguistics, epistemology, or metaphysics. If these paradoxes can be resolved by spreading the supervenience base of mind over a nexus of brain–body–world relations, we should be willing to acknowledge that mind–brain supervenience is really only a convenient approximation.

Rob Wilson (2001) is aware of these problems, but tries to save the concept of intrinsic supervenience by adding more distinctions. He presents decisive arguments against the assumption that the supervenience base is both (1) *determinative* and (2) *physically constitutive* of the entity that supervenes on it. Using arguments similar to the ones I have traced back to Mill, he shows that usually those items that are thought to be physically constitutive of mental states (i.e., brain states) are not entirely determinative of those mental states. He is, in other words, too aware of the nonatomistic nature of causal relations to simply assert that brain states cause mental states all by themselves. Nevertheless he still wants to claim that the properties of the brain are "physically constitutive" of mental properties, even though they do not "determine" mental properties. Thus he divides the causal nexus that produces mental states into three parts: (1) the core realization, (2) the total realization, and (3) the background conditions.

Wilson wants this distinction to apply to a variety of different systems including "psychological, biological, economic, computational, chemical etc." Consequently, he does not always fully spell out how these distinctions apply to the mind–body problem. It seems clear, however, that he sees the brain states as the core realizations of mental states, and that this is synonymous with saying that they physically constitute the mental states. For Wilson, however, the core realizations are not sufficient to produce mental states; they are only "most readily identifiable as playing a crucial causal role in producing or sustaining" the mental states. (This distinction frees Wilson from the need to accept the "brain in the vat" theory of mental states, although he does not specifically mention this.) The core realizations are able to produce mental states only because they are part of a total realization that is sufficient to produce the mental state. Wilson also admits, however, that even the total realizations might not be quite as total as all that:

Strictly speaking then, it is only the physical states constituting a total realization, *together with the appropriate background conditions*, that metaphysically suffice. . . . This might be taken as suggesting that even total realizations, considered simply as complex configurations of matter and energy, are metaphysically context-sensitive in much the same way that partial realizations are. (Wilson 2001, p. 11, italics in the original)

Wilson does give intuitively compelling examples of this distinction from several different sciences. But the criteria he gives for drawing the lines that separate these different parts of the causal nexus actually support a pragmatist position more than they support a "realist" position.

His argument against what he calls "irrealism" is "it is not simply up to us to determine what constitutes a system or the system of relevance." This is, of course, the most common misunderstanding of pragmatism (popularized even by admirers of pragmatism, such as Rorty). But what leads to errors in the attempted performance of a human activity is not up to us either. The assumption of mind–brain supervenience has been an extremely useful one for neuroscience so far, just as the assumption of absolute space was extremely useful for Newtonian physics. Any physicist or neuroscientist who had assumed otherwise at inappropriate points in the history of science would have made many errors in her predictions. This is why it was not a matter of consensus or arbitrary choice that made Newtonian physics superior to Cartesian physics or mind–brain supervenience superior to mind–kidney supervenience.

Epistemological factors, in other words, are not arbitrary and can shape this three-way distinction every bit as effectively as ontological factors. When Wilson defines the core realization as "the specific part of [a system] that is most readily identifiable as playing a crucial causal role," the obvious questions are "readily identifiable by whom?" and "crucial to whom?" (Wilson 2001, p. 10). It makes no sense to think of these sorts of properties as being completely intrinsic to the object being studied. Wilson's only criterion for distinguishing between total realizations and background conditions is equally dependent on who is studying the system. While talking about the circulatory system he says, "While we would expect physiologists to offer a more precise specification of both the core and total realizations of this system, we wouldn't expect them to contribute much to our understanding of the background conditions of these realizations" (ibid., p. 11, fn.). In other words, background conditions are those parts of the causal nexus that are of no interest to whoever is studying them, which means that what counts as the realization or supervenience base varies depending on the goals and purposes of those doing the studying.

Also—a point I will develop at greater length elsewhere—this leaves open the possibility that the supervenience base of mind fluctuates in ways that are dependent on the goals and purposes of *the mind being studied*. This was most famously expressed by Heidegger's claim that when the hammer is ready-to-hand, it is not distinct and separate from the person doing the hammering. If he is right about this, it would mean that the question

"What does the mind supervene on?" would have different answers at different times. When a person is hammering, her mind would partly supervene on the hammer, but when she is playing a violin, her mind would supervene partly on the violin, and so on. For the mind would then be seen as a field of purposive activity radiating into an environment rather than a piece of biological stuff with a permanent border, size, and weight.

Perhaps, after all of this, you may grant that it is a metaphysical fact that mind–brain supervenience is not absolute. However, you may still believe that this metaphysical fact has no significant cash value. After all, the claim that temperature supervenes on molecular motion may not be absolutely true, but this fact makes no difference to the practice of science. Couldn't mind–brain identity be a similar kind of claim? Garson gives the following argument why mind–brain supervenience appears to be as straightforward as the temperature–molecular motion example.

> So for example, I am having a conscious experience of a green field. One of the things that is causally relevant to my having this experience is that there is a big sheet of green paper out there causing the experience. But is *that* causal nexus part of the supervenience base of my experience? To ask the supervenience question in the case of the green paper is to ask *not* what causes the experience, but rather to ask whether I could have that very same experience without the green sheet of paper. And of course I could. It could be a monitor turned to green, or a blank wall under a certain neon sign, or. . . . (Garson, Pers. comm.)

This example appears at first to be an exact parallel with the molecular motion and fire example. Several different things can heat the boiling water, but the molecular motion occurs regardless of how the water is heated. Therefore the temperature supervenes on the molecular motion. Garson (and the common consensus) says that lots of different things can cause the same experience of green, because they can all cause the same brain state. Therefore the experience supervenes on the brain state.

We can uncover the problem with this analogy by first noting, rather pedantically, that the experience produced looking at a green sheet of paper is not the exact same experience as looking at a green monitor or a blank wall under a neon sign. They are, in a sense, members of the same genus but they are still noticeably different from each other. Very well, you may say, how about looking at two identical pieces of paper from the same package on two separate occasions? Wouldn't that produce the same experience with two different external objects? Well, no, because the second experience would be conditioned in some way by the fact that you had seen a piece of paper exactly like this once before. Or it might be conditioned by the fact that you were tired, or had recently had a fight with a loved one. No, you may object, I'm not talking about the thoughts about the experience, or the emotional reaction to it, I'm only talking about the patch of green that is present in my visual field right now. If you make this objection, you are committing yourself to the position that experience is made up of discrete independent moments, each of which supervenes only on whatever is happening in the brain at that point in time.

Kim specifically makes this commitment when he says that mental states supervene only on the internal states of the organism that has them, and then defines "internal" as "neither rooted outside times at which it is had, nor outside the objects that have it. . . . an internal process would be a causally connected or continuous series of internal events or states involving the same object or system of objects" (Kim 1993, p. 184). Strictly speaking, this definition doesn't exclude the possibility of brain–body–world supervenience, for the brain–body–world is a system of objects. But Kim clearly isn't considering this possibility. By a system of objects, he means a network of brain cells. The assumption he (and almost everyone else) is making is that the network of brain cells in the skull constitute a closed system, which follows certain laws that are in principle comprehensible without making reference to the rest of the world. Strictly speaking, of course, there is no such thing as a closed system. But the fact that we can temporarily isolate certain systems is what makes scientific knowledge possible. It is why, for example, we can think of boiling water as a substance with the intrinsic causal power to cook other substances, and why we can say this predicate called "boiling" supervenes on a certain rate of molecular motion.

But is there any reason to assume that the brain can fruitfully be isolated as a closed system? What sort of architecture would the brain have if it functioned as a closed system? There could be many possible answers to this question, but there are, I think, only two that have been seriously considered by scientists and philosophers.

(1) The brain stores and manipulates sense data, which are completely independent from both the outside world and each other. This would mean that once the sense data were in the brain, they would no longer

have any contact with the outside world, and thus the brain and its contents would be a closed system (although not a very systematic one).

(2) The brain has causal independence as an experience-producing engine because it operates something like the way computers operate.[3] Specifically, this view of the mind presupposes that the structure of the brain is *rigidly modular*. By "modular" I mean that not only is the brain itself seen as a closed system, but also each of its parts is seen as a closed system that relates to the rest of the system by clearly defined input and output channels. A system of this sort must relate to the world by taking in information as a series of discrete and independent bits, because that is the only way that the information can flow unchanged from output to input throughout the system. If this were the case, most of the rules that govern how the brain responds could be ignored when considering an individual experience. This is because these neurological background conditions would function in ways that did not affect what was being processed within a particular perceptual module. (That is what makes the module a module.) This would mean that if we really wanted to understand a particular experience, the key thing would be to understand what was happening from moment to moment inside that neurological module. In this view of the brain, experience would not be made up of sense data in the Humean sense. But it would fundamentally consist of a sequence of discrete bits of information, each of which would only partially reveal the object(s) in the outside world that caused it to appear in the brain.

If we accept either of these positions, a variety of different objects could cause the same experience. The brain could, in other words, make one response to a variety of stimuli. A color photograph of a tree and the tree itself would produce the same tree-experience. Two different square green objects could create identical experiences of a green color-patch. This view of the mind also assumes we can identify a given experience with a single brain event. This is why Anglo-American philosophers of mind in the 1950s and 1960s could speak about pains as being identical to C-fibers firing (or something of the sort) without anyone questioning the essential rightness of the claim.

If this were the way the brain operated, then perhaps it would be a closed system upon which human experience supervened. But there are numerous problems with this view of experience. We can start (as Wilson did in his 2001) by pointing out that a pain is almost certainly not identical to a C-fiber firing. No one believes that a single C-fiber isolated in a petri dish is having a pain experience. Thus neither identity nor even supervenience could be claimed for the C-fiber firing itself. So what else is necessary? No one really knows, of course, but the assumptions those philosophers of mind made were (1) all the other events that constituted the causal network responsible for any single experience are brain events, and neuroscience as an autonomous discipline could eventually tell us what they were, and (2) these other brain events could be isolated from the pain experience itself as "background conditions" by means of ceteris paribus clauses. An experience of this kind is seen as not only distinct from the thing in the outside world that causes it, but also from whatever other brain events are occurring at the same time. Such an experience was often called a "raw feel," because supposedly we do not need to run it through the process of relating it to other experiences in order to know that we have it.

For sense-datum theory, raw feels provide a foundation upon which all knowledge rests. But sense-datum theory is supposedly a theory that no one takes seriously any more. Fodor claims that the modern objections to sense-datum theory are best described as "poverty of the stimulus" arguments. These arguments correctly lead us to assume that an individual stimulus–sense datum[4] cannot create knowledge by itself. But Fodor also claims that if our sensory experience is created by informationally encapsulated modules within our brains, there can still be a distinction between knowledge and experience. This distinction, Fodor claims, enables us to claim that the experiences produced by those sensory modules is what gets us in contact with the outside world (see Fodor 1985).

But a look at the history of philosophy seriously weakens this optimistic claim. Kant's objections to Hume were met only by denying us access to the outside world, and modularity theory's Kantian solution compels us toward something like Kantian idealism. Both modularity theory and sense-datum theory still see knowledge as dribbling into the brain a piece at a time, regardless of whether they refer to that piece as a sense datum or a bit of information. Because modularity theory claims that the cognitive worth of information comes from how it is processed by the cognitive machinery in the brain, it makes direct knowledge of the world in itself highly problematic. The usual claim is that "most" of the cognitive worth derives from how it is processed, but that there is something in the outside input that also contributes to the knowledge (somehow). But no one has ever been able clearly to explain exactly how this is accomplished.

I will argue in the next chapter that this tension between atomistic empiricism and holistic idealism is an inevitable consequence of Cartesian materialism. Most of the problems that lead to skepticism come from the fact that neither of these alternatives is satisfactory. The fact that both accept Cartesian materialism is what makes these two positions seem to be the only possible alternatives.

6 Experience, Sense Data, and Language: Putting Experience Back into the Environment

Philosophy has always acknowledged a distinction between knowledge and experience, but this distinction also implied an unavoidably close relationship. Experience is the most private thing each of us possesses, and yet it also serves an essential function of some sort in the acquisition of intersubjective knowledge. Experience has to possess this ambiguous status because of the presuppositions of Cartesian materialism, and this ambiguity produces many of the traditional problems that lead to skepticism. Because Cartesian materialism says the mind is the brain, it requires us to assume that the only way that the mind can have experience of the world is to somehow get the world inside the brain. Because this is clearly impossible, what with the world being so big and the brain being so small, it is very hard to avoid concluding that knowledge is impossible.

Yet Cartesian materialism seems so unquestionable that, when combined with logic and the empirical sciences, it became the basis of the theory of knowledge that dominated philosophy in England, the United States, and Austria for the first half of this century. This theory of knowledge was called logical positivism or logical atomism, when it was hostile to epistemology, and logical empiricism when it began to explicitly formulate an epistemology. The following description is an idealized caricature that leaves out numerous details that distinguish its various adherents from each other, and deliberately emphasizes only those aspects of their positions that reveal their commitment to Cartesian materialism. The original adherents would not have put so much emphasis on Cartesian materialism, because it would not have occurred to them that anyone would question it. But as far as I can tell, my shifts in emphasis do not actually contradict them in any way. Their theory, redescribed to serve my purposes, goes something like this:

Our sense organs bring us direct knowledge of the outside world, and the laws of logic are necessarily true. We learn about the world by carrying bits of knowledge from our sense organs through message cables to the brain, where the self lives. We then manipulate these bits of knowledge with the laws of logic and are thus able to make inferences about those aspects of the world that do not impinge on our sense organs. If we make incorrect use of logic or have too few sense data to work with, our minds can create imaginary entities that unsuccessfully attempt to explain what we experience. These entities have no ontological status whatsoever, and the language that talks about them makes no reference to anything that exists in the real world (i.e., these terms have intension but no extension, sense but no reference). However, if we are sufficiently rigorous about gathering and logically processing our data, we can discover those entities that exist in the outside world totally independently of any of our thoughts about them. This is because the sense data provide a completely reliable foundation for our knowledge, and the laws of logic enable us to build unassailably constructed inferences from that foundation. The physical sciences were constructed out of sense data using logic in this manner. Although it is likely that a few human errors were made in the construction of these sciences, it is virtually certain that these errors were few in number, and so for all practical purposes we can assume that essentially everything the sciences say is true. All other forms of human inquiry are in contact with reality only in so far as they are methodologically and theoretically compatible with the unchanging body of knowledge discovered in this way by the physical sciences.

Ironically, this brain-based view of the mind is every bit as indebted to Descartes as the "ghost in the machine" theory described by Ryle. Descartes believed that the soul contacted the body through the brain. Cartesian materialists made only a relatively slight modification to this position by saying the soul *is* the brain. For Descartes, the brain was the turnstile that knowledge had to pass through to get to the soul; for the Cartesian materialists the brain was knowledge's final resting place. Both positions, however, were lumbered with the same doomed epistemological question: "How does the world get into the brain?" The only answer available, given these presuppositions, is "a piece at a time, by means of sense data that are carried through the body to the brain by means of message cables." On closer inspection, even this answer doesn't really work. The world itself does not get into the brain, only an impression or copy of the world. We thus are compelled to accept idealism, and conclude that we never get to see the real world, only a world of appearances. This position is so irritatingly counterintuitive that it is eventually rejected even when no one can find any good arguments against it. But because the atomistic empiricism described above is the only alternative we have to idealism, we usually slowly drift back toward idealism again.

Although there are still many scientists who subconsciously see knowledge as sense data that dribble into the mind through self-contained observations, almost every professional philosopher today considers this position to be a dead horse. We are all supposedly holists today,[1] and agree with Quine that our sensory experience does not confront us a piece at a time, but as a body. But it is, I claim, difficult if not impossible to avoid the alternatives of sense-datum theory versus idealism as long as we accept Cartesian materialism. If we reject the assumption that each moment of experience is directly given to us as a self-contained sense datum, and continue to accept Cartesian materialism, the only alternative to sense-datum theory is some kind of Kantian idealism. If the world cannot get into our heads a piece at a time, Cartesian materialism forces us to conclude that the world never gets into our heads. Some contemporary holist philosophers may be willing to simply go back to Kant and graft on insights from modern science. There are interpretations of Sellars that imply this: the dust jacket of *Science, Perception, and Reality* says that Sellars "defends the thesis that the world of common sense and ordinary language is a phenomenal world in Kant's sense." But there is also another position, arguably ascribable to Dewey,[2] that escapes Cartesian materialism by taking experience out of the head and putting it into the world.

This position is not dualist, for it accepts that whatever is physically responsible for conscious experience is analyzable into a set of physical causal interactions. These physical interactions have to have some sort of borderline; they will not include the entire universe. From the physical interactions within that borderline, the pattern that we call consciousness will emerge. When I say that consciousness emerges from this causal network, I don't mean anything spooky. I just mean that the entire causal network will be conscious, but not any one part of it. None of this is new or controversial. But important new philosophical possibilities open up when we ask the question "Where do you draw the line?" Cartesian materialism assumes that we must draw the line at the cranium. Chapters 2 and 3 of this book have given arguments why there are good reasons for extending the border beyond the cranium into the rest of the body. Chapter 4 opens the possibility of extending the line beyond the skin, because the line between intrinsic and relational causal properties is a pragmatic one, and relational properties that cause experience inevitably extend out from the organism into its environment. Even externalists like Clark and Wilson have so far been willing to say only that *cognition* emerges from certain environmental interactions with the brain and body. The force of tradition, however, makes it seems undeniable to them that *experience* must emerge only from interactions among cranial neurons, not interactions between brain and body. But once you are willing to deny that unjustified assumption, the dichotomy between experience and the world dissolves, and there is no longer any need to answer the question "How does the world get into the brain?" That question is unavoidable if we assume that consciousness emerges only from the causal interactions between neurons, or even if we expand the supervenience base of consciousness out to the skin. If we are conscious only of what is happening in our brains or bodies, we have to create a copy of the outside world inside of us in order for us to be aware of it. We are then forced to conclude that we are aware only of the copy, not the original. But if experience emerges from brain–body–world interactions, the problem doesn't even come up. There is no need to make a copy of the world inside the head in order for us to be aware of our environment if our consciousness is partly embodied by the environment itself. Mind, instead of being an emergent property of the brain, becomes an emergent property of a "behavioral field" that ripples and fluctuates throughout the environment–body–brain nexus. My subjective experience is thus embodied by my world in essentially the same sense that it is embodied by that part of my world that is my brain.

This idea, as counterintuitive as it may sound, is not completely without precedent. Gibson was not quite comfortable with the idea of emergent properties, so he claimed that visual experience existed in the light. But unless he was claiming that light would somehow be experienced even with no one there to see it (by God, perhaps?), he must concede that visual experience emerges from interactions between light and the organism that perceives it. Once we grant this possibility, there is no principled reason to exclude the objects in the environment that reflect the light.

Although Dewey is never quite as explicit as the above paragraphs, his rejection of the fact–value distinction strongly implies something like this. For Dewey, unlike Hume, values are not feelings that take place within us. They actually reside in the world itself. Dewey points out that before we begin any inquiry, we experience a world full of things that we care about, and those cares presuppose goals to be strived for and dangers and unpleasantries to be avoided. Those goals and purposes shape our experience by pointing beyond our bodies and brains. Our experience would be incoherent without these references to the outside world, just as it would make no sense to talk about the function of lungs without making any reference to oxygen.

Dewey claims that experience does have parts, but these parts are not bite-size chunks conditioned by how much can be fit into the brain at any given time. They are experienced as moments in a flow, like the different courses of a dinner, or the sequence of interactions in a conversation. Sometimes an entire hour can be experienced as a whole, like a trip to the grocery store, sometimes each individual volley in a tennis match can be experienced as separate if a player or observer is focusing intently enough with that goal in mind. But in each case the parts are determined with reference to function and purpose, just like the parts of any other biological system.

It is just plain false to say that a digestive system could be divided into parts that consisted of identical one-inch cubes; if it were so divided it would be chopped tripe, not a digestive system at all.[3] The parts of a digestive system are those subsystems that perform specific functions that contribute to the digestive process: the stomach, the teeth, the small intestine, and so forth. To divide our experience into parts based on how much can be inside the brain at any moment is as irrelevant to the natural parts of the experience as dividing the digestive system into one-inch cubes. There is also no need to assume that smaller parts are more fundamental than bigger ones, because we are not trying to establish Cartesian certainty by claiming that what is immediately given here and now provides a foundation for inferences to the rest. Or perhaps more accurately, the here-and-now is no longer considered to be punctate and infinitely divisible. It is an emergent property that is of different lengths depending on the experiential interactions it emerges from.

Once we see experience as a biological concept defined by function, it can have borders that go beyond the brain without encompassing so much as to be meaningless or trivial. It won't be terribly useful to assume that an experience supervenes on the entire causal nexus that made it occur. This would require us to say that each of my experiences supervenes on the big bang, or on an assassin's bullet that failed to kill my parents.[4] Today almost everyone in philosophy recognizes that biological concepts are not merely causal, but functional as well. Functions presuppose purposes and goals. We identify a heart by recognizing it as the organ whose purpose is to pump blood, and blood as the fluid whose purpose is to carry nutrients and oxygen. Dewey portrays experience as fundamentally purposive, in opposition to the position that Dewey calls sensationalistic empiricism, which sees experience as discrete sense data that are intrinsically irrelevant to the goals of the perceiver. Thus, for Dewey there is no such thing as a raw feel; all experience is constituted by its relationship to the world and goals of the experiencer. Whatever is happening in the brain is certainly necessary to produce experience, but there is no reason to assume it is sufficient.

If experience supervenes only on those causal connections that fulfill the purposes of the experiencing organism, this would definitely extend the supervenience base outside of the brain and body and into the environment. But it would also narrow the number of causal connections contained in the supervenience base to something manageable and significant. Some of these causal connections would fulfill deliberate, conscious purposes, such as those connections between the hand and the hammer, or the hammer and the nail. Other connections would fulfill purposes essential to the life of the organism whether the organism was aware of them or not, such as those between the lungs and oxygen. But neither the big bang nor the assassin's bullet would be included among these causal connections, because such a connection would have no recurring biological significance. Since consciousness is fundamentally a biological phenomenon, this would be a legitimate and principled way of drawing the boundaries of supervenience. It would also be open to revision as new data was discovered, unlike the mind–brain identity, which tends to prejudice researchers against the data discovered by scientists like Brothers, Pert, Berglund, Gibson, and the others I have cited in this book.

A biological definition of supervenience would not limit us to the borders of the skin, for *ecology* is a biological science, every bit as much as is anatomy or physiology. Ecology studies ecosystems, which outline the interelationships between organisms and their environments, and the only part of the physical world surrounding an organism that counts as its environment is that with which the organism has a purposive relationship. From the physicist's point of view, one pile of sticks and grass within the

vicinity of a bird may be pretty much like another. It is the purposive relationship that the bird has with one particular pile that makes it a nest, and
thus part of the bird's environment. If our experience emerges from our
purposive relationship with our environment, surely it makes the most
sense to say that this is what our experience supervenes on. Each organism sets up a distinctive symbiotic[5] relationship with certain aspects of the
physical reality in its spatial vicinity, and it is only these aspects that
become part of that organism's environment, in this technical sense. This
is why ecology, the study of environments, is a biological science and not
a physical one.

The fact that the self emerges from its relationship with its environment
does not mean the self is identical to its environment. The fact that two
entities are ontologically dependent does not always imply that they are
identical, or even that the border between them is blurry. It is certainly
true that no one can be a parent unless they have a child. But we would
never infer from this that there is no difference between a parent and a
child. On the contrary, if there were no differences between parents and
children, it would be impossible for either to exist. In this and many other
cases, the ontological dependence actually *requires* the two entities to be
distinct. This point is both important and far too frequently ignored. But
once we acknowledge that the constituting relationship is a dynamic one,
this implies that the borders of the two relating entities could fluctuate as
the activity that defines their relationship fluctuates. This is exactly what
I (and Dewey and Heidegger) claim happens in the relationship between
self and the world. At any given moment, a self has a world, and that
world, by definition, is distinct from the self that relates to it. But because
that relationship is in dynamic flux, it becomes impossible to draw a completely accurate and enduring border between the self and the world. In
Heidegger's famous example, the carpenter and the hammer are (literally)
one when the hammer is ready-to-hand and being used. But when the carpenter is in his car and driving, he is one with the car, not the hammer.
As Dewey says, the distinction between self and world is a "distinction of
flexible function only, not of fixed existence. . . . one and the same occurrence plays either or both parts, according to the shift of interest" (Dewey
1896, p. 1). For certain activities, such as neuroscience, drawing the border
between the self and world at the skull is an effective simplification. For
other activities, the skin is a more effective border. But there is good reason

to assume that these borders shift, depending on the goals of both the minds being studied and the minds doing the studying.

Clark (1997) discusses a 1934 monograph by Jakob Von Uexkull that "introduces the idea of the *Umwelt*, defined as the set of the environmental features to which a given type of animal is sensitized" (p. 24). *Umwelt* is also a technical term in Heidegger's *Being and Time*, where it is usually translated as "environment." Clark and Von Uexkull stress the very Heideggerian point that not everything in the spatial vicinity of an organism is part of its umwelt. This is because an organism's cognitive system is designed to relate to only those parts of the surrounding area with which it has what Heidegger might call concernful dealings. This is especially obvious for organisms whose concerns are relatively simple and unchanging. A tick's umwelt, according to Von Uexkull, consists of only three elements: (1) the smell of butyric acid, which tells the tick it should loose its hold on its branch, so it will fall on a warm-blooded animal, (2) tactile contact, which tells the tick to run about until, (3) heat is detected, which initiates boring and burrowing. The numerous other factors that would be part of our umwelt if we are in the same spatial area— the smell of the flowers, the color of the sky—are not part of the tick's umwelt at all.

We may smile patronizingly at the simplicity of the tick's umwelt, but we must remember that the difference between the tick's and ours, great as it is, is mainly a difference in degree. We see only a small part of the electromagnetic spectrum as light, and hear only a small range of vibrations as sounds. And there are—must be—vast domains of being that are not only imperceptible to us, but unintelligible as well. Like all organisms, the possibilities of what we can sense and think are limited by what might possibly serve our purposes. The real difference between the tick and us is not that we sense the world "as it really is" and the tick senses only what it needs to know to fulfill its goals. The difference is that we have a much vaster and more flexible range of goals, and our senses and thoughts are thus also proportionately more vast and flexible.

Language and Thought as Biological and Functional Categories

Once we recognize that environment is a biological category, and accept Ruth Millikan's claim that language and thought are also biological categories (Millkan 1984), we can dissolve one of the toughest problems in philosophy of language: Putnam's Twin Earth problem. Although the primary concern of this book is to argue that sensations and experience do not exist solely in the head, many of the points I have made can be applied equally effectively to the internalism–externalism debate in philosophy of language. Like many philosophical problems, this debate can be resolved by questioning one of the assumptions that frame it: the idea that a language-speaker's mind and her environment can be seen as independent from each other. Concrete illustrations of the tight relationship between environment and language will also make it easier to see that an equally tight relationship exists between environment and subjective experience (when we return to that subject in the next section of this chapter). For I believe that Millikan's biological view of language implies that nonverbal experience has a relationship with its environment that is essentially the same as the relationship between language and the world to which it makes reference.

Millikan argues that the environment within which an organism dwells and functions has a special symbiotic relationship to the organism that is not shared by the rest of reality, including most of the reality that is in the organism's immediate spatial vicinity. This symbiotic relationship sometimes makes it difficult for an ecological analysis to determine where the organism stops and the environment begins.

Most crabs molt when about to grow out of their shells, secreting a substance that hardens to become a new and bigger shell. Birds, however, build their nests out of materials that they find in the environment, although some complete these nests by lining them with their own breast feathers. The crab's shell is considered to be part of the crab. Why is the bird's nest not considered part of the bird? . . . The distinction between what is spatially "inside" and what is spatially "outside" the bird, as such, has no significance for the study of the avian biological *system*. (Millikan 1993, pp. 158–159, italics in original)

But even though the line is blurry, it is clear that Millikan's observations do not require us to refer to everything within a given spatial radius around an organism as part of that organism's environment. The avian biological system, like the tick's biological system, contains only those external elements that are closely related to the bird's biological functions. This close relationship is still ontologically essential when an organism becomes sophisticated enough to have perceptual representations, rather than mere responses to stimuli.

If you eat both mice and frogs, it is not economical to have completely different perceptual processing mechanisms, for example, separate eyes, for perceiving these. Similarly, if you eat mice and flee from snakes. If you have a complex structure such as an eye, clearly you should use that same eye for as many of your various purposes as it can be made relevant to, avoiding specialized adjustments that will make it unsuitable for multipurpose use. This has important consequences when we consider the obstacles confronting the design of any apparatus with a sophisticated capacity reliably to make icons showing affordances of distal objects. To be as useful as possible, such an apparatus must enable recognition of the affording distal object or property and its relevant relation to the animal over as wide a range of object–animal relations as possible (not just dead center under the animal's nose) under a variety of mediating conditions (under various lighting conditions, sound echo conditions, etc.), despite distractive intrusions affecting proximal stimulation ("static" such as wind noise or shadows or extraneous smells). (Millikan unpublished)

Note that the purpose of the perceptual organ is still to mediate object–animal relations, even though there is a wider range of such possible relations that can be maintained by a single signal received by the higher mammal's eye than by the sensors of the tick. Even the signals received by the tick are, in Millikan's terminology, intentional icons. Like language icons, they have a certain mapping relationship with the environment of the organism that determines their function. But the more sophisticated icons produced by more sophisticated intentional systems (such as language) can relate to the same aspect of the external world in service of a variety of different purposes. As Millikan puts it: "The intentional icon that has a dozen or a hundred uses depending on the particular state of potentiation of the nervous system, all of which uses require it to be aligned with the world in exactly the same way, becomes at the limit an any-purpose, hence purely fact-representing, icon" (ibid.).

I won't go into Millikan's elegant and detailed story of how the ability to create fact-representing icons becomes the basis for fundamental concepts like space and substance, and eventually becomes the basis for linguistic concepts such as inference and negation. The only point I need to make here is that this story, like the rest of Millikan's theory of language, explains the intentionality, the aboutness, of representation by describing the functions performed by causal relationships between an organism and its environment. Because it limits itself to those causal relationships that perform a function for the organism, it is not vulnerable to the usual objection made against causal theories of reference: that there are too many causal relationships between Paris and thoughts that "Paris is the capital of France," and consequently merely saying there is a causal relationship tells us nothing useful. Only a relatively small number of those causal relationships are functionally designed to relate my thoughts to Paris, and it is possible and useful to say that my thoughts about Paris supervene on those causal relationships between me and Paris that help perform linguistic functions. In some cases, those thoughts may be mediated by perceptions of Paris, or perceptions of postcards of Paris, or books I have read written by experts on Paris. But they will not be mediated by the molecules of air that once blew through the streets of Paris and that are now being inhaled by my lungs. Even though those molecules do help create a real causal relationship between me and Paris, it is not a causal relationship that serves the sorts of functions that make thought possible.

The conflict between internalism and externalism in philosophy of language has usually assumed that there are only two possibilities. To say that the intentional content of a thought or proposition is broad is to say that it supervenes on mind-independent reality. To say that it is narrow is to say that it supervenes on the brain. Both sides usually refer to mind-independent reality as "the environment." To understand the alterative I am proposing, it is essential to remember that this is *not* the way I am using the word "environment." Environment, as I have defined it, is not mind independent. Its borders and qualities are constituted by its relationship to the mind (goals, projects, functions) of the organism that dwells in that environment. My alternative to these two positions might be called a theory of middle-sized content, because I claim that intentional content supervenes on the environment, the umwelt, of the thinker or the speaker, and not on either the isolated brain or on mind-independent reality. The umwelt of a language speaker extends out beyond the brain to include the causal relations that make linguistic functions possible. But it does not include those aspects of reality that have no impact on the thinker or speaker of the proposition.

For those who are not familiar with the Twin Earth thought experiment:[6] Oscar and Twin Oscar live on two planets called Earth and Twin Earth. These planets are identical except that on Twin Earth, water has a different chemical structure—it is XYZ rather than H_2O. This difference has no obvious macroscopic consequences. But careful scientific analysis could eventually reveal the difference, although it hasn't during the lifetimes of the two Oscars. So the question is: When Oscar and Twin Oscar use the word "water" are they both referring to the same thing? And/or does the word have the same meaning for both speakers?

By the posits of the Twin Earth thought experiment, the differences between H_2O and XYZ exist in the external world, but they have no impact on the umwelts of Oscar and Twin Oscar. This is true even in the very sophisticated sense of umwelt applicable only to language-using organisms. The umwelt of language users includes the causal connections that enable us to access the knowledge of experts. The Twin Earth example posits that Twin Lavoisier has not yet discovered that Twin Earth water has a molecular structure of XYZ. For once that discovery is made, the two earths would not be twins, and in more ways than one. There would be scientific papers on XYZ, discoveries of new chemical compounds that used the molecular structure of XYZ for a variety of industrial purposes that could never be accomplished by H_2O, and other repercussions literally too numerous to mention. But without the two Lavoisiers, the two Oscars also have identical umwelts as well as identical brains. Because intentional content supervenes only on the organism–umwelt relationships that make language functions possible, the two Oscars mean the same thing by the word "water."

Let us suppose that half of the water on our earth is radically different from the other half in subatomic ways that are impossible to measure by any tools that human beings could ever build, use, or possess. For all we know, this could be true. Does this have any effect whatsoever on how we should classify water? Of course not. Suppose these differences are measurable in principle, but through bad luck, humans just never figure out how to do it. Same situation, as far as the meaning of the word is concerned. But once Lavoisier and Twin Lavoisier appear on their respective scenes and discover that the molecular structures of water and twater are H_2O and XYZ respectively, Oscar and Twin Oscar mean different things by the word "water." This is because what they both mean by water includes "what the experts would tell me about water if I asked them," and because their worlds now contain different experts, the meanings of the two words are different.

Putnam (at least the early Putnam) would have objected to this theory of content by saying that our word "water" refers to the natural kind H_2O, whether we (or our experts) know it or not, and that Twin Oscar's word "water" refers to the natural kind XYZ, whether he (or his experts) know it or not. I don't believe in natural kinds myself, or perhaps I should say that I believe that all kinds are equally natural. The idea that certain kinds are not "interest relative," and therefore deserve the honorific "natural kind" is a position that Putnam now rejects, and with good reason. My arguments against intrinsic causal powers are equally effective against natural kinds, because to say that something is a member of a kind usually implies that it has certain causal powers that define that kind. (The concept of "essence" may be a somewhat more rarefied way of saying the same thing.) If you don't find my arguments against natural kinds effective, there are plenty of others.[7]

Putnam himself said many years later that the existence of natural kinds was actually incompatible with materialism, which is why Locke considered sortal designations to be fit only for the marketplace and the wake (Putnam 1983, p. 205). If orthodox physicalism is to be consistent, it must claim that the only natural kind is the quark (assuming quarks are the fundamental particle that everything else is made of). All nonquark discourse is merely about ways of grouping and relating quarks into the functional categories that serve the purposes of relatively provincial categories like those of chemistry, economics, European history, dentistry, or baseball. Putnam now says that the only essences he accepts are "the product of our use of the word, the kinds of referential intentions we have: This sort of essence is not 'built into the world' in the way required by an *essentialist theory of reference itself* to get off the ground" (ibid., p. 221; italics in original).[8] This means Putnam does not privilege even physics as having categories that are built into the world (see also Putnam 1978, pp. 123–138). Consequently, he should accept an argument like the one below, which applies to functional kinds like "automobile," as being equally applicable to so-called natural kinds.

British English refers to what Americans call the "hood" of a car as the "bonnet" of a car. Let us suppose that there is an embargo on American cars shipped to England, and this means that there are now no American cars in England (or advertisements about them, etc.). Does this mean that the word "bonnet" now only refers to the front covers of Astin Martins, Rolls Royces, and so forth, and that "hood" only refers to the front covers of Fords and Chevys? Of course not, because if someone heroically broke the blockade, the British would unhesitatingly refer to the front of that single American car as a "bonnet." Consequently "bonnet" means the same thing as "hood," and both refer to the same entities. For the same reason "water" and "twater" are the same thing, and the Twin Earthers are perfectly justified in not adopting the Earth philosopher's habit of referring to them with two different names. To give an example that is a little more obviously isomorphic with Twin Earth: suppose there are only Fords in Maryland and only Chevys in Wyoming. Does this mean that "car" means "Chevy" in Wyoming and "Ford" in Maryland? Of course not, and for the same reason "water" does not mean H_2O on Earth and XYZ on Twin Earth.

If there were such a place as Twin Earth, water would refer to both H_2O and XYZ until experts on either planet discovered the difference between the two compounds (at which point the two places would no longer be twins). For it is the theories of experts that determine the ultimate meanings of the words that refer to the entities in the domain of their expertise. There is, however, no reason to assume that all experts would say that XYZ wasn't water in such a case, even if some experts did. Even if chemists decided that H_2O and XYZ had to be considered two different substances, they would probably end up being considered the same in the discourse of geologists studying erosion, or of hydraulic engineers. The reason that the latter experts have a different set of kinds from chemists is that they have a different relationship to their environment from chemists. They are trying to answer different kinds of questions, and perform different kinds of tasks. It is this relationship to their environment that determines the meanings of the words they use, and the ontology they posit, not (merely) because there are different things going on inside their brains.

There are many different stances one can take toward the world, depending on what one wants to accomplish, and each of these prompts us to see certain causal connections as intrinsic to substances, and others as relations between substances. One such stance sees the brain as a substance that possesses all of those intrinsic causal powers that make mental functions possible. There are many mental functions, however, that are best seen not as intrinsic causal powers of the brain, but as relationships between an organism and its environment. One such function is propositional thought, whose intentional nature requires a reference to something in the outside world. When the part of the outside world to which such thought relates is seen as the environment shared by the language-speaking community, the special relationship between organism and environment becomes the basis for a compromise position between hard-core internalism or externalism. An organism's environment (or *umwelt*, as Heidegger and Von Uexkull would say) does not include all of reality, not even all aspects of reality within an organism's immediate vicinity. It only includes those parts of the outside world with which the organism has some functional relationship. This functional relationship can be as simple as the relationship between lungs and oxygen, or as complicated as that between language and its intentional content. Language gets its content through that functional relationship between a language community's speakers and their shared environment. Those aspects of reality that are not part of a language speaker's umwelt are outside that speaker's "frame of reference," and differences that make no difference to any member of the language speaker's community cannot be referred to by that community.

By the conditions of the thought experiment, until Twin Lavoisier appears, the umwelts of Earth and Twin Earth are identical, even though potentially they are different. Consequently, if there is no difference between the behavior of water in the umwelt of Earthers, and the behavior of twater in the umwelt of Twin Earthers, "water" means the same thing on both planets. The case is not significantly different from the circumstances in which we refer to all water in this world with the word "water," even though certain water molecules may be different from each other in ways that are impossible for us to detect. Now that Putnam acknowledges that essences are a function of our use of the word, he must also accept this solution to the Twin Earth problem.

Meaning is not in the head, nor is it independent of the head. As Putnam once said, the head and the world together jointly make up the head and the world (Putnam 1981, p. xi). But this implies that the world is an environment with a symbiotic relationship to the organism that possesses the head, not what Putnam now dismisses as "a ready made world" that exists independently of those who think and speak about it.

Subjective Experience and the Environment

Problems of meaning and reference arise in philosophy of language at least partly because of the Cartesian materialist assumption that we can only know what is happening inside our heads. It seems obvious that language must set up some sort of relationship between the head and the world. The

philosophical and scientific challenge is figuring out exactly what that relationship is, given that what happens in our heads is irreducibly private,
and what happens in the world is irreducibly public. There seems to be no
such problem with understanding subjective experience, however. By definition, it has no relationship to the world. It is private and securely locked
between our ears. To understand everything there is to know about it, all
we need to do is introspect, and supposedly everyone knows how to do
that. But these assumptions seem unquestionable only because our awareness of subjective experience is shaped by the conceptual filter we inherited from Descartes. When we introspect believing that our introspection
is unmediated, what we are doing is experiencing the world in terms of
the epistemic projects defined by Cartesian and empiricist epistemology.
Once we recognize that this view of experience is shaped by our presuppositions, it leaves open the possibility that other theories may be more
accurate.

If Dewey is right, experience is not the sort of thing that can enter the
brain in the form of sense data. Instead, it is constituted by neurological
activity that interacts with extraneurological factors to create what Millikan calls intentional icons. For language-using creatures, some of these
intentional icons acquire a flexibility in multitasking that prompts Millikan to call them fact-icons. Words and/or sentences are clearly the prototypical fact-icons, and perhaps there are others. But the important point
for our purposes is that intentional icons are constituted by their relationship to the environment *even more* than fact-icons are. Fact-icons, by
definition, have some measure of independence from each of the various
organism–environment relationships that they participate in. Intentional
icons are far more closely bound up with a single relatively reflexive
body–world relationship. Consequently, there is far less reason with intentional icons to privilege some particular activity in the skull as being
somehow distinct and independent from the rest of the causal nexus that
embodies that relationship.

The paradigmatic example of an intentional icon is the neurological
activity triggered by the light stimulus that causes a frog to extend its
tongue when it "sees" a fly. It is, of course, the neurologist's job to answer
the question "What is going on in the frog's brain when it sees a fly?" The
fact that something measurable and recurrent takes place in the frog's brain
every time it sees a fly is good evidence that if the frog is conscious, the

brain activity must be part of the supervenience base of its experience of the fly. But it is only Cartesian materialism that leads us to the assumption that the brain activity is the *entire* supervenience base. J. J. Gibson did not share that assumption, and there is really no reason to deny the Gibsonian[9] alternative claim that the frog's experience supervenes on both the light and the neurological activity. Although Gibson did not acknowledge this, once we have started down that slippery slope, there is also no reason to remove the fly from the supervenience base, or anything else in the frog's environment with which it has a similarly symbiotic relationship.

If the frog could make a variety of decisions about what to do when it sees the fly, the frog would have a fact-icon that could in some sense be seen as referring to flies in those different situations. This level of independence possessed by fact-icons, of which words and propositions are the most sophisticated examples, do create the temptation to think that fact-icons are somehow distinct from the world, and thus perhaps identical to certain kinds of brain states. But there are externalist arguments in this chapter, and others made by philosophers of language like Putnam, Burge, and Millikan, that this level of independence from particular experiences does not permit us to claim that a word or proposition is identical to a particular kind of brain state. However, these kinds of arguments are even stronger when applied to the neural components of nonverbalized experience. In the frog's case, the light, the fly, and neurological activity are not sharply distinguishable parts of the causal nexus that produces the frog's experience at that moment. An organism that possesses language can use the same symbolic icon in service of a variety of different purposes. But the environmental relationship of the nonverbal experiences we share with animals is far more seamless. The frog's ability to capture a fly does not require that the frog have a concept of the fly as independent from itself, anymore than it needs a concept of neuron or reflex. In much the same way, a person hammering has no distinct concept of hammer, until she stops hammering and starts talking to herself about hammering. So the need to separate the brain events from the body or world events in the *experience* of hammering is far less than it is in *thoughts or words* about hammering.

Admittedly, when we perform skillful activities, we do have more flexibility than frogs. But I would not unhesitatingly make the same claim about a hawk's ability to track a mouse through tall grass, or a bloodhound's ability to distinguish one scent from another. The cognitive processes of nonverbal animals are essentially the same as what happens to us when we have "subjective" (i.e., nonlinguistic) experiences. Dewey wants to claim, I think correctly, that it is the interaction between brain, body, and world that creates such experiences, not just the brain activity all by itself.

When we look directly at an object "without doing anything else," it is natural to assume from this perspective that we are encountering the fundamental building blocks from which the rest of our experience is made. In fact, most sensory experience is not passive in this way; it is usually involved in some kind of motor control. We keep our eye on the ball so that we can hit the ball or catch it, and there is no reason to believe that the inputs from our somatosensory system have no affect whatsoever on the visual sensation that Sellars would describe with the coined adverb "a-white-moving-ball-ly". Motor control always uses the muscles and thought processes to achieve some specific purpose that divides up experience in an idiosyncratic way. Musicians must be able hear sounds and feel their muscles in a different way from other people in order to be able to make their instruments play at exactly the right tempo and intonation. And so they hear movements, accents, dynamics, and vibrato, and not just sound (the way an animal[10] would) or music (the way a sympathetic but untrained listener would).

Notice, however, that the musician's and the athlete's experience of performing skillful activities are not raw feels. They have a qualitative character, what Thomas Nagel might call a "what it is like." This qualitative character is irreducibly private. In Michael Polanyi's words, it contains an element of "tacit knowledge" that we know but cannot tell (Polanyi 1966). But this qualitative character, unlike a raw feel, is not epiphenomenal. Without it, the musician or athlete could not successfully perform the skillful activity. Knowing how to play a violin means recognizing exactly what a properly tuned note sounds like, and what it feels like to adjust your muscles to produce that properly tuned note. No set of sentences or mathematical equations can communicate those qualities at an intersubjective level, they have to be felt. But feelings of this sort are not discrete audial or tactile sense data that reside only in the skull. Not only do we have to have those experiences to perform the activities, we have to perform the activities to have the experiences. Imagining ourselves doing these activities may involve only brain activity.[11] But imagining a skillful activity is qualitatively very different from actually doing it, and the most plausible explanation for that difference is that our bodies have to actually interact with the world for the complete experience to happen.

The Cartesian meditation of universal doubt is one particular skillful activity, with its own way of constituting experience. It is taught as a rite of passage in introductory philosophy courses, and its goals and procedures divide up experience in a way that is as real as any other. But it is no realer, and the paradoxes that arise from giving that perspective a privileged status have led us into serious epistemological errors. Once we acknowledge that the Cartesian perspective does not provide a foundation for the rest of our knowledge, we no longer have any reason to confine experience to our minds and thus separate it from the rest of nature. The idea that we start from experience that exists only in our minds, and from this infer the existence of a universe of dead clockwork, no longer holds up if the Cartesian meditation technique does not reveal certainty. Instead we experience, not sense data that remind us of objects, but the objects themselves in a world with which we interact: tables and chairs in which we sit, and people with whom we have relationships, people whose likeability or cruelty or beauty is every bit as predicable to them as is their height or weight.

Without these Cartesian presuppositions, we do not experience facts as being in the world and values as feelings that exist only in the head. We experience the totality of facts, values, and ourselves as a whole that exists in a world. We have no reason to doubt this experience, once we have deprivileged the Cartesian perspective that supposedly makes us certain about what is happening inside the brain and forces us to infer what is happening outside the brain. *This means that experience emerges from (is embodied by) the world, not just our neurons.* When we inquire into the world, we discover the system whose natural parts are the body, the brain, and world. But we have no reason to assume that the brain can produce experience without the other two, any more than the lung can perform its proper function without oxygen.

Minds, Worlds, and Reality

Cartesian materialism, when it acknowledges that it would not be scientific to simply assert the consciousness of brains as a brute fact, sees consciousness as an emergent property of brain structure. Chapters 2 and 3 of this book argue that there is no principled reason to assume that the brain is the only part of the body that embodies the structures responsible for consciousness. Now we have discovered that this slippery slope has carried us out beyond the skin, into the realm of behavior and the world. We must remember that Ryle, who saw mind as being totally a function of external behavior, has already paved our way for this passage, so we shouldn't be too surprised to be here. But there is no denying that the trip is a bit dizzying, so much so that we may confuse where we have arrived with similar but significantly different destinations.

First of all, none of this commits us to the existence of telepathy. I am not saying that we "magically" become aware of the outside world. The connections between the environment and the brain I am speaking of are purely causal and physical. It is no more mysterious to claim that consciousness emerges from brain–world physical interactions than to claim that it emerges from the physical interactions between neurons. It is, however, no *less* mysterious, and the mystery is more noticeable only because we have gotten used to the idea of minds emerging from neural interactions. Unfamiliar mysteries are more disturbing that familiar ones, but that does not mean they are either more or less comprehensible. As Chalmers and others have pointed out, the emergence of consciousness from anything physical, whether neurons, environment, or silicon, is not easily comprehensible if we accept our current concepts of the physical and the mental. In the next chapter, I will deal with how Chalmers's "hard problem" changes radically once we acknowledge that Cartesian materialism cannot be taken for granted. But for the moment I will just say that Cartesian materialism is no worse or better on this score than the alternative I am proposing.

This Deweyan theory of experience also does not imply Kantian idealism, although it would if it were joined with Cartesian materialism. If we replace independent sense data with a self-contained perceptual system that was located entirely in the brain, the world would only be able to penetrate such a system sporadically, if at all. Any attempt to describe those moments of penetration would make them look uncomfortably like sense data. But if the system in question was already located in the world, there would be no need for the world to penetrate it. Anyone with a knowledge of neuroscience and a poetic soul has surely imagined a fetal brain slowly maturing into consciousness as its neural networks are tuned appropriately.

The abstract pattern that produces consciousness, only vaguely known to us now but surely knowable in principle, would gradually adjust its numerous intelligible parameters until it came into full focus. The only thing I am saying is that there is no reason to assume that all of those parameters would be confined to the brain or even to the body of an organism, once it is interacting with a world. Consciousness could be a pattern that, like a vibration started by throwing a stone in the water, ripples through the world even though there is a biological creature at its center. Like all analogies, this one ignores numerous differences. The pattern that is consciousness would be far more complex than the simple circles that emanate from a stone, and the "ripples" of consciousness probably come back to the center and thus become causes as well as effects. But the important point here is that a pattern, particularly a dynamic one, can be embodied by different stuffs at different times. Once we recognize that consciousness is a pattern, rather than a piece of meat in the skull, there is no reason to assume that the embodiment of that pattern is nothing but the brain.

But don't we still end up with some sort of Kantian perspective that says the whole universe ends up existing in our minds? No, for there is an important difference between a universe and a world or environment. It's not that far from ordinary usage to say that we recognize that we each have a world that is not all there is to reality. My world is that part of reality in which I am at home. It contains items that I have an extended interactive relationship with. Many of these items are not conscious beings, which is why this theory does not imply the more preposterous forms of panpsychism. Anyone who has read David Skrbina's exhaustive survey (Skrbina 2003) would hesitate to dispose of the numerous forms of panpsychism with a single argument. But there is one form of panpsychism I will unhesitatingly renounce: the far-fetched speculation that consciousness is also possessed by rocks and trees and toasters, even though they offer no behavioral indication that they have it.[12] There is no reason or evidence for positing the existence of experiential centers in the above-mentioned objects. We experience other human beings as conscious beings (and sometimes dogs, cats, etc.), because it is a useful assumption that enables us to act skillfully in our world with relatively few errors. A person who experienced rocks and trees as conscious beings would undergo so many disappointments and unfulfilled expectations that they could not function effectively in the world without abandoning that assumption. It is therefore reasonable to trust our assumptions about who is conscious in the world and what isn't, even though we may occasionally be fooled by audioanimatronic dolls, and people in comas.

However, because consciousness is a product of a system, it is also possible to designate parts of that system that are not conscious. Even mind–brain identity theorists will acknowledge that the individual neurons are not conscious. Similarly, the claim that the brain–body–world nexus is conscious does not imply that all of the parts of that nexus are conscious. It does imply, however, that each of these objects plays a role in constituting our conscious experience, even though they are not con- scious themselves. Because our experience of an object is partly embodied by the object itself, it is every bit as real as the object itself. We experience the objects in our world as being beautiful or barren or opportunities for climbing, not as naked dead things utterly lacking in value. This experience of them is as real as their shape or color, for these values emerge as a result of real relationships that exist between us and them. When we experience something as an object with value, it does possess a kind of "otherness." We could not desire the beautiful object, or flee from the fearful object, if we thought that we were the same thing as the object. But this relationship of otherness is in constant flux. The desirable object becomes a possession, and thus is experienced as mine, and consequently part of who I am. The fearful object is vanquished or driven out of my world, and thus negated. These, and many other purposeful interactions too numerous to catalog here, determine where the self stops and the world begins.

Consequently, to say that the mind emerges from the brain–body–world nexus does *not* mean that there is no world, only a mind. The line between the self and the world must always be drawn somewhere for any conscious being *at any given moment*. But this does not imply that there is a single place that the line can be drawn for all conscious beings, or for a single conscious being throughout its history. Although it is often convenient for the neuroscientist to draw the line between the world and the mind at the skull or the skin, this does not mean that this division will suit all other purposes. But the line will always be drawn somewhere. That is what it means to live in a world.

The first thing we encounter when we stop all our other projects and reflect upon this world is our bodily sensations, but these sensations are not discrete bits. They are part of a complicated perceptual and motor system that enables us to act in response to the outside world and/or passively endure or enjoy it. To fully understand why we have these sensations rather than others, that perceptual motor system has to be related to the long-range projects and goals that motivate the distinctions we make between the significant and the ignorable. It is because of these projects that I encounter the particular objects that make up my world: my computer, the street on which I live, the United States government, other selves whose worlds overlap with (and cocreate) my world in varying degrees, the writings of Heidegger and Dewey that I am paraphrasing as I write this. My world also includes indications of its own incompleteness, and these are the evidence for the reality that exists beyond my world. I know, for example, that there is dirt under my house, but although this fact is part of my world, the dirt itself is not. Each of us also knows that the other people we encounter have worlds of their own, which include items and processes that are not part my world, such as an educational history that enable them to tell elms from birches. We also know that other people encounter other people, and so on ad infinitum. Perhaps our worlds include possible people (the epistemological equivalent of the ideal observer in ethics) who could go to places that no one has ever actually been, such as the outside of our solar system, or the inside of a quark (if they have insides). We thus see that although my world is much bigger than my brain, it is not infinite, and there is a reality that extends beyond it.

Because our goals and purposes are more complex and flexible than those of the tick described above by Von Uexkull, the boundaries between one's world and the rest of reality are in constant flux. Even within those parts of reality in which I am at home, there are still fluctuations as to what constitutes my world at any given moment. When Descartes had the original insightful experiences that inspired his *Meditations*, his reality probably consisted primarily of his brain states, and perhaps certain body states as well. But once he sat down to write about these insights, his world also contained his desk and his quill. When he got up from his desk to ride across town to dinner, his world probably had about as much geography in it as yours or mine.

More important, reality continually impinges upon our comforts and requires us to establish new relationships that incorporate these impingements into our worlds. This is why we find idealism so counterintuitive.

Reality is so clearly beyond us, and so constantly challenging us, that it is absurd to say that it exists in our minds. But this is equally true even if our minds exist in our worlds, and not in our skulls. Our worlds are not invulnerable to outside encroachments by reality. We encounter strange travelers and phenomena who upset the world we are used to; that is an inevitable part of the human condition. But there is no reason to infer from this that the world that we lived in before these upsets occurred was an illusion that our brains projected across reality like a magic lantern show. The relationships that constitute our environment evolved from our interactions with the reality around us and are embodied by those inter-actions. When we learn to interact with the new phenomena that we found upsetting at first, there is no need to account for this by saying that we now have a copy of the world in our heads. The new interactions, like the previous ones, are interactions between a brain, a body, and a world.

Dan Dennett makes this important point about the relationship between a conscious being and the world it inhabits.

Wherever there is a conscious mind, there is a point of view. . . . A conscious mind is an observer, who takes in a limited subset of all the information there is. An observer takes in the information that is available at a particular (roughly) contin-uous sequence of times and places in the universe. For most practical purposes, we can consider the point of view of a particular conscious subject to be just that: a point moving through space-time . . . for instance . . . we explain the startling time gap between the sound and sight of different fireworks by noting the different transmission speeds of sound and light. They arrive *at the observer* (at that point) at different times, even though they left the source at the same time.

What happens, though, when we close in on the observer, and try to locate the observer's point of view more precisely, as a point within the individual? The simpler assumptions that work so well on larger scales begin to break down. (Dennett 1991, pp. 101–103)

I think there is no way that those of us who agree with Dennett on this point can avoid several other conclusions. Dennett's point is that there is no reason to assume that this model will work once we get inside the brain. But there is also no reason to assume that it will always work inside the skin, or that there is a constant and unchanging line between where it works and where it doesn't work. At any given time, there is a region within my world in which I am engaged with my tools; the region within which everything is ready-to-hand for me and thus not observable. And this region, I maintain, is *me* in the most unambiguous sense possible. The

pattern of activity that occurs within that region is primarily what embodies me: it includes, but is not limited to, the activity in my brain and body.
When I observe something, or relate to it in any other way, it becomes
part of that region of activity, and thus, in a nontrivial sense, part of me.
As a poetic metaphor, this statement is almost common sense. But the
arguments that Dennett and I have put forth against Cartesian materialism create a slippery slope that disposes of any reasons to avoid taking it
literally.

The experience of having something enter my world is a fundamental
aspect of having experience. So is the experience of having something
move from the edge of my world toward the center. But the difference
between these two is broad and blurry, for James was right when he said
that consciousness is always surrounded by a fringe (James 1890, ch. 11).
The dirt under my house is not really a part of my world, but it is closer
to my world than the dark side of the moon (unless I am an astronomer,
in which case the dark side of the moon could be near the center of my
world if that were my specialty). If my world is constituted by the goals
and activities that engage me at any given moment, its borders would fluctuate as they fluctuate. The borders between my world and the rest of
reality would be, as Dennett said in slightly different context, contentious
and gerrymandered.

To map the embodiment of my consciousness would be to map the
dynamics of the numerous interactions that take place in my world, and
to do so would require not just talking about the computational regions
described by variations in neurosynaptic voltages. The synaptic voltages
would make no sense without relating them to the world, and I see no
reason to deny the ontological implications of this epistemological fact. As
neuroscience has become more interdisciplinary, this has become harder
and harder to ignore. The following example is almost certainly only the
tip of an increasingly harder to avoid iceberg.

In *Friday's Footprints*, psychiatrist Leslie Brothers shows how certain neurological data reveal a brain system consisting mainly of the cingulate
gyrus, the amygdala, and the orbital frontal cortex. This system is designed
to enable humans and other primates to interact socially. This accounts
for the fact that a variety of otherwise unrelated malfunctions occur when
the amygdala is either stimulated or damaged. When human subjects
receive electrical stimulation of the amygdala, they experience feelings of

insecurity that they describe in specifically social terms, such as "being at a party and not being welcome" (Brothers 1997, p. 49). A patient with a disease that damaged the amygdala showed both a socially inappropriate loss of sexual inhibitions and an inability to read the emotional meaning of facial expressions, although she had no trouble identifying the faces (ibid., p. 54). Other patients with damaged amygdalas showed an inability to interpret the social and emotional significance of voice tones. Monkeys who had their amygdalas removed lost all of the abilities necessary to communicate with other monkeys socially: "they had blank facial expressions, poor body language, and lack of eye contact" (ibid., p. 62). Rhesus monkeys without amygdalas were usually killed by their old social groups when placed back among them.

A knowledge of primate social interactions is essential in order to make any sense out of this constellation of pathologies. (A fact that might be easy for some neuroscientists to ignore, because being primates themselves, they acquired this knowledge as children and/or genetically.) Consequently, this provides even more impetus for the trend among neurophilosophers to believe that psychology will coevolve with neuroscience, rather than be eliminated by it. Imagine an alien neuroscientist who lives alone on his planet like an extraterrestrial Prospero, but with no Miranda, Ariel, or Caliban. He consequently has no knowledge of social interactions. Imagine him kidnapping a terrestrial primate and trying to discover the function of the amygdala by conducting experiments on that solitary caged creature. There is no way the alien would ever be able to figure out why one organ was in charge of this particular amalgam of (1) behavioral changes that related to reproduction, (2) certain sounds and not others, (3) certain images and not others, and (4) an apparently arbitrary set of body movements. (In fact, early experiments by humans on caged monkeys were unable to figure out the significance of the amygdala.) Of course, the alien's task would be even more difficult if he was studying the primate's brain in a vat. To increase our understanding of any socially significant system in the brain, we will have to increase our understanding not only of physiology but of social science as well. If we don't know in detail what this system is doing, we can't even ask ourselves how the system does it. To understand what this system is doing we have to see it as part of a greater system that includes—surprise!—a brain, a body, and a world.

The dramatic quality of Brothers's examples makes it easy to see this point, but it is equally true of almost all other neuroscience. Would it have been possible to discover that there is a certain part of the brain that is dedicated to seeing faces if we did not know what a face is? Could we understand why face recognition is so important without concepts like "kinship" and "predator"? Could we have made any sense out of the function of the retina without considering its relationship to light, or the importance of embodied organisms to see things?

Although arguably there are times when it is not appropriate to go from an epistemological argument to an ontological argument, I can see no reason to refrain from that move now. The complex social behavior of primates is one of the reasons that we think of them as being conscious. If we assume that there is usually a reasonable correlation between the criteria we use for making judgments and the way things are, then this complex social behavior is at least partly responsible for the fact that primates are conscious. Because this behavior requires a world with other primates to relate to, and the neural behavior makes no sense unless it is embedded in such a world, I believe that we should conclude that it is the brain, body, and world that embody consciousness and not the brain alone.

Perhaps you are not convinced by my redefinition of the borders of physical–mental supervenience. Perhaps you still believe that the mind is the brain. Or perhaps you accept my arguments that extend supervenience to the skin, but are willing to go no further. But I hope I have at least convinced you that the claim that the mind is the brain must be justified by arguments and evidence; it cannot be assumed as a brute fact, or even as the only serious contender. In the next chapter, I will argue that once we acknowledge that physical–mental supervenience is up for grabs, any attempt to justify one position or another brings us face to face with what philosophers call the zombie problem. This question (also referred to as the "hard problem") is often considered to be purely academic in the worst sense of the term. But that is only because mind–brain identity is assumed to be a brute fact. Once we need to justify one form of physical–mental supervenience over another, the zombie problem becomes unavoidable. What criteria can we use to choose among the possible candidates? There seems to be no possible answer to that question, given the assumptions that usually shape the debate. However, the Deweyan theory of experience I have begun to describe in this chapter redefines the concept of subjective in such a way as to make a solution possible. It does so by radically redefining the relationship between the subjective and the objective.

7 The Return of the Zombies

No one would ever be able to make a successful horror movie about philosophers' zombies. Hollywood zombies are, of course, dramatically different from ordinary people. They shuffle, drool, stare into space, and do horrifying things. But philosophers' zombies behave exactly like ordinary humans, except that they lack consciousness. There's nobody home, no little light on inside, but no way for anyone to detect this fact.[1] The zombie debate among philosophers is over whether this concept involves some sort of contradiction or confusion, like talking about round squares or Oxford University as being something more than a particular set of buildings, people, and activities.

Dennett, who believes that zombies are a by-product of confused thinking, probably speaks for most practicing scientists when he says that the zombie question "sums up, in one leaden lump, everything that I think is wrong about current thinking about consciousness" (Dennett 1996, p. 322). I sympathize with this description, because like Dennett I have no strong interest in philosophical questions that have no impact on the practice of science. But I would be a bit more charitable, for I do feel that the hard problem is a genuine anomaly given many widely held presuppositions. I do feel that most philosophical dialogue about zombies goes nowhere interesting, despite the care and intelligence of those contributing to it, and that most people looking for a scientific explanation of consciousness can safely ignore the current philosophical literature on the subject. But the problem is real, for it stems from the four presuppositions mentioned in the first chapter, which are, I feel, both unavoidable and fruitful. The appearance of triviality, in contrast, arises from uncritical acceptance of Cartesian materialism.

Before the zombie question can be made to deal with issues of scientific interest, however, we must rescue zombies from the philosopher's definition in much the same way that we rescued the word "epiphenomenal." As I said in the first chapter, it is useless to talk about things that are absolutely epiphenomenal, but useful to talk about being epiphenomenal with respect to a particular functional system. Similarly, although it is scientifically useless to talk about a zombie that is exactly like a human but lacks consciousness, it can sometimes be useful to conduct thought experiments that posit zombies that differ from us in other ways, and then consider whether those differences have any effect on the existence of consciousness. When we do this, we are bringing into philosophical and scientific discourse something similar to a Hollywood zombie: a creature that tempts us to label it a conscious being, but which nevertheless is clearly missing something. In the case of the Hollywood zombie, what is missing is a certain clearness of eye, control of salivary glands, and so forth. We can help clarify our concept of consciousness by positing zombies that are missing other more philosophically interesting characteristics, and then asking ourselves whether we believe the missing item is either functionally essential or epiphenomenal with respect to consciousness. The most extreme philosopher's zombie is a being that isn't missing anything except consciousness itself. But very few philosophers who actually defend the possibility of zombies are that hard core. Chalmers has talked about his "zombie twin," which is exactly like him, down to the last quark, but is not conscious. This sort of zombie is a useless concept scientifically, as far as I can tell. Chalmers himself admits that such a zombie would be logically possible, but not physically possible. This means that scientists, who are only interested in physical reality, can safely ignore them. But there are other kinds of philosophical zombies that are relevant to scientific research, because they help clarify the distinction between the functionally essential and the epiphenomenal.

In a discussion of zombies in his 1995 article in *Journal of Consciousness Studies*, Güven Güzeldere artfully sums up the debate by describing three distinct kinds of zombies: behavioral, functional, and physiological. This distinction rests on what each of these concepts considers to be epiphenomenal about consciousness. A behavioral zombie is one that behaves exactly like a human being, but lacks what Güzeldere calls a "functional-computational structure on the basis of which they could have a true psychological description" (1995, p. 328). A functional zombie is one that possesses a functional-computational structure identical to that of a conscious being, but is nevertheless not conscious. A physiological zombie is one that lacks consciousness even though it is exactly like us in every biologically relevant detail. Güzeldere notes that each of these categories is a subset of the one that follows it. A functional zombie would by definition duplicate perfectly the behavior of the behavioral zombie, and the physiological zombie would be functionally equivalent to a functional zombie. I think that these three categories accurately describe the outlines of the debate as it has gone so far. But I want to make finer divisions within the category of physical zombie, and discuss a significant relationship between functional and behavioral zombies. When we do this, we will see that there is scientific research that cannot be fully understood unless we face the zombie problem head on.

Why Physiological Zombies Have Scientific Significance

Physiological zombies are usually thought of as being equivalent to zombie twins, but this assumption ignores another important possibility. The further question remains: *What* aspect of our physiology embodies our conscious experience? Any attempt to answer that question, once we acknowledge that we can't simply take Hippocrates' word for it, leads us back to a new version of the zombie problem. The usual assumption is that science has proven that if we duplicated either Chalmers's brain or the brain of his zombie twin and put them in a vat with a life support system, there would be no change in the consciousness (or lack thereof) of either. The relationship between brain and body is thus seen as roughly analogous to that between horse and rider. The body is alive but not conscious, and only the brain has the kind of life that produces consciousness. But the facts described in the first five chapters show that this assumption, although far from disproven, is also far from undeniable.

Let us suppose that someone completely models the neural activity in the cranium that is responsible for consciousness, and claims that he has created a conscious being. Another person expands his model to include all of the connections in the rest of the nervous system as well. Person A says, "all that extra stuff is not essential," and person B says, "yes it is." How do we decide who is right? Person A says, "My machine is conscious, because a brain in a vat would be conscious, and my machine models the behavior of a brain in a vat." But why should we go with person A just because Cartesian materialism says that a brain in a vat is conscious? No one has ever proven this, and I don't see how anyone possibly could. This is the presupposition that makes the zombie problem appear scientifically trivial, and it is completely unfounded. The fact that almost everyone believes in Cartesian materialism should cut no ice whatsoever: science is not supposed to take commonsense intuitions for granted.

On the other hand, how do we decide between person B and person C, who says that we must also model the chemical flow of hormones in the cerebral spinal fluid? Both of their theories expand beyond common sense in plausible ways, as good scientific theories should, but how can we tell which one is better? Suppose when we observe the behavior of one of these new systems, a little light goes on in our minds and a voice says, "Aha! this one must be conscious!" So what? Why should that be any more decisive than a flutter in the stomach, or a pattern in tealeaves or animal entrails? When we suggest a radical new theory about anything else, we can make a prediction about what will happen based on that theory, and if we all observe that this prediction, and others like it, are successful, we eventually decide that the theory is true. But the only prediction that makes any decisive difference in a theory of consciousness is not observable by anyone except the subject of the experiment. Person A's machine knows that it is conscious, if it is, but we can't take its word for it, assuming it can speak. Otherwise any simple text-based program with stored answers to questions like "Are you conscious?" would be conscious. We are therefore forced to fall back directly on our own commonsense intuitions. This is why the Turing test relies entirely on the human ability to make decisions based on whether we feel someone or something is behaving like a conscious being.

Science, of course, relies on intuitions of its own to tell good methods from bad ones, and the development of those intuitions is part of what it means to acquire expertise. But in this arena science seems to be no better equipped to answer the question than the person-on-the-street, which makes one wonder whether science has made any real progress at all. To use the Turing test to determine the truth about the nature of consciousness is rather like using a public opinion poll to decide whether or not Columbus landed in America in 1492. No one would ever choose between theories in any other scientific discipline using nothing but a naked appeal to common sense. Yet that seems to be what usually happens when questions about thought and consciousness arise.

Consider, for example, the famous Chinese nation argument that appears in Block 1978. Block points out that in principle we could duplicate the functional structure of the brain by having the entire nation of China manipulate flash cards in the same functionally essential pattern that occurs in a conscious brain. And yet, Block claims it is obvious that the resulting pattern would not be conscious. Many people, myself included, have responded to this claim with "That sure isn't obvious to me!" But what sort of experiment could we possibly run, and what sort of findings must it reveal, to prove that I am right about this and Block is wrong (or vice versa)? This thought experiment can't prove what Block wants it to prove, because there is no reason to assume that our commonsense intuitions are worth anything when taken out of their natural abode and placed in a possible world as loony as this one. But those of us who believe that Block is wrong are equally powerless to prove him wrong. If we can't imagine anything but common sense as a way of telling zombies from conscious beings, why do we have any reason to assume that a science of consciousness is even possible?

Functional and Behavioral Zombies

This problem becomes even more obvious when we examine the relationship between functional and behavioral zombies. Güzeldere says that the behavioral zombie is a philosopher's fancy, because it would have to be manipulated by a miracle or a deity. But in fact AI is already on the verge of confronting the problem of behavioral zombies, thanks to some recent achievements. AI is now operating out of two radically different paradigms, neither of which has so far replaced the other. The symbolic systems hypothesis (sometimes called good old-fashioned artificial intelligence, or GOFAI) models the behavior of conscious beings by analyzing them into functional structures that use the principles of logical inference. Connectionism models the behavior of conscious beings using a network of connected nodes that are functionally similar to the actual structure of the brain.

The functional structures of GOFAI and connectionist systems are radically different from each other, so much so that there is no real consensus on exactly what the differences are. Some claim that the hardware–

software distinction, which is essential to GOFAI, is not even applicable to connectionist systems. But there is no denying that the similarities between brains and connectionist systems must be seen as in some sense functional, rather than purely physical, for the latter are, after all, made out of silicon rather than protein. In this same sense in which brains and connectionist systems are functionally similar, brains and GOFAI systems are functionally very different. When contemporary cognitive neuroscientists make an abstract map of what was going on in the brain, it usually resembles something that could be modeled in silicon by a connectionist system. Such a map is structurally very different from the flow charts that are used to divide a GOFAI computer system into modules. But although GOFAI and connectionist systems are *functionally* very different, they have at the very least the capability of being *behaviorally* very similar.

GOFAI's proudest achievement so far has been the creation of Deep Blue, a chess-playing program that has beaten a world champion player. There is no question, however, that the functional processes used by the minds of a human chess champion are radically different from those used by Deep Blue to simulate them. Deep Blue relies on a search algorithm that considers a much broader range of possibilities for each move than a human being ever could. It is able to do this because the electrical signals used by a computer travel at the speed of light, and the signals that travel through human neurons travel at only about two hundred miles an hour. Consequently, however the human mind manages to play skillful chess, it doesn't do it by implementing the same program as Deep Blue. If it did, it would take thousands of years to decide on a single move. Although no one has yet built a connectionist system that can play chess as well as Deep Blue, the current assumption is that the chess masters themselves are such systems. If this assumption is correct, this would mean that when Deep Blue is competing with a chess champion, what we have are two functionally different systems, one connectionist, one GOFAI, which are behaviorally equivalent.

During Descartes's time, I think that most people would have assumed that any machine that could play chess was conscious. But living around the rational machines of the computer age has caused us to raise the bar for what counts as conscious, so let us consider the following thought experiment. Let us suppose that the GOFAI labs succeed in building a machine (call it Super Blue) that can not only play grand master level chess, but also pass the toughest sort of Turing test imaginable. Let us suppose the connectionist labs also create a machine that passes the Turing test (call it Super Net). We don't really need Super Net to create this problem, if connectionist theory is correct in assuming that we are Super Nets. But let's posit it anyway, to make the following development possible. The connectionist lab, in order to decrease the competition for funding, claims that Super Blue is not really conscious at all, because it does not have the same functional structure as a biological conscious being. It is, the connectionists claim, only a behavioral zombie, and this is proven by the fact that there are not only physical, but functional, differences between Super Blue and a conscious being. The GOFAI lab responds by saying that these differences are not functional, but only epiphenomenal, and have no more significance than the fact that both Super Blue and Super Net are made out of silicon rather than protein.

How can we possibly decide between these two claims? This is not a trivial question. Because the whole point is to create a conscious being, what we are trying to decide is the success or failure of each lab's entire project (to say nothing of the fact that money is at stake). Do we really want to say that the only factors that determine consciousness are those that can be measured without opening up the machine's black box? This is rather like saying that people do not suffer if we cannot hear them scream. Can we say that it is purely a matter of arbitrary proclamation or semantics? Then why not proclaim that certain races are not conscious, and thus morally legitimatize slavery?

The Roots of the Problem

What both of these examples show is that if we can simply posit the identity of mind with one particular hunk of biological stuff, or one particular functional structure, the zombie problem is only of philosophical, rather than scientific, significance. But once there is more than one contender for the title of mental embodiment, the decision between the two contenders becomes stunningly arbitrary, given the assumptions that make the zombie problem possible. Many important scientific discoveries have been made operating on the assumption by physiologists that the mind is the brain, and the assumption by AI researchers that what the brain does is manipulate symbols using the rules of logical inference. But these assumptions are no longer unquestionable, and once we question them, the zombie problem rears its confusingly ugly head.

The fact that zombies reveal problems for scientists does not mean that the scientists can find the answer in the laboratory. Nor does it mean that these problems can be solved by a specialized philosophy of consciousness. When a problem is impossible to answer in principle, it is a waste of time to treat it as a self-contained question. Given the current set of presuppositions, there is obviously no theory of consciousness that cannot be disarmed by the statement "But I can imagine a machine possessing X and not being conscious." To look for one would be to confuse a conceptual problem with a research problem, rather like measuring every triangle one encounters in hopes of finding one whose angle sum was less than 180 degrees. It therefore cannot be a weakness of any particular theory of consciousness that it is vulnerable to this objection, and consequently when a scientist hears a philosopher make this criticism of his theory, the scientist can safely ignore it.

What the philosopher needs to do, rather than annoy the scientist with objections that are impossible to satisfy, is to question the other concepts that are presupposed in the formulation of the problem.[2] We have already questioned the concept of causality in chapter 4, which is one of the reasons we now have very different zombie problems than the ones we started with. In the next section of this chapter, and some of the chapters after that, we will explore alternative epistemological theories that I believe can help to solve these problems. When the zombie problem is seen from an epistemological perspective, it is often called the problem of "the explanatory gap" between our theories and our subjective experience. I am proposing that we examine our presuppositions about both sides of the gap. The gap is, I maintain, as much a by-product of the nature of theories as it is a by-product of the nature of consciousness.

Zombies, Experience, and Skepticism

Oxford ordinary language philosophy considered commonsense to be the final court for deciding what is acceptable philosophically. Contemporary naturalized philosophy, in contrast, refers to commonsense ideas about the self and consciousness with the pejorative term "folk psychology." This label was chosen to emphasize that folk psychology, like any other kind of folk knowledge, is in principle vulnerable to revision in response to scientific discoveries. But even naturalized philosophy must use folk psychology as a starting point. At the moment folk psychology is the only theory we've got that can account for many regular occurrences in daily life. We cannot use neuroscience to explain why someone goes to the store to buy milk, when they want milk and believe that the store carries it.

Nor are the folk referred to in this label merely the so-called people on the street. When we talk about how scientists ought to do science, we must use folk psychological categories when we say that they *want* to find the truth, and that they (we) *believe* that following the scientific method will help them find it. There is, of course, a huge difference between the way people appear in the folk psychological image and the way they appear when studied in laboratories and under microscopes. But the scientists doing the comprehending still see *themselves* in folk psychological terms when they are formulating explanations about what they have discovered, and when they are evaluating the scientific work that they do. So if we wish to understand how our theory of explanation leads us to consider the possibility of things like zombies, we must look at those aspects of folk psychology that science shares with folk psychology. Although the hermeneutics of folk psychology is a long way from being a quantifiable science, it is somewhat easier when we limit ourselves to the folk psychology shared by practitioners and admirers of science, since scientists, like Oxford dons, share a common culture thanks to the specialized training that they receive. In this chapter, I will try to show that at least some of the seductiveness of the zombie question can be accounted for by considering the implications of certain principles that science adapted from common sense.

At the beginning of the last chapter, I described how the Cartesian materialist sense datum theory I described gave rise to the problem of skepticism. It also gives rise to the most widely known arguments for the zombie problem as well. Sense datum theory claims that our subjective experience is directly given to us, and our knowledge of the objective world is inferred from the subjective. The difference between feeling our subjective experiences and knowing about the world seems so fundamental, so irreducible, that it seems to be completely responsible for the hard problem. The only way to be aware of feelings is to feel them, and we cannot ever feel anyone's feelings but our own. So why shouldn't it be possible for everyone except me to be a zombie? This is the assumption that supports the following arguments from Chalmers.

Conscious Experience, by contrast, forces itself upon us as an explanandum and cannot be eliminated so easily. (Chalmers 1996, p. 109)

Experience is the most central and manifest aspect of our mental lives, and indeed is perhaps the key explanandum in the science of the mind. Because of this status as an explanandum, experience cannot be discarded like the vital spirit when a new theory comes along. (Chalmers 1995, p. 206)

If it were not for the fact that first-person experience was a brute fact presented to us, there would seem to be no reason to predict its existence. (Chalmers 1990)

Locutions like "forces itself," "central and manifest," and "brute fact" clearly imply Chalmers's belief that experience is in some sense directly given to us, in a way that the rest of our knowledge is not. Anyone who rejects what Sellars (1963) calls the "myth of the given" has no reason to take these arguments seriously. But the hard problem cannot, alas, be dissolved merely by disposing of these arguments. There is clearly some sort of difference between our awareness of the objective and our awareness of the subjective. All of our concepts about knowledge and how it relates to the world presuppose this difference. We probably could not make sense of anything we say or do if we tried to do without it. If we cannot account for that difference by saying that the subjective is directly given and the objective is inferred, we need to come up with another explanation for it.

Given that we don't have a direct awareness of subjective experience, how do we know what sort of subjective experiences we are having? And how is our knowledge of subjective experience different from our knowledge of the external world? There are certain ways of relating to subjective experience that appear at first to be not significantly different from the way we relate to the objective world. When we learn folk psychology, we acquire what I call the concept of the third person first person (3P1P for short). The 3P1P enables us to think about and classify mental states in terms that can be communicated to other people, and these are the same concepts that enable us to make sense out of our own mental life, rather than just experience it. But there are also certain aspects of 3P1P concepts that make them very different from any other concepts we have. We know what pains are, we know how people behave when they have them, and we know what it is like for us to have them. But we also know, because it is a necessary part of the 3P1P concept, that it is very different for other people to have pains than it is for us to have them. When I see you drop a rock on your foot, we both know that you have dropped a rock on your foot. But there is something in our respective experiences of this fact that is very different, and none of the arguments against your "direct awareness" of your pain exempts us from the need to acknowledge this difference.

We make a variety of inferences and descriptions based on this difference, and almost all of these descriptions and inferences underline the difference between what is subjectively felt and what is intersubjectively knowable. To determine what we know and what we don't, we have to separate the subjective from what can be communicated in what Sellars (1963) calls the "space of reasons." If we can't tell the difference between the subjective and the verbally expressible, it would be impossible to communicate to other conscious beings. The primary purpose of the concept of the subjective is to aid us in making this distinction, particularly if one is in a knowledge-seeking profession. This is one reason why the subjective cannot be explained in principle, and that this fact is particularly difficult for philosophers and scientists to ignore. By definition, the subjective is that part of our experience that cannot be explained. Conversely, anything that could be communicated to our fellow inhabitants of (visitors to?) the space of reasons would by definition not be subjective. So there is a kind of conceptual necessity for the claim that no explanation can ever account for subjective experience. The purpose of explanations is to separate the subjective from the objective, so if something can be captured in an explanation, then by definition it can't be subjective.

We also have much higher expectations for an explanation of consciousness than for explanations of anything else. Part of the reason for this is that because our consciousness is always with us, we are far more aware of the gap between *explanans* and *explanandum* with consciousness than we are with other concepts and their objects. What we really want from a theory of consciousness is to explain our consciousness and have nothing left over, and no theory can ever do that with its subject matter. We don't expect this from theories about other things. It doesn't bother us that there will always be an explanatory gap between our concept of dog and individual dogs like Fido and Rover. Fido will have a distinctive pattern to his fur, and flecks of dirt on his feet from his morning walk, Rover will be bigger and taller than Fido and have a slightly crooked left incisor that he inherited from his sire. None of these factors is accounted for when we classify Fido and Rover as dogs, and this doesn't bother us, because we can sense that the concept of dog somehow captures what Fido and Rover have in common. We expect the concept of dog to leave out Fido's and Rover's individual characteristics; that is part of its job. The more dogs we see, the less we expect the concept of dog to account for in an individual dog.

Suppose, however, that Rover was the only dog we had ever seen or heard tell of. We would have no way of knowing whether that crooked left incisor was a characteristic of Rover or of dogs in general. Increase this problem by several orders of magnitude and you at least partially account for the explanatory gap between consciousness and explanation. For an essential assumption of the 3P1P is that we have only one exemplification of conscious experience to account for—our own—and nothing else that is a member of a genus that remotely resembles it. How can we possibly develop a general concept when we are studying what is experienced as one awesomely unique case? No matter what we say about consciousness there will always be something we have left out, just as there will always be something left out when we say Rover is a dog. But with any explanation of consciousness we will always feel that something essential has been left out, because it is impossible with consciousness to tell the difference between essence and accident. This is at least part of what we are experiencing when we notice that something is being left out of any theory of consciousness. A theory of consciousness is not conscious; it does not sit thoughtfully in hyperspace wondering how many people will eventually believe it is true. So there will always be an explanatory gap between it and its subject matter. But that is not a failing of theories of consciousness in particular, but of all human theories possible and actual.

Although the subjective is defined by its relationship to the objective, it is not merely a negative category. We can and do speak of pains, fears, sensations, hopes, desires, and other inhabitants of subjective space. So the 3P1P concept of subjectivity is not a negative concept like "gentile," which refers to non-Jews without saying anything specific about them. Our 3P1P concepts have a lush and vivid variety to them, referring to tickles, itches, tastes, smells, remorse, elation, colors, shapes, and sounds. Furthermore, the 3P1P concepts have the ability to change and refine the subjective experiences themselves. They do not just describe or refer to the subjective experiences, the way the concept of dog refers to a dog. The sound of a minor ninth chord is a subjective sensation, with a distinctive qualitative presence. But I can recognize that sound when I hear it only because I've studied the theory of jazz harmony. There are plenty of people who experience all jazz chords as essentially the same, and there was a time when I was one of them. Learning how to recognize that chord involved setting up a dynamic relationship between the vibrations of the instrument and my perceptual system. It is possible to set up that relationship without using the 3P1P concept. There are musicians who can play minor ninth chords (and play them at the right time so that they make elegant musical sense) but cannot tell you what a ninth chord is. But it is impossible to understand the verbal concept "ninth chord" if you have never had the perceptual sensation of ninth chord. When the musically illiterate but skillful musician learns to recognize the ninth chord he has been playing for years, it could be argued that in some sense the sensation itself has not changed, it has merely been identified. But when someone to whom all jazz chords once sounded the same learns to recognize a ninth chord, and to distinguish it from major seventh and diminished chords, then the 3P1P concept is actually creating a new sensation that it can refer to. This is what Paul Churchland (1979) calls the plasticity of perception.

Learning to recognize and distinguish such qualities, and learning what muscles should be moved in response to them and when, is an essential part of acquiring any physical skill. If there has not been this change in our perceptual concepts, but only a change in our verbal concepts, the person will only be able to talk about the skill, he will not be able to do it. This perceptual plasticity occurs in all sensory modalites throughout our lives. If the doctor needs this information, a person in pain can develop a whole new set of concepts to distinguish different kinds of pain, and tell when the pain is stabbing, searing, burning, a slow ache, and so forth. But although the ability to recognize and classify pains requires being able to make a judgment with a specific content, there is more to being in pain than being able to make such a judgment; you and I can both make such a judgment about my pain, although I will probably find it of greater interest than you, but my pain hurts me and doesn't hurt you. What is this factor that differentiates my awareness of my pains from your awareness of my pains? Admittedly, this difference is not always as absolute as is widely believed. Anyone who has had to care for a suffering loved one knows that what one feels in that situation is nothing like altruistic concern, and far too strong to be called mere empathy. But the difference is still real, and the contemporary view attributed to Sellars that "All awareness is a linguistic affair" has no effective way of accounting for this difference.

Dennett's *Consciousness Explained* (1991) attempts to account for this difference by eliminating it, for he describes all perceptions as kinds of judgments. This is the subtext behind his attacks on the claim that the existence of blindsight proves that it is possible to separate qualitative experience from information. For Dennett, qualitative experience without information is a contradiction in terms (p. 322). His rejection of qualitative experience is also the primary motivation for his extended attack on external images in chapter 10, and the critique of the concept of "filling in" with the qualitative stuff he derisively labels "figment" (p. 344). Dennett could claim that in these critiques he is consistently applying the Sellarsian dictum that all awareness is a linguistic affair. But in doing so, he is being more royalist than the king, for he blurs a distinction that Sellars himself thought was extremely important.

Sellars, like most analytic and postanalytic philosophers, embraced the assumption that questions about knowledge and thought are primarily questions about language. But unlike most of his contemporaries, Sellars was also aware of the limitations of this assumption. In the following quotation, he almost admits that there is something wrong with his approach, without actually suggesting that there is any other way of dealing with these questions.

> Not all "organized behavior" is built on linguistic structures. The most that can be claimed is that what might be called "conceptual thinking" is essentially tied to language, and that, for obvious reasons, the central or core concept of what thinking is pertains to conceptual thinking. Thus, our common-sense understanding of what sub-conceptual thinking—e.g., that of babies and animals—consists in, involves viewing them as engaged in "rudimentary" forms of conceptual thinking. We interpret their behavior using conceptual thinking as a model but qualify this model in ad hoc and unsystematic ways which really amounts to the introduction of a new notion which is nevertheless labeled "thinking." Such analogical extensions of concepts, when supported by experience, are by no means illegitimate. Indeed, it is essential to science. It is only when the negative analogies are overlooked that the danger of serious confusion and misunderstanding arises. (Sellars 1975, p. 305)

When Sellars wrote about perception, his commitment to the principle that all awareness is linguistic often prompted him to equivocate about "organized behaviors" that were not built on linguistic processes. He claimed that the apparently unified processes of seeing an object in front of us consists of two distinct processes, and (as he often said in class) the only reason that these processes occur simultaneously is that people can chew gum and walk at the same time. The first process consists of the occurrence of a sentence in the mind, saying something like "lo, a pink ice cube over there," and is completely cognitive. The second process consists of a manner of sensing, an occurrence in the mind of a process Sellars called "sensing a-pink-cubely." Sellars usually describes this second process as completely noncognitive, but he never felt completely comfortable with this description. Consider, for example, this passage from Sellars 1963, which offers an explanation for how linguistic knowledge can be derived from prelinguistic experience:

While Jones's ability to give inductive reasons today is built on a long history of acquiring and manifesting verbal habits in perceptual situations, and, in particular, the occurrence of verbal episodes, e.g., "This is green," which is superficially like those which are later properly said to express observational knowledge, it does not require that any episode in this prior time (i.e., before Jones had language) be characterizeable as expressing knowledge.

. . . (Footnote 5 added in 1963) My thought was that one can have direct (non-inferential) knowledge of a past fact which one did not or even (as in the case envisaged) could not conceptualize at the time it was present. (Sellars 1963, p. 169)

Note that this passage equivocates on whether sensory experience is knowledge or not. The original passage says sensory experience is "not . . . characterizeable as expressing knowledge," the footnote says sensory experience is "direct (non-inferential) knowledge."

In *the Structure of Knowledge*, Sellars attempts to clarify this distinction between thought and sensing by saying that musicians and composers have two different ways of thinking about their art. They can think *about* sound (i.e., linguistically) and they can also nonlinguistically think *in* sound. He then makes the following conclusion from this, which seems to contradict many of his other statements.

There is much food for thought in these reflections. . . . But the fundamental problems which they pose arise already at the perceptual level. For as we shall see, visual perception itself is not just a conceptualizing of colored objects within the visual range—a "thinking about" colored objects in a certain context—but in a sense most difficult to analyze, a *thinking in color* about colored objects. (Sellars 1975, p. 305)

Sellars was certainly right that this sense was most difficult to analyze, and the more he wrote on this subject, the more obvious the difficulty became.

This paragraph actually seems to be implying that Sellars believed that sensations are different from both the linguistic and the nonlinguistic thoughts we have about them. This seems to leave us with three categories of mental events, exemplified by (1) linguistic thoughts about sound (2) nonlinguistic thinkings in sound, and (3) audial sensations. One wonders how many more mediating entities would have to be posited if we continued along these lines. What function would the completely noncognitive sensation perform if we had both linguistic and nonlinguistic concepts? Why not just say that the world caused the nonlinguistic concept, and eliminate the noncognitive sensation as an unnecessary middle person? Clearly there was a tension in Sellars's thinking on this point that was very difficult for him to resolve.

This tension is completely absent, however, in Rorty's interpretation of Sellars. His initial description of the problem nicely captures the essence of Sellars's distinction between knowledge and sensation.

> Sellars invokes the distinction between awareness-as-discriminative behavior and awareness as what Sellars calls being "in the logical space of reasons, of justifying and being able to justify what one says." Awareness in the first sense is manifested by rats and amoebas and computers; it is simply reliable signaling. Awareness in the second sense is manifested only by beings whose behavior we construe as the uttering of sentences with the intention of justifying the utterance of other sentences. (Rorty 1979, p. 182)

But Rorty's description of the relationship between these two kinds of discriminative behavior ignores Sellars's ambivalence, describing him as being, like Dennett, firmly committed to the idea that all awareness is linguistic.

> Either grant concepts to anything (e.g., record-changers) which can respond discriminatively to classes of objects, or else explain why you draw the line between conceptual thought and its primitive predecessors in a different place from that between having acquired a language and being still in training. (Ibid., p. 186)

Rorty imagines Sellars placing this dilemma before those who reject the claim that all awareness is a linguistic affair. But it can easily be placed before Sellars himself during those times he is trying to salvage some kind of noncognitive consciousness for sensations–experience. There is no point in criticizing Rorty's Sellars scholarship; the texts are ambiguous enough that his resolution of the ambiguity is as accurate as any. But the other resolution of the ambiguity—saying that there are two different kinds of awareness, which follow different rules—can be more fruitful if we combine it with certain insights from Dewey.

Dewey wanted to claim that experience is not just vaguely perceived knowledge, but something different in kind from knowledge; something constituted by our habits, skills, and abilities, and necessarily linked to our goals, aspirations, and emotions. Throughout its history, philosophy has concentrated on understanding the architecture that made rational thought possible: that is, language. Language is the thing that separates us from the brutes, and entitles us to the Aristotelian honorific "rational animal." For that reason, most philosophers associated conceptual thought with the abstract and the spiritual, and it was thus considered to be the thing that made us conscious beings. Felt experiences were considered to be thoughts that were deficient in some way: They were confused thoughts, waiting to be brought into focus, or atomistic bits of thought waiting to be assembled into scientific theory. Dewey's radical claim was that although "knowing is one mode of experiencing" (Dewey 1910/1997, p. 229), experience in general had more fundamental rules of organization that were all its own. "By our postulate, things are what they are experienced to be; and, unless knowing is the sole and only genuine mode of experiencing, it is fallacious to say that Reality is just and exclusively what it is or would be to an all competent knower" (ibid., p. 228).

Until very recently, it was usually assumed that both sensations and thoughts were constituted by processes that were essentially the same and essentially linguistic and propositional. Positing sensations–qualitative experience as being significantly different from concepts–language sounded mystical and ineffable, because the sole model we had for cognitive activity was a linguistic one. Dewey made an important contribution by showing the advantages of assuming that thought and experience were different processes that were cognitive in different ways. Unfortunately, because he could not explain the two different mechanisms that distinguished knowing from feeling, he had to assert this claim as an unproven postulate. But modern connectionist neuroscience has now caught up with Dewey's vision, and shown that there are cognitive processes that are nonlinguistic, and that enable us to do many things in ways that are very different from language-based cognition.

Many books and articles on the philosophy of cognitive science contain paraphrases of the principles of connectionist neuroscience, followed by discussions of their philosophical implications. Anyone who has not read one of those paraphrases can skip ahead to the last chapter, where my paraphrase of those principles will develop and emphasize those aspects of connectionism that support the central thesis of this book. Those who are familiar with the philosophical discussions on connectionism, however, will already know the reasons why connectionist processing is considered to be fundamentally nonlinguistic (Rockwell 2001; Churchland 1989 and 1995; among many others). The fundamental computations in connectionist nets are not logical inferences, nor could anything in them be legitimately called a word or a sentence. Instead of using logical inferences, connectionist nets use a completely different form of mathematical relationships called *vector transformations*. For the moment the only point that needs to be made is that vector transformations are completely different from the logical inferences that connect words and sentences. The nearest thing to verbal translation of the behavior of a trained connectionist net would be the single sentence "When you get input that resembles this, do something that resembles that" repeated and strung together by a branching tree of conjunctions and disjunctions. But this description would be completely empty, and equally applicable to every connectionist net. The "content" of the connectionist net, the information that gives it its cognitive power, is determined by how the computational space is divided up, and this is expressible only in multidimensional geometry, not in any language made up of sentences. This is one reason why connectionist nets are so much better at modeling the knowledge that we "know but cannot tell," such as perceptual pattern recognition and the "knowing-how" skills that require muscular coordination.

Although there has been some controversy over whether the regions of computational space in a connectionist neural network are describable as representations, no one would claim that their interactions were fundamentally describable as a language. Even those who believe that a language-of-thought theory is the best description of higher cognitive processes acknowledge that connectionism successfully implements "lower" processes like perception and motor control. This means that no language-of-thought theorist denies that there are many activities that are describable as cognitive in some sense that is clearly not linguistic. The controversy between language-of-thought theorists and connectionists is over whether connectionism can eventually reduce or eliminate a language of thought. No one is claiming that things could go the other way around, and we could eventually describe connectionist nets with a language-of-thought theory.

In chapter 1, I said consciousness must be an emergent property of some kind of system. What I am suggesting now is that this system consists of two distinct but closely related subsystems, each of which is responsible for a different kind of awareness. One sort of consciousness enables us to occupy the logical space of reasons, explanations, and communication. The other enables us to perform the kind of discriminative signal processing manifested by rats and amoebas, and modeled by connectionist nets. The first kind makes possible the sort of awareness that is a linguistic affair. The second kind makes possible what Dewey calls experience and Sellars calls sensations.

There are passages in Dewey that are strikingly parallel to Sellars on this point. "[T]o be a smell is one thing, to be known as a smell, another; to be a 'feeling' one thing, to be known as a 'feeling' another" (1910/1997, p. 81). If we substitute "a-pink-cube-ly" manners of sensing for smells and feelings, this claim is identical with the Sellarsian distinction between thoughts and sensations we discussed earlier. There are numerous distinctions between Sellars's concept of sensation and Dewey's concept of experience, but there is enough in common between them to provide a foundation for a non-Cartesian form of dualism. This would be a very relative sort of dualism, of course. Both linguistic thought and nonlinguistic connectionist experience are implemented in physical systems, which differ only in structure, not in fundamental substance. Contemporary neuroscience strongly implies that linguistic structures are also specific implementations of certain connectionist structures. But it appears plausible that connectionist structures that don't implement language are experienced differently by us than those that do, and that this could account for the qualitative dichotomy between thought and experience.

Sellars often said that the sensing part of a perceptual act was noninferential, but he did not mean by this that it was "given" in the way that classical empiricism said that sense data were given. On the contrary this claim became the basis of one of Sellars's most important critiques of sense datum theory. What he meant by this was exactly what he said: perceptual sensations are noninferential because you can't make inferences from them. It really is impossible to make an inference from a particular "sensing a-pink-cube-ly," even though it is fully justifiable to make an inference from the mental sentence that accompanies it. To think otherwise (as did the sense datum theorists) is to make a category mistake along the lines of trying to make an inference from a walnut (as opposed to making inferences from a sentence about a walnut). The fact that you cannot make logical inferences from a sensation bars the sensation from ever entering the space of reasons. But this does not mean that the sensation is not cognitive in the broad sense that connectionist cognitive science defines "cognitive." For if a sensation is the product of a series of appropriate vector transformations it might enable us to move skillfully through the world even if it was not accompanied by any sentences that would enable us to talk to ourselves (and others) about it. It might, for example, help me in reaching skillfully across the room to pick up the pink ice cube and put it in my drink, even though I was completely absorbed in the discussion of some other topic. To do this, however, it would have to be something other than a single "a-pink-cube-ly" manner of sensing that was joined at the hip to a sentence like "lo, a pink ice cube." It would instead have to be like what Dewey described as experience: a moment in an experiential process that was constituted in part by its relationship to a series of ongoing projects in the world.

Rorty's grouping of computers with rats and amoebas in the above-cited quote shows that he considers the distinction between the linguistic and the nonlinguistic to be merely the distinction between the complex and the simple. Computers are of course much simpler than we are (at the moment). But regardless of their simplicity they are still devices designed to help us function in the logical space of reasons. In contrast, a connectionist system can be as complex as a logic- or language-based computer, and far more skillful at what it does best. It is a common mistake to assume that only simple functions can be performed without verbal processing, and thus we describe sensations with the pejorative term "raw feel." One of the things we have learned from the philosophical analysis of neural networks is that their kind of discriminative signal processing can be more complex than what most computers do, and that in us it is far more complicated than in rats or amoebas. Human beings are not different from animals only because we have language. No nonhuman animal can learn a complicated noninstinctive dance step, or play a musical instrument. The fundamental principles that govern this kind of processing are not linguistic, which is why humans with "know-how" can often do things that they cannot explain, even to themselves. Even animals possess cognitive processes that enable them to be skillful enough to avoid predators, remember where they have stored food, and recognize kin, all without any help from that awareness that is a linguistic affair.

If this kind of vector-transformation-based cognition is capable of producing consciousness when it reaches a certain level of complexity, then the higher nonlinguistic animals would be to some degree conscious in this sense. For humans, this kind of consciousness would provide the qualitative background in which our linguistic consciousness would dwell. Language might be the factor that enables us to have what Rosenthal (1986, 1990b) calls higher-order thoughts that pick out individual items in our qualitative space and make them present-at-hand.[3] But if I'm right about this, a language-processing machine would not be able to produce consciousness all by itself, no matter how many Turing tests it could pass. Language would perform a supplementary function that enriched our awareness of the qualitative experience produced by vector transformations, but by itself the language-producing machine would be a zombie. This is almost the reverse of Dennett's position on animal consciousness. Dennett claims that animals are not conscious because they lack linguistic processing. I am saying that linguistic processing enriches and deepens consciousness, but by itself it cannot produce consciousness.

If the vector transformations produced by connectionist nets could generate conscious experience without language, this experience would be as fundamentally private as language is fundamentally public. Consequently, any attempt to incorporate this kind of knowledge into the logical space of reasons would be necessarily doomed to failure. We could not completely capture the experience of this kind of discriminative processing by describing its structure and function in linguistic terms. This processing is distinct from linguistic processing, just as language is distinct from anything else it describes. Thus we would experience an explanatory gap when we compare the linguistic component of perceptual judgment to the manner of sensing that accompanies it. There is obviously more there than simply the observation sentence, but what? Words fail us, but that is because we have other cognitive processes that make words unnecessary. These cognitive processes have no need for the logical space of reasons, although they are frequently guided and corrected by our frequent visits there, and from the advice and communications we receive from those who share that space with us. But the processes themselves are not designed to convince anyone of anything, they are designed to move me skillfully through the world. The Cartesian materialists might be correct in claiming that I could in principle *understand*, those processes by putting my brain under a cerebroscope, and describing all of those processes in intersubjective terms. My own view is that understanding those neural processes is necessary but not sufficient for understanding mental processes. But knowing how to describe and understand any sort of biologically embodied skill would necessarily be a different ability from the one being described.

When seen from the third person logical space of reasons, any nonlinguistic cognitive process will always appear different from the way it does to the person who actually possesses those abilities. So every third-person description of those process will appear to be vulnerable to the objection "But I can imagine a machine doing X and not being conscious." What we are imagining during such a thought experiment is the exact perspective that the logical space of reasons is designed to create. This experience, profound and unshakable though it may seem, is actually based on a subtle misunderstanding. When I contemplate an item, whether organism or machine, from the objective third-person point of view, it will, by the very nature of that perspective, seem like an object, an unconscious thing. But that doesn't mean that what I am contemplating is not conscious from its own point of view. Objectivity makes everything appear to be an object, including entities with subjective points of view. This is what accounts for both the illusion of solipsism and the hard problem.

And—to return to the recurring theme that unites this book—this description of the subjective–objective distinction has no necessary connection to the distinction between the inside and the outside of the skull. Although connectionist nets are often thought of as being in the brain, the same vector transformations that give them their cognitive power also govern the dynamic system that is the brain–body–world. (See the final chapter of this book.) It is these dynamic interactions through time that determine each of our personal perspectives, and it is the uniqueness of these personal perspectives that have to be ignored when communicating objective information in the space of reasons. Some of those uniquenesses (such as the fact that my pain hurts only me) have been classified by the

3P1P in such a way that they can be recognized immediately. Others, involving the differences in our personal history, are more idiosyncratic, and learning how to recognize them is part of the skill involved in learning how to communicate and argue effectively. But my personal history takes place in the world, and involves my body's interactions with the world. It does not take place in my skull.

When we communicate with each other, we do so while living through personal histories that are very different from each other. This difference between individual histories is part of what accounts for the difference between the objective and subjective. But there is another factor that makes this dichotomy impossible to bridge even in principle. The experiences that constitute those personal histories are embodied by dynamic interactions between the environment, body, and brain. These interactions are describable by the math of vector transformations, and in many cases it is possible to communicate something about those experiences to those fellow beings with whom we share the space of reasons. But it is the vector transformations themselves, not what we say about them verbally or mathematically, that constitute our subjective experiences. Although all objective awareness is a linguistic affair, there are many aspects of subjective private experience that cannot ever be communicated to anyone else, because no one else is embodied by that particular constellation of vector transformations that is in each case "Mine," as Heidegger would say. These experiences are consequently not expressible in words, and therefore never enter into the space of reasons. This is all that is needed to account for the difference between the objective, which can be communicated, and the subjective, which cannot. We do not need to explain the difference between the objective and the subjective by saying that each of us is imprisoned within his or her skull, and that subjective experiences are those mental phenomena that are embodied only by what is taking place inside that skull.

8 The "Frame Problem" and the "Background"

Up to this point, I have been writing as if the world that cannot be communicated in the space of reasons was unique to each person. Dewey, however, sees us as being fundamentally social creatures, so much of what is necessarily private is not also necessarily idiosyncratic. The "common sense" we all share consists not only of a set of shared concepts, but of a domain of shared experience. Without this domain of shared experience, the language of common sense, and all other language, has no semantics; no way of referring to the world. This is why Dewey claimed that if students did nothing but memorize sentences that stated facts, they were not really learning anything at all. If the new words were not accompanied by new experiences, they would be meaningless to the students, even if they were able to correctly recite them for examinations. When Dewey ran an elementary school, he did not divide the students' learning up into classes determined by subject matter. Instead the students would perform goal-directed activities—one well-known example was making cereal—and their knowledge of chemistry, agriculture, and so forth was related directly to what they needed to know to successfully achieve those goals (see Tanner 1997). Dewey believed that without such connections to embodied activities in the world, the ability to recite facts was not knowledge about the world at all. His belief received strong empirical support from laboratory research that occurred a decade after his death.

The AI research based on the symbolic system hypothesis made a go-for-broke commitment to what I earlier called the myth of the machine-in-the-machine. These researchers assumed that a thinking machine could function without a body and a world, provided it stored the sentences that we use when we think, and then manipulated them appropriately using the laws of logic. Because the AI community put itself on the line by actually attempting to build the machine-in-the-machine, their failures produced dramatic evidence of the inadequacies of that myth.

The person who has documented these failures in greatest detail is Hubert Dreyfus, whose achievement is especially impressive because he predicted how and why many of these failures would occur before they actually happened. His descriptions of these failures are complex and detailed, but I will be focusing on what I consider his most essential point: the fact that "understanding requires giving a computer the background of common sense that adult human beings have by virtue of having bodies, interacting skillfully with the material world, and being trained into a culture" (Dreyfus 1972, p. 3).

Dreyfus claimed that one of the biggest mistakes of symbolic systems AI was to substitute the propositions that are caused by experience for the experience itself—a strategy that should have worked if all awareness was a linguistic affair. These AI researchers saw common sense as a particular set of concepts. Their assumption was that once these concepts had been reduced to a body of information and a list of rules expressed in sentences (propositions), the symbolic machine would then be able to manifest common sense by making logical inferences from these propositions. Unfortunately, common sense seemed to be the one thing that computers couldn't be taught. AI researchers tried to translate common sense into a set of propositions and store all the propositions in their machines' memories. But it became clear to almost everyone after a while that this was a doomed project. It was necessary to program in even statements as obvious as "when you put an object on top of another object, and move the bottom object, both objects move," one of many statements that never has to be verbalized by anyone who has a body and has used it to move things in the world. And when one takes into consideration the numerous other things that humans "just know" without making specific inferences, the idea that we have this kind of information somehow stored in our brains becomes highly implausible. For example, everyone you've ever met knows that George Bush wears underwear, but almost no one has ever consciously or unconsciously thought that sentence (unless they have been reading the philosophical literature on this subject). Or an even more convincing example used by Jim Garson: Everyone believes that a hippopotamus is smaller than the Washington Monument, but it is absurd to think that this fact could be explained by positing that we have always had this sentence stored in our brains.

In an attempt to make the storage process more efficient, some researchers tried to formulate the simplest most universal principles, and infer all other commonsense conclusions from those. Unfortunately, the "abstract" principles were every bit as ad hoc as the specific sentences, and at best seemed likely to reduce the list from trillions to billions. (Presidents wear standard business attire? Animals are smaller than buildings?) Other researchers, like Roger Schank, tried to store the information in stories called "scripts" or "frames." There was a time when what AI researchers called the "frame problem" was considered to be within the grasp of a few decades of research. But according to Dreyfus, most researchers today will admit when pressed that most of AI's greatest accomplishments have resulted from finding ways of working around the frame problem. By limiting themselves to what are called "toy worlds," whose boundary conditions are simple enough not to trip up the brittle inference structures of symbolic systems, these systems can often perform functions that bear a superficial resemblance to human thought. But Dreyfus gives convincing arguments that regardless of how impressive these may be as engineering feats, the principles they follow cannot be used to account for the human ability to think and use language.[1]

Admittedly not everyone finds these arguments convincing. There are still two prominent research programs that are using the symbolic systems method for modeling common sense. Douglas Lenant is still trying to compile a dictionary of common sense to solve the frame problem. He admits that this dictionary, which he calls CYC, will have to be "10^5 times larger than today's expert systems" (quoted in Dreyfus 1972, p. xviii). He has continued to compile this system for over ten years, and remains optimistic. There is also a project that gathers data about the assumptions of common sense by using a Web site called Project Open Mind (www. openmind.org). People who visit this website are given sentences like "Bob bought some milk" and then asked to write up to five things that someone should already know in order to fully understand that sentence (such as "Bob probably used money to buy the milk," "Milk is a kind of food," and "Bob probably bought the milk at a store"). The Open Mind Common Sense project is clearly a much more efficient method of gathering data then the CYC project. It has so far acquired over 850,000 assertions from approximately 15,000 contributors in a very short period of time, and this is clearly only the beginning.

The CYC database, despite its limited size, has become effective enough to be used by the U.S. military and at least one search engine. And the Open Mind project might very well succeed for the same reason that the Deep Blue chess-playing computer was able to beat Gary Kasparov. It is using computers to do what they do best: acquire vast amounts of data, and search through it at literally the speed of light. If this database eventually becomes sufficiently large and well organized, and is able to thus mimic human common sense in a convincing manner, this will be an impressive and useful engineering accomplishment. But there is no reason to think that such a program will tell us anything about how *humans* acquire common sense. As I mentioned in chapter 7, a human brain could not possibly search a database of this magnitude the way a computer searches a database. While computers can send signals at the speed of light, neural signals travel at around 200 miles an hour. This would slow down the search process to the point that if we made commonsense decisions by consulting a language-based database, we couldn't decide whether a hippopotamus was smaller than the Washington Monument during a single lifetime. Thus even if a computer were able to compile enough information to acquire something like common sense, we could not infer from this that human common sense could be stored as information inside a disembodied brain.

John Searle (Searle 1992, ch. 8) makes a similar point with a series of compelling examples from ordinary language. He argues that even the simplest easy-to-understand sentences are incomprehensible without a special kind of commonsense experience, which he calls the "background." When someone says "cut the cake" we know that we should remove a slice with a knife. When someone says "cut the grass," we know that we should run a lawnmower across the lawn. No one would ever run a lawnmower across the top of a cake, if we asked them to cut the cake, or take a slice out of the lawn with a knife, if we asked them to cut the grass. Similarly, when I say to a waiter in a restaurant "I'd like a steak and potatoes" the waiter will know that I want the steak cooked and brought to my table on a plate, not raw, or delivered to my house, or stuffed in my pocket. And yet none of this information is contained in the sentence "I'd like a steak and potatoes." We might think, when first considering this problem, that the reason we know the correct meaning of the sentence "I'd like a steak and potatoes" is that we have learned this from going to numerous restaurants in the past. And this is true as far as it goes, but the key question is *how* did we learn this? The failed attempts by symbolic AI researchers provide dramatic evidence that we couldn't have learned all of it by storing this background knowledge in previously learned sentences with a subconscious command like, "Oh, the waiter is bringing the food to my table. I guess he always does that, so I better store that fact for future reference." Obviously, we consciously do that sort of thing a great deal of the time. But there have to be other processes that take place and/or activities we perform that give us another sort of knowledge—a knowledge that enables us to know instantly that a hippopotamus is smaller than the Washington Monument, even though that sentence was clearly never thought by us prior to our being asked.

Much of this book (especially chapters 6 and 7), deals with the problems that arise from assuming that concepts and experiences are the same sorts of things. But the fact that they are different does not mean that they are independent of each other. Searle's examples show us that language needs experience even more than experience needs language. Animals can have some sort of experience without language, but without experience language is too ambiguous to be useful. The only reason we are able to communicate to each other at all is because we share a certain range of experience. But that experience cannot be completely captured in language. The language points to it, and presupposes it for its communication function, and consequently it cannot contain it. In this sense all language shares something in common with what are called indexical terms, like "here," "now," and "this." It is impossible to determine whether the sentence "here is the grocery store" means the grocery store is down the block, or twenty feet under water, or on the third floor of the Empire State Building, unless you share the appropriate context with the speaker of that sentence. Insofar as we all share a context that doesn't change during the history of our discourse together, we don't need a separate word to perform the indexical function. In a specific but very broad sense, we are all here now together in the lived world of our spoken language. Consequently, we can fool ourselves into believing that a sentence like "Sally cut the grass" communicates its meaning all by itself, without the benefit of that shared lived context. But the falsity of this assumption is dramatically illustrated the few times that communication breaks down because of a lack of shared context.

There is a (probably true) story about an aborigine in the Australian army who attempted to enter the enlisted man's club while wearing the regiment's field uniform (which had short pants) instead of the dress uniform (which had long pants). The military policeman (MP) at the door said, "You can't come in here wearing shorts." So the aborigine unzipped his shorts, handed them to the MP and walked into the club. The aborigine's mistake did not come from a failure to understand the meaning of any of the individual words. In fact, the aborigine correctly interpreted the literal meaning of the MP's words. If we were to evaluate meaning totally on those terms, we would have to say that it was the MP who did not express himself correctly. The aborigine's mistake arose from not having a shared history with the MP, for whom the only sensible meaning for the sentence was "you can only come in here wearing long pants." Now that we have a new formulation for the sentence that makes the aborigine's misinterpretation impossible, it's tempting to think that if only we speak more precisely, incidents like this will never occur. This is precisely what the symbolic systems AI researchers assume when they build machines, label various combinations of those machine's inner states as "words," and sincerely believe that those machines are using language. When we do this, however, we ignore the fact that those machines' languagelike abilities derive from the fact that we use them as tools in the context of our lived experience. For whatever happens in *our* heads that is partly responsible for our language abilities has even less autonomy than the so-called computer languages. The quasi-indexical reference to lived experience is what gives our languages the semantic power that computers lack. Although Searle doesn't state this conclusion himself, this is compelling evidence against the assumption that knowledge consists of sentences in the head.

Of course, describing this lived experience is harder than criticizing theories that don't account for it. But Searle and Dreyfus both offer positive theories of lived experience, showing how it provides the background of meaning that makes language possible. The rest of this chapter will compare and contrast their theories with my Deweyan theory, and argue that the most consistent interpretation of their positions implies that experience emerges from a brain–body–world nexus.

Searle versus Dewey

The key difference for our purposes between Searle and Dewey is revealed by the following passage:

Intentional phenomena, such as meanings, understandings, interpretations, beliefs, desires, and experiences only function within a set of background capacities that are not themselves intentional. (Searle 1992, p. 175)

Dewey, as I interpret him, would have removed the word "experience" from the list at the beginning of the sentence, and used it to replace Searle's phrase "a set of background capacities that are not themselves intentional." In other words, Dewey believed all intentional phenomena take place within a background of experience, which was itself irreducibly intentional. One might say that for Dewey reality was intentional all the way down, but this would be misleading because Dewey did not believe that you could find the ultimate nature of reality by going all the way down. He did believe that analysis was an important part of most kinds of inquiry, but because he believed in emergent properties he also recognized that analysis would inevitably be unable to tell the whole story about everything. And below a certain level of analysis, that which is realest to us, lived experience, would inevitably get bypassed. More important, for those with a scientific turn of mind, experience was not the only thing that got bypassed. This absolute faith in analysis that prompted many to deny the irreducibility of experience would also, if applied consistently, deny legitimacy to biology as well, including the neurophysiology that most people think of as the "physical" basis of consciousness.

Searle has two main arguments against the intentionality of the background, one of which I will call the *intrinsicality* argument, and the other the *Darwinian* argument.

Searle's Intrinsicality Argument

The intrinsicality argument claims that physical characteristics are somehow intrinsic to things, but intentional characteristics are not. Consequently, underlying all of this intentionality, which is only relative, there has to be some sort of purely physical reality, which is absolute. This argument was developed at greatest length in Searle's *The Construction of Social Reality*, but is also concisely stated in *The Rediscovery of the Mind*.

To understand this argument fully, it is essential to understand the distinction between features of the world that are intrinsic and features of the world that are observer relative. The expressions "mass" "gravitational attraction" and "molecule" name features of the world that are intrinsic. If all observers and users cease to exist, the world still contains mass, gravitational attraction and molecules. But expressions such as "nice day for a picnic" "bathtub" and "chair" do not name intrinsic features of reality. Rather they name objects by specifying some feature that has been assigned to them, some feature that is relative to observers and users. If there had never been any users or observers, there would still be mountains, molecules, masses and gravitational attraction. But if there had never been any users or observers, there would be no such features as being a nice day for a picnic, or being a chair or a bathtub. (Searle 1992, p. 211)

Despite the fact that some form of this distinction is very widely accepted, there are a lot of things wrong with it. It's true that there would be no chairs if there had never been people who could sit in them. But it's also true that there would be no hearts if there had not been circulatory systems in which they could pump blood. Searle denies this (ibid., p. 208), but he also says that we can imagine a world filled with chairlike objects and no people to sit in them, and that in such a world those objects would not really be chairs. Suppose there were no hearts, but certain trees grew a fruit that was molecule for molecule identical to the beef hearts that one sees in butcher shops. If those objects had never been part of a circulatory system, they would not be hearts any more than the aforementioned chair-like objects would be chairs. And from there, it's impossible to avoid the conclusion that there would be no brains unless there were nervous systems that they could participate in, and no nervous systems unless there were bodies. So Searle's plan to ground the study of consciousness in the so-called intrinsic properties of the brain is a nonstarter.

Part of Searle's confusion comes from the fact that he conflates *relative* features with *assigned* features. Chapter 9 of Searle 1992 says repeatedly that once we accept functionalism we must accept that any system what-soever could implement any program. In this view, we transform systems into programs simply by naming them, the way tigers became tigers because Adam said that's what they were. But this is not what the people Searle is paraphrasing are actually saying. When Ned Block says we could implement a computer program using cats and mice and cheese (quoted in Searle 1992, p. 206), what he is saying is that one could get almost any object and *build a system around it* that could implement the program. Once one decides to build a computer program using cats, the doors have to open at exactly the right time, the mice have to run away at the right time and so on. Certain features would perform essential functions in the system and the tolerance for how they could vary would be very small. Other features would be epiphenomenal and could vary considerably; it probably wouldn't matter whether the cats had black fur or white fur. But all this would be determined by real characteristics that the whole system actually possessed, not by a programmer's proclamation. The fact that a heart is not intrinsically a heart does not mean one can simply assign the role of being the heart to any organ in the body one chooses. And when one observes the world of human practices, the chairness of chairs is not up to that observer to assign. Chairs are chairs, just as hearts are hearts, because there is a network of relationships in the real world that makes them that way. Certain entities are constituted by relationships that do not obviously refer to or presuppose the existence of human beings. But even such entities as the chemical elements presuppose certain relationships to laboratory procedures and measurements. It would make no sense to say that this substance is still sulfur, even though it does not behave the way sulfur would behave in a laboratory.

One can effectively dispose of this particular objection by saying that consciousness is a relational property and not an intrinsic physical one, so Searle's demand for a physical study of the intrinsic nature of consciousness is misguided. But defending Dewey's concept of experience requires a stronger claim: that the relational characteristics that define things in terms of biological functions, or human goals and values, are every bit as real as the characteristics described by physics. If experience is constituted by relationships that exist between intrinsically physical things (as Searle believes), it's hard to avoid the conclusion that what is actually out there is "really" physical and inanimate. This would mean that whether something is living and biological (or beautiful or useful) is a matter of relations between those intrinsically physical things, and that relative existence is less real than intrinsic existence. Fortunately for our side, there are many arguments against the idea that physical properties are intrinsic, some of which come from Searle himself. Searle specifically says, "in order to have one belief or desire, I have to have a whole network of other beliefs and desires" (1992, p. 176). This means that he must also reject the existence of intrinsic properties. If we assume that at least some of our beliefs express facts about the world, then there must be a similar relationship that exists between those facts, that is, in order for one fact to be true, a network of other facts must also be true, and no one fact can be intrinsically true in and of itself.

Not surprisingly, this is every bit as true of the facts of physics and chemistry as of anything else. It is not just an intrinsic fact about a particular piece of stuff that it is sulfur. To say that something is sulfur means that it is imbedded in a complex network of relationships to the other elements, which is articulated by its position in the periodic table of the elements. It would make no sense to say that this lump of stuff is sulfur, but that none of the other facts described in the periodic table are true. Why is that significantly different from a heart being a heart because of the relationship that it has to a circulatory system? Searle also says that language is meaningless without a background of experience we share because we have bodies and are part of a culture (ibid., p. 185). This is because, as Searle says, "Sentence meaning radically underdetermines the content of what is said" (ibid., p. 181), and this fact is inescapable because "each sentence we add is subject to further misunderstandings unless fixed by a background [which includes cultural and bodily experience]" (ibid., p. 183). So this means that the entire network of chemistry concepts, including the periodic table itself, has no intrinsic meaning, but is instead dependent on its relationship to a background of lived embodied activities that include laboratory experiments, journal publications, and so forth. If this is true of statements like "Sally cut the grass," or "he ordered a steak with potatoes," why should it be any less true of statements about the facts of physics and chemistry?

But wouldn't this mean that the facts of chemistry are not really true, but are only true in a manner of speaking? No, sulfur really is sulfur because of the way things are in the world we interact with, and hearts and chairs really are hearts and chairs because of the way things are in the world we interact with. All this means is that sulfur is *no more real* than hearts and chairs. The belief in the uniquely intrinsic quality of physical properties can only be justified by saying something like "When everyone else talks about the world, the concepts that they use are dependent on their goals and purposes. But when physicists talk about the world, their concepts touch reality itself, unsullied by any goals or provincial perspective." There is simply no reason to privilege the discourse of physicists in this manner.

Physics, like any other human activity, requires dividing the world up into categories that enable the goals of that activity to be achieved. If you want to track the behavior of the planets, or predict how light will disperse, there is no other set of concepts that you can use and still achieve those goals with maximum effectiveness. But that does not grant intrinsicness to these concepts, any more than the fact that the concept of heart is necessary to zoology makes the concept of heart intrinsic.

It does seem intuitively obvious that if all conscious, purposeful beings disappeared from the universe, the physical properties would still be there. But this so-called intuition has essentially nothing to support it. For one thing, there are certain concepts in physics that may not be possible to separate from purposeful activity. Energy, for example, is often defined as "the ability to do work." I have never seen a definition of "work" that makes no reference to purposeful activity, and cannot imagine what such a definition would look like. The concept of entropy is also usually defined by saying that an increase of entropy in a system decreases its ability to do work. It thus is probably just not true that energy and entropy would still exist if there were no purposeful beings in the universe, and without energy and entropy, we would not have much of a physics left.[2] But even if these problems were solved, we still have the problem of basing a claim on an unperformable thought experiment. This claim is not a scientific fact: I am certain there is no article in any scientific journal describing an experiment that begins "We eliminated all of the conscious beings in the universe, and discovered that all of the physical properties remained." For all we know, the entire universe could very well completely disappear once all of the conscious beings were gone. There is no evidence that it will disappear, but there is also no way of acquiring evidence that it won't. The only thing we do know is that if this experiment is ever performed, none of us will be around to discover the result. It is, to say the least, misleading to call a position "realist" when it is based on an experiment that has no "cash value," because it is impossible to perform in principle.

Consequently, I believe we are justified in dismissing Searle's distinction between the observer–relative and the intrinsic, or as he described it later, between institutional facts and brute facts. This means that we can join Dewey in bridging the gap between experience and nature that was the subject of his book of the same name. There is no longer any reason to think of the world as being really made out of dead matter, with observer-relative qualities and values being projected over this dead matter like a magic lantern show that radiates out from the brain. All of our experiences are experiences of our relationship to our world, and because both ourselves and the world are real, there is no reason that this fact supports skepticism, or the belief that our experiences are illusions. On the contrary, our experiences become the realest thing we have, because they are constituted by our relationship with the world. Insofar as we are at home in the world, and what we encounter is ready-to-hand, we *are* the world. And insofar as reality impinges onto our world in ways that we cannot cope with, we experience the world as being different from ourselves. In either case, however, our experience is constituted by our relationship with the world, not just by the neurological activity in our brains or the sentences in our heads. Because there are no absolutely intrinsic characteristics, these relational properties are as real as anything can be.

Searle's Darwinian Argument

Searle also uses another argument for why the background of intentional experience must be nonintentional, which is derived from a popular interpretation of Darwin. The fact that we evolved from natural selection supposedly proves that all intentional explanations are, Searle says, either metaphorical or false when applied to purely biological organisms. For example, we may say that in order to survive, a plant turns its leaves to the sun. But Searle claims that what is actually happening is completely described by two closely related explanations.

(1) The mechanical hardware explanation: Variable secretions of auxin cause plants to turn their leaves towards the sun.
(2) The functional explanation: Plants that turn their leaves towards the sun are more likely to survive than plants that do not. (Searle 1992, p. 230)

The first point in the Searle quote above is a restatement of the intrinsicality argument. Searle is describing the chemicals in the plant itself (the "variable secretions of auxin") as having the intrinsic causal power to turn the leaves of the plant toward the sun. Searle's second argument explains the plant's behavior by reference to a broader environmental context, but removes all references to intentionality from that context. Searle claims that it is just a purely physical fact that plants that turn their leaves toward the sun are more likely to survive than plants that do not: no reference to goals and purposes is needed to explain what is happening in purely scientific terms. Can Darwinian science actually eliminate the need for intentional explanations by relying on discoveries of what tends to increase survival chances? There is a popular impression to that effect, but it does not stand up to careful scrutiny.

One of the reasons that most attempts to unseat this belief have failed is that they have tried to find some aspect of human behavior that was completely untouched by our evolutionary history. No one has come up with an example of this yet, to my knowledge, and my guess is that they probably never will. But the assumption shared by both parties in this argument is that if we find an evolutionary factor that was *a* cause of some aspect of human behavior, it must therefore be *the sole cause* of that behavior. But this does not follow, for reasons I explained in chapter 4. (See also Rockwell 1998.)

Let us suppose (as many people do) that the evolutionary reason that Mozart had a powerful enough brain to compose his music was that his ancestors came down from the trees and became predators instead of gatherers. Because they were small primates rather than large canines or felines, they did not have enough strength or speed to catch prey by muscle power alone. Consequently, those primates from that group who had large brains were more likely to survive than those who did not. Several thousand years later, one of the ancestors of those primates consequently had a large enough brain that he could use it to help him compose symphonies. This story is exactly analogous to the example Searle gives of a functional explanation for why plants turn their leaves to the sun. Both stories are true as far as they go. But it's clearly false to confuse the claim that this is *a* cause for Mozart's writing his symphonies with the claim that it is *the* cause. What this interpretation of Darwin does is to confuse pragmatic causality with what I call compleat causality (see chapter 4).

When we are studying the evolutionary history of humankind the pragmatic cause that we are looking for (and will probably find) will be an evolutionary one. But that does not mean that the cause that is of most interest to that particular project will be the only real cause. Mozart's symphony writing, like every other event in the universe, was caused by a network of interacting events, none of which could have caused the symphony writing all by itself. Evolutionary theory does not possess, not even in principle, the conceptual resources to account for all such events that make up the behavior of organisms. People (and animals) do many things that have nothing to do with whether they will survive and/or produce offspring. Genetic evolutionary theory, by its own presuppositions, is forced to be completely silent as to why they do one of those things rather than another, because the only question it permits itself to ask is "How did the presence of this trait increases the probability of survival and reproduction?" Consequently, it cannot explain, for example, why Mozart chose to use his brain to compose symphonies rather than make a fortune in commercial real estate, because Mozart would have survived and reproduced regardless of which of these two professions he had followed.

Some people object that Mozart probably would have lived longer and had more offspring if he had gone into real estate, and therefore the Darwinian cause could not have been responsible for his composing. But this objection is too easily disposed of, for it assumes that these Darwin-inspired arguments can only be beaten by getting us completely out of the evolutionary loop, that is, by finding a human activity or characteristic for which the evolutionary events are not part of the causal nexus at all. Because of this shared assumption, Darwinians can respond to this kind of objection by saying that although Mozart's brain evolved to help his ancestors hunt grazing animals, it has now been exapted for other purposes. But if this evolutionary story is supposed to completely account for human behavior, the unavoidable next question is: why was it exapted for that purpose rather than some other? If the answer is "because Mozart enjoyed composing more than selling real estate," then Darwinian explanations have not completely replaced intentional ones. Unless *all* those new purposes are *completely and exclusively* related to the goal of physical survival and/or reproduction, this kind of evolutionary theory cannot give a complete explanation as to why an organism did one of these things rather than the other. In other words, the entire causal nexus has to consist of evolutionary explanations in order for intentionality to reduce to Darwinian selection.

Can this be done? This Darwinian metaphysics is not threatened by the fact that it would be too difficult or expensive to find all the evolutionary causes. But it does require us to say that if someone had the time, money, and omnipotence to completely research the topic, the fact that Mozart wrote symphonies, rather than sold real estate could be explained by causes that were either purely physical or purely Darwinian. (Of course, the latter are a subspecies of physical explanation, which is what gives this Darwinian metaphysics its appeal or repugnance.) So the question we need to ask: is this possible even in principle? The answer, once the question is stated this clearly, seems to me to be negative.

For one thing, Darwinian explanations are *in principle* incapable of explaining why *an individual* did one thing rather than something else. We use the intentional stance to explain individual people's behavior all the time. But once Sally has produced enough offspring to ensure that her genes survive, orthodox Darwinian evolution has nothing to say about the rest of her life. Because we could no longer say "Sally went to the refrigerator because she wanted ice cream and believed there was ice cream in the refrigerator," we would have to say "Sally went to the refrigerator because her neurons fired in a way that triggered certain muscular actions." No one believes that an explanation of that form could replace an intentional explanation. If I told you I hit you in the face because a signal came down from my brain and triggered the neurons in my arm, you would not consider that to be an acceptable explanation no matter how detailed it was. What you want is an explanation that makes reference to my beliefs, desires, and emotions, such as "I know you were flirting with my wife, and I wanted to teach you a lesson." Neither the Darwinian or the physical explanation can possibly have sufficient explanatory power to replace the intentional explanation. It is not just that we don't have the ability to get a complete explanation. The problem is that the Darwinian explanation has ground to a halt, and the physical explanation is going in the wrong direction.

Dennett's Darwinian Argument: Genes versus Memes

Searle claims that when science studies the brain, or the lower animals, it should limit itself to these kinds of nonintentional explanations. He does, however, insist that intentional explanations are still valid (in fact essential) when applied to conscious beings. This special pleading for consciousness is not, however, acceptable to the numerous other people who use this argument, such as Quine, Dawkins, E. O. Wilson, and Dennett (whose *Darwin's Dangerous Idea* is almost entirely devoted to this topic). The usual interpretation of this argument is that all intentional explanations are metaphors and/or illusions, and that physical explanations are the only true descriptions of reality. As Dennett puts it "the various processes of natural selection, in spite of their underlying mindlessness, are powerful enough to have done all of the design work that is manifest in the world" (Dennett 1995a, p. 60). Because Deweyan experience is constituted by relations and transactions whose function is defined by our intentions and purposes, it may seem inevitable that when intentionality goes, Deweyan experience becomes an epiphenomenon of physical reality. This eliminativist attitude toward intentionality is arguably attributable to Quine, E. O. Wilson, and Dawkins. But Dennett's position is far more complex than this. Dennett claims that intentionality is a concept that emerges only when we take what he calls the "intentional stance" toward the world. In his earlier writings, it often seemed that Dennett saw the intentional stance as a useful fiction superimposed over a fundamentally physical world which, because it was so useful, was somehow more than a fiction. But more recently, especially in his 2003 book *Freedom Evolves*, he has been aggressively defending an ontologically robust intentional stance against the more simplistic forms of genetic determinism. It is thus necessary to make a separate response to Dennett's position, which I believe is quite close to Dewey's, once we add the fine print and qualifying clauses revealed by a careful reading of Dennett.

Athough Dennett speaks provocatively in Dennett 1995 (*Darwin's Dangerous Idea*, hereinafter DDI) about the impact of the "universal acid" of Darwinism on the concept of intentionality, he still insists that "Darwinism doesn't falsify or eliminate the concept of intentionality at all. It grounds intentionality" (personal communication). A closer look at DDI provides plenty of quotes to confirm this. He says that Darwin's universal acid will not explain away minds, purposes, and meanings, but leaves them "still standing, but just demystified, unified, placed on more secure foundations" (1995, p. 82). He paraphrases and endorses Dewey by saying that "we must not suppose that we can make sense of an uninterpreted version of evolution, an evolution with no functions endorsed, no meanings discerned" (ibid., p. 403), and later says that Dewey's point is that "there is no substitute for the intentional stance" (ibid., p. 421).

But if intentionality itself is still standing after exposure to Darwin's universal acid, what exactly was eaten away by it? Dennett criticizes several other Darwinians who defend the "greedy reductionism" that claims that gene selection by survival of the fittest can completely explain or control our behavior (in ch. 16, sec. 3, of DDI among many other places). But he seems somewhat more ambivalent about whether *memes* can control our behavior. Memes are cultural constructs (often linguistic) that "survive" by replicating themselves in our brains in much the same way genetic patterns replicate themselves through DNA. If we saw Sally's going to the refrigerator as arising out of the evolutionary battle between memes, it might be the case that Sally's behavior could be accounted for by explanations like "the 'slimness' meme and the 'comfort' meme were competing with each other, and the comfort meme survived that particular struggle and was thus able to reproduce itself in Sally's neurons.[3] Therefore Sally's neurons sent signals to her muscles, which moved her body towards the refrigerator." Could the behavior of conscious beings be completely accounted for by such explanations? Are such explanations intentional or nonintentional? Dennett's answer is, I feel, somewhat equivocal.

Dennett says in *Consciousness Explained* (1991) that consciousness itself is a meme that creates "a Joycean virtual machine" that enables us to focus on and revise other brain activities. It seems unlikely, however, that this virtual machine is all there is to the self. It is merely the device that inspires the "searchlight" metaphor used to describe the faculty of attention, and this metaphor should not be extended to the point where we could imagine the searchlight existing independently of the various other memes that create experiences, memories, and so forth. (See Rockwell 1996 for a further development of this distinction.)

What then is the relationship between the self and the memes that constitute it? Dennett seems to be considering two possible answers: (1) consciousness is nothing but a loose coalition of memes, and therefore there is no single meme that is the self; (2) consciousness is itself an emergent "meta-meme," with some characteristics not possessed by any of the memes that it is made of. Option (1) would be closer to an eliminativist position on the self but option (2) would be closer to the position advocated by Dennett's mentor Ryle.

Although Ryle is best known for his attacks on the dualism that sees the self as a separate "ghost in the machine" he was equally critical of the eliminativism of his fellow behaviorist B. F. Skinner. This is easily seen in section 3.5 of Ryle 1949 entitled "The Bogy of Mechanism":

The discoveries of the physical sciences no more rule out life, sentience, purpose, or intelligence from presence in the world than do the rules of grammar extrude style or logic from prose. (Ryle 1949, p. 79)

Men are not machines, not even ghost-ridden machines. They are men—a tautology which is sometimes worth remembering. (Ibid., p. 81)

Ryle's criticism of substance dualism is expressed by his famous story of
the visitor who says "You've shown me everything at Oxford except for
one thing. Where's the university?" But this story can also be used to justify
Ryle's objection to the Skinnerian claim that people are nothing but mechanisms. Ryle believes that B. F. Skinner is making the same mistake as a
man who visits Oxford and says "I have a list here of all the buildings,
people, and things on campus. You notice that the university is not on
this list, which gives us scientific proof that there is no such thing as the
university." In another words, Oxford is not a separate entity from its
buildings and people, but this does not mean that Oxford doesn't exist.
Ryle was thus both antireductionist and antidualist about the mind, and
Dennett's position leaves open the possibility of making a similar distinction. After all, if memes are emergent entities with characteristics not possessed by any of the cells they are made of, there is no reason to deny the
possibility that a mind possesses emergent (and arguably intentional) characteristics not possessed by any of the memes that it is made of.

There is a similar ambivalence about the relationship between memes
and the self in the writings that follow *Consciousness Explained*. In DDI,
Dennett criticizes Dawkins for saying "We alone can rebel against the
tyranny of our selfish replicators" by replying "This 'we' that transcends
not only its genetic creators but also its memetic creators is, we have just
seen, a myth" (p. 366). Yet further on, he says "Persons . . . are not bound
to answer to the interests of their genes alone—or their memes alone. That
is our transcendence" (p. 471). It appears here that Dennett is mainly criticizing the idea that the transcendent self is some sort of ghost in the
machine, or organ within the brain. What he is saying is that the self is
created when certain memes "join to make common cause, creating a
larger beneficiary out of parts" (p. 471). This beneficiary, however, has genuinely real emergent properties not possessed by any of the parts, which
result in what Dennett calls autonomy (and which looks very much like
what Robert Kane calls autonomy in his 1996 defense of free will). That is
why a self can make decisions that are not bound by the "selfish" interests of the memes that it emerged from.

On the other hand, in Dennett 2001 and 2002, he seems to be drifting
toward a more eliminative position. In Dennett 2001, he says "If my body

is composed of nothing but a team of a few trillion robotic cells . . . there seems to be nothing left over to be me" (p. 13). It is hard to tell whether Dennett is describing his own position here or Darwinism in general. Because Dennett believes that memes are necessary to explain human behavior, he must also acknowledge that the behavior of memes cannot be reduced to the behavior of cells. He does say in the previous quote that this is the way things *seem*, which may imply that this might not be the way things *are*. But he also says that the fear of this disappearing self is deep "only in the sense of being the most entrenched, the least accessible to rational criticism." Later he asks rhetorically "Does this realization amount to a loss—an elimination—of selfhood . . . ? Those who are closest to the issue . . . often confront this discovery with equanimity" (Dennett 2001, p. 25). If we *discover* that the self has been eliminated, this implies that the self really has been eliminated.

It appears that Dennett still feels that careful equivocation is the best strategy for describing the ontological status of the mind or self. If the mind is real in the same sense that Oxford University is real, that's a pretty robust ontological status. No one would refer to Oxford as a loose coalition of buildings and people. It might very well be, however, that it is more appropriate to refer to a mind as a loose coalition of memes, depending on how tightly we define the word "loose." Recent scientific discoveries have indicated that the relationship between the mind and its parts is certainly much looser than Plato or Aristotle ever thought it was. But exactly what degree of looseness defines the borders between heaps, aggregates, coalitions, and structures? Which degree of looseness forces us to dispense with the concept of intentionality, and which one permits us to accept it? Can the beliefs and desires described by the intentional stance actually exist, if the memes do not constitute a self to do the believing and the desiring? Can the individual memes themselves have beliefs and desires, or are they just lifeless forms of self-replicating software?

I have not done justice in this brief survey to the many nuances of this problem, especially those explored in Dennett 2003. But the complexity of the issue gives us good reason to refrain from confidently asserting that the physical world is ontologically fundamental and the world of intentions and purposes is ontologically dependent. We can, of course, make the (a)theological speculation that there was a time when there was no intentionality in the world, and that intentionality, and/or the appearance of it, eventually emerged through the random shufflings of genetic roulette. But we should not pretend that this kind of metaphysical speculation can ever be scientifically proven or disproven. We cannot really imagine such a world without also imagining ourselves, as intentional beings, looking back on it. The only thing we can know is that we now live in a world that is impossible to understand without the point of view that Dennett calls the intentional stance. Sometimes Dennett seems to say that the physical stance is more ontologically fundamental, and other times he implies that the intentional is every bit as real as the physical. We Deweyans claim that even the so-called physical stance is a point of view that we take because it frequently serves our purposes to do so, and therefore the physical stance is less ontologically fundamental than the intentional stance. The only point I wish to make in this section is that Darwinian science cannot settle this question. Evolutionary theory is fully compatible with the Deweyan claim that the reality we live in is fundamentally intentional and purposive. We can acknowledge that our world can be divided into parts, some of which can be manipulated because they are what we call "lifeless," "purely physical," or "present-at-hand," without accepting the implication that these physical parts are the fundamental constituents of reality.

Dreyfus, Clark, and Conscious Experience

Dreyfus's *What Computers Still Can't Do* offers a detailed critique of symbol-based AI computer systems, and then ends by offering some alternatives to its traditional assumptions. Dreyfus describes this section of the book as a "phenomenological description" and adds somewhat deferentially that "such an account can even be called an explanation if it goes further and tries to find the fundamental features of human activity" (p. 233). What Dreyfus calls a phenomenological description is more than similar to what is called a functional description in computer science. The functional description enables a programmer to describe precisely what a program does, which is the first step to figuring out how to write that program in code. This is done by creating a block diagram that assigns each distinct function the program must perform to a separate block, and joining these functions together in a flow chart. Dreyfus provides a similar sort of description of human experience, but uses it to show that conscious processes *cannot* be divided up and interrelated using the presuppositions of symbol-based AI without seriously misrepresenting how we experience ourselves and our world. This was not, however, a mere act of destructive criticism designed to justify a retreat to dualism and an abandonment of AI. Although Dreyfus did not feel confident enough to offer a specific physical alternative to symbol-based AI when he made this phenomenological description, he clearly intended it to be a criterion and guide for any physical system that embodied thought and/or consciousness. Because there have been many new developments in both theory and engineering since Dreyfus wrote this phenomenological description, it can still serve that purpose. One of the goals of this section is to show that the metaphysical commitments we would have to make to account for the phenomenology Dreyfus describes would be just the sorts of claims I have been making in this book. This is especially obvious when we evaluate his responses to the most recent developments in AI, which have had some successes because they have managed to free themselves of some, but not all, of symbol-based AI's most self-destructive presuppositions.

One of Dreyfus's most perceptive phenomenological observations is the contrast he makes between perceptual experience and the bits of information worked with by computers. Dreyfus points out that while each bit of computer information is firmly distinct from every other bit, this is never true of moments of perception. In Merleau-Ponty's words "The perceptual 'something' is always in the middle of something else; it always forms part of a 'field'" (quoted in Dreyfus 1994, p. 240) Furthermore, the object being perceived is not only surrounded by an indeterminate outer horizon, it also has what Husserl calls an inner horizon: "When we perceive an object we are aware that it has more aspects than we are at the moment considering" (ibid., p. 241). Because none of these moments is clearly separated from the others in our experience, it seems plausible that the experience presents itself to us a whole, and we break it down into parts depending on how we choose to relate to it at any given moment. Symbolic computer models, in contrast, operate by building the whole out of the details. It is thus not surprising that symbolic machines were so bad at perceptual pattern recognition, and that when a new machine came along that was noticeably better, it operated on distributed holistic principles, rather than on assembling a perception from sense-data-like parts.

Connectionist systems are far superior to symbolic ones at escaping the toy world limitations of most artificial intelligence. They repeatedly outperform symbolic systems at perceptual tasks, where the machine must classify and identify things such as colors, shapes, words, or letters. Like the perceptual experience revealed by Dreyfus's phenomenology, the "information" stored in a connectionist system is not independent bits that must be combined and manipulated, but regions of computational space that must be divided and connected. The word "information" is in quotes, because points in computational space do not have the kind of independence possessed by bits of information, even though they can be used to achieve similar results. For those who have not heard the basic story of how connectionist networks perform cognitive functions, I will once again recommend that they turn to the description given in the last chapter of this book. The following quick description is only meant to underscore why connectionist networks are fundamentally holistic, rather than manipulators of atomistic information.

Any set of N amount of numbers can be mapped as a point in an N-dimensional Cartesian space. Consequently, the numbers describing the input signals of an array of ten neurons in a neural network can be seen as describing a point in ten-dimensional space. These signals can be fed into other arrays with different numbers of neurons, each of which combines their signals into different combinations and/or "weights" by stimulating or inhibiting specific signals at each stage. After going through several such stages the system produces an output: a set of signals that appears on an array of neurons at the end of the system, and the numbers that describe this set of signals describe another point in computational space. Because a set of numerical values is called a vector, and connections systems operate by receiving one vector and outputting another, the basic cognitive principle used by connectionist systems is called *vector transformation*. There are much more complicated forms of architecture that can be built with this principle, especially when the flow of current circles back to produce what are called "recurrent" networks. (See P. M. Churchland 1995, ch. 5.) But the main point for our purposes is that in a trained net, the points in one region of computational space are related to the points in another region, and this is how the net learns how to identify individuals and interrelate categories. It is thus a process that starts with a whole, that is, a multidimensional computational space, divides that whole up into regions, and then uses intermediatary computational spaces to establish relationships that create new wholes. This is the exact opposite of the process used by a digital computer, which takes in information a bit at a time, and then assembles and manipulates it to create a pattern with discrete parts.

If a connectionist system was responsible for the emergence of human experience, it seems plausible that it would resemble Dreyfus's phenomenological description of perception. For regions of computational space are not sharply divided. A connectionist pattern recognition system does have many clear-cut cases of what it is trained to recognize firmly in the center of each space. But it also has more borderline cases on the fringes of that space. There is thus not a sharp line between one region of computational space and another, which is why no connectionist system is ever completely error free. When it does make an error, however, it is usually a close call, and not the kind of radically false error that computers usually make and people almost never do. This is because computers, being logic-based machines, operate on the law of the excluded middle, which makes it difficult for them to recognize the similarities between various non-Ps when they are in the process of identifying P. A connectionist machine, however, *must* classify things by similarities, which means it will probably classify an input as a cat with a computational space that is adjacent to the space that is used to classify something similar (such as dogs), and very far away from the space that is used to classify something different (such as birds or vegetables or numbers). Although no one has ever used a connectionist system to synthesize an entire visual field, this ability to work with regions separated only by continua would make connectionism a natural for producing such phenomena as the "fringe," and the inner and outer "horizons."

Dreyfus, however, refuses to see the arrival of connectionism as a solution to all of AI's problems. His critique of current connectionism in many ways parallels my critique of Cartesian materialism, and often refers back to his phenomenological alternatives to the traditional assumptions at the end of Dreyfus 1992. He points out that a connectionist network cannot generalize in a useful way unless its inputs are constrained in very specific ways that are idiosyncratic to a laboratory situation. Left to run free on its own, a connectionist network could not train itself, it would simply establish associations between any similarities that were somewhere near its starting weights. And from a purely "objective" point of view, the network would not be making mistakes because "everything is similar to everything else and different from everything else in an indefinitely large number of ways. We just do not notice it" (Dreyfus 1996, par. 53). But the question remains, how can these associations be channeled in directions that have any cognitive worth without the teaching algorithms and other artificial impositions of the laboratory?

Dreyfus says that two factors are necessary: the constraints of body structure (ibid., par. 60), and a lived situation that is constituted as a function of human needs (Dreyfus 1992, p. 272). In other words, what is necessary for a brain to create human experience is to be part of a system that includes a body and a world. Dreyfus states the mutual dependency between self and world in no uncertain terms. "When we are at home in the world, the meaningful objects embedded in their context of references among which we live are not a model of the world stored in our mind or brain; *they are the world itself*" (ibid., p. 266). In this same paragraph Dreyfus makes it clear that this is even true of "my experience . . . my private set of facts," and thus, as far as I can tell, commits himself to the most radical version of the thesis in this book: that even the most private, subjective, qualitative aspects of human experience are embodied in the brain–body–world nexus, and not just in the brain alone. If I am correct in interpreting Dreyfus this way, he joins me in disagreeing with Andy Clark. Clark is willing to make only a partial commitment to the thesis described in the title of his book *Being There: Putting Brain, Body, and World Together Again*. Clark gives detailed arguments for showing that language and other forms of cognitive activities could not be seen as self-contained languages of thought within the skull. But as I pointed out in chapter 1, he deliberately refuses to apply the implications of his argument to consciousness: "Thoughts, considered only as snapshots of our conscious mental activity, are fully explained, I am willing to say, by the current state of the brain" (Clark 1997, pp. 215–17).

Clark's use of the "snapshot" metaphor is the last gasp of sense-datum theory. Suppose we duplicated all of the brain states of a laboratory subject looking at a green patch for two seconds and then ran them continuously in a repetitive loop. There is no reason to believe that we would get an idiot consciousness that had a continuously repeating experience of "Green Patch! Green Patch! Green Patch!" Given the lack of biological evidence for sense-datum theory, the most plausible speculation is that there would be "nobody home" in such a brain-loop, because experience requires a personal history of interactions with a world. If this is true, then all three parts of the brain–body–world nexus are essential in embodying even what we consider to be most subjective and private: the background of human experience that supports, but cannot be communicated in, the space of reasons. This background is a holistic network, not a string of snapshots, and our interaction with this background is what produces the feelings, values, and purposes that make us care about this rather than that, and that give our lives their distinctive qualitative feel.

But so what, you may ask? Can we do any sort of science based on that assumption? Or is it just an audacious speculation that may or may not be experimentally confirmed someday? Will it make any difference in how science is actually done now to admit that all of this might be true? I believe that it already has made a difference, which can be found in the body of research that is often called dynamic systems theory. This new paradigm takes the computational power of state space transformations and applies it to the entire organism and its environment, rather than limiting it to the brain, as connectionist AI so far has done. This gives it a biological accuracy and computational power whose potentials we are just beginning to explore, and which I will discuss in the last chapter of this book. First, however, I need to make another digression to answer one of the most common objections I have received in correspondence: if we are partly embodied by our world, how can we ever be mistaken about it?

9 Dreams, Illusions, and Errors

There are still certain aspects of knowledge and experience that have to be accounted for by any possible alternative to Cartesian materialism. One thing that any epistemology must do is to explain the existence of errors. The traditional brain-centered picture has a very plausible explanation for errors, which goes something like this. True theories are a distinct species whose essential characteristic is that they refer to entities in the outside world. False theories, in contrast, are a different species because they refer to entities that exist only in the mind–brain. Those entities are called illusions, and they cause errors by getting in the way of our experience of the reality in the world. On the other hand, if we accept that the self is already in and constituted by the world, it is not obvious how we can account for the existence of errors. Is it possible to develop a coherent theory of errors that has no need for those entities called illusions, which both exist and don't exist because they exist "only in the head"?

Perhaps the experience that inclines us most toward believing that illusions are what cause errors is the experience of dreaming. Descartes himself thought that it was possible that all of our experiences could be dreams, which he believed would have meant that our minds had no contact with the external world at all. This was the inspiration for his "evil genius" thought experiment, which in turn inspired the Cartesian materialist "brain-in-a-vat" thought experiment described in chapter 5. However, I will be arguing in this chapter that the fact that we dream does not require us to accept that we are embodied only by our brains, or that a disembodied brain in a vat would have the same experiences as an embodied brain in a world.

However, to effectively "think outside the box" on this subject, we have to start by carefully studying the box we are trying to escape. This means that we need to look carefully at the Cartesian concept of error. Almost everyone on both sides of the big debates in the history of western philosophy accepted certain crucial Cartesian assumptions about the nature of error, even when they saw themselves as actively criticizing everything else Descartes was saying.

Cartesian Materialism and the Empiricists

Both Descartes and the empiricists believed, despite their numerous other disagreements, that regardless of what caused us to have an experience, the experience itself had an integrity that located it completely inside the mind–brain. This is what supposedly made such experiences a suitable foundation for knowledge. If I see an object in front of me as yellow because I have jaundice, I have made an error if I believe that there is yellow pigment in that object. But that doesn't mean that the experience of yellow contains any error of its own. Descartes stated this point by saying that error is a property of judgments, not of the ideas themselves. No idea by itself compels us to make an error; it is the judgment about its relationship to other things that produces errors: "Now as to what concerns ideas, if we consider them only in themselves and do not relate them to anything else beyond themselves, they cannot properly speaking be false" (Descartes 1641/1911).[1]

Descartes had two main points wrong, however. First of all, both he and the British empiricist writers who critiqued him conflated two importantly different prototypes for the word "idea." For Descartes, an idea was a mathematical truth grasped by the inner light of reason. For the empiricists, an idea was a sensation grasped by means of the sense organs. It took Kant to clarify the debate by pointing out that each side was talking about something slightly different. Kant rejected Descartes's concept, which he labeled "intellectual intuition," and this rejection became the basis for the logical positivist view of knowledge described in chapter 6. Kant, in other words, agreed with the empiricists that there was no such thing as intellectual intuition, and that only the sense organs gave us intuited experience. He thus replaced Descartes's distinction between judgments and ideas with the distinction between concepts (which we arrived at by making logical inferences and other forms of judgments) and percepts (which, like Descartes's ideas, provided some sort of foundation for those judgments).

But second, what both Descartes and the logical positivists had wrong was the assumption that we could ground our inferences in certain ideas or percepts because they were immediately given to us. However, much of what we have learned about biology since then (see chapter 2 for a sample) indicates the relationship between percepts and concepts is much more dialectical than this. They are constantly reconditioning each other, and neither can provide a foundation for the other. During waking life, we have the perceptual sensations we have because of the relationship that has grown up between outside stimuli and the conceptual structures that are waiting to receive them. During dreaming, it seems likely that some sort of relationship between body and world is also operating, even though the connection is comparatively erratic and unpredictable.

Admittedly, the question of what embodies consciousness during dreaming is an empirical one. For that reason, I cannot, as a philosopher, deny the possibility that when people dream, their experiences are embodied entirely by their brains. But even if that were true, it would not imply that our *waking* experiences are embodied by our brains. If there is someone who every night dreams he is a butterfly and then wakes every morning and discovers that he is a Chinese poet, that particular person would have no way of knowing that he was not in fact dreaming he was a Chinese poet but actually a butterfly. But it is an empirical fact that our dreams are not like that. They are incoherent jumbles, which vary in style and content from night to night. The most likely reason for this incoherence is that when we are dreaming, our brain's contact with the world is tenuous and arbitrary. Perhaps—just perhaps—our brain has no connection to the outside world whatsoever while we are dreaming. If this is the case, our dreams are embodied by just our brains, which would account for why they are so different from those experiences that are embodied by the entire brain–body–world. But precisely because dreams are so different from waking experience, we cannot infer from the cerebral embodiment of dreams to the cerebral embodiment of all experience. Even if there were unassailable proof that our dreams are embodied only by our brains, this would not imply that the rest of our experiences are embodied only by our brains.

There is, however, plenty of anecdotal evidence that sometimes dreams are causally affected by the outside world. Consider the scene in the movie *Mask*, where Jim Carrey's character Stanley dreams that a beautiful woman is licking his face, and then wakes up to discover that his dog is actually licking his face. That scene strikes a responsive chord because most of us have had the experience of incorporating events from the world into our dreams. The relationship between Stanley's tactile experience and his belief system was so chaotic that the resulting visual experience and accompanying story was a confabulation that was out of joint with the rest of his experience (although it did have a relationship to his desires). But the tactile experience was still causally connected to the world; it was not spontaneously generated by the brain.

However, even if there is a causal connection between dreams events and the outside world, the fact that this connection is so tenuous and arbitrary tempts us to use the distinction between causation and embodiment, which was criticized in chapter 4. Perhaps in the case of dreams, there is a distinction between percepts and judgments. Percepts would be those mental events that are embodied by the brain, and judgments would be mental events about percepts that speculate about the nature of what exists outside the brain. Both Cartesians and Cartesian materialists would say that Stanley was mistaken when he believed that a woman was licking his face, but there would have been no error if he had known that he was only dreaming that a woman was licking his face. Is it possible that in the dream world, at least, we can preserve the distinction between percepts and judgments? Yes, it is possible, but there is another alternative that deserves serious consideration. As I interpret Dewey and James, they would claim that we cannot separate Stanley's experience of the dream from his judgments about the dream. He had that dream-experience because he made those judgments, and vice versa. And although his judgment contained a serious error, there is only a difference in degree between that error and the waking "error" that the pattern of quarks in front of us is a chair or a tree. Hopefully the reader will find that claim less counterintuitive as my arguments unfold.

The Pragmatist Alternative

If we take Dewey's position that an experience is always constituted by a goal-directed activity, this would mean that our percepts were actually produced by registering information in terms of how it related to the goals of that activity. This is significantly different from the empiricist view that each moment of experience was completely independent of all the others.

And it is only this alleged independence that gave credence to the idea that a single moment of experience can be directly given to us (i.e., complete and self-contained within the confines of the mind–brain). The information theory that is central to modern cognitive science provides far more support for Dewey's position than for the atomism that Dewey derisively labeled "sensationalistic empiricism." Fodor was importantly wrong when he said that "information theories are, on the face of them, atomistic about content" (Fodor 1994, p. 6). This is because information theories do not imply that "all that matters to whether your thought is about dogs is how it is causally connected to dogs" (ibid.).

A thermometer gives us information about the temperature not just because of how it is causally connected to the temperature. If this were all that were needed, there would be no significant difference between a thermometer and a teakettle. A thermometer delivers information by positing a set of numerical values for a range of possible temperatures, and then informing us which of those possible temperatures describes the environment right now. The causal connection with the outside world is thus necessary for us to receive information, but it is not sufficient. Nor does information theory require there to be a measurement of a quantity when information flow takes place. A thermostat does not need to assign a numerical value to a temperature. For certain activities, it could work just as well if the calibration on the dial said things like "cold, cool, warm, hot, very hot." It is an information-using device because it responds to the temperature in a room by choosing from a set of possibilities, each of which requires a different response within the context of a purposeful activity.

Our perceptual faculties register information in much the same way as a thermometer or thermostat, but instead of deciding among possibilities located along a single axis, they comprehend what we are interacting with by locating it within a multidimensional state space. Pages 102–108 of Churchland 1989 gives an idea of how information-rich such a multidimensional space can be, and also points out that we usually do not respond to receiving information about where a perceived object is within such a space by saying something like "lo, a pink ice cube." On the contrary, we respond to each perception with a set of behavior patterns, which normally help to fulfill a purpose of some sort. The behavior itself also exists within a range of possibility spaces, and acquiring skill is setting up consistent and useful correlations between perceptual space and behavioral space; or to put it more colloquially, learning how to do the right thing at the right time (or more technically again, responding appropriately to what is perceived in one's environment). Any living being, even a plant, is capable of setting up these kinds of correlations between what stimulates it and how it responds. Despite what Skinner believed, such correlations are never an atomistic laundry list. They are always part of a systematic whole that can be comprehended only if one is aware of the goals of the system: the optimal equilibrium (or set of equilibria) that the system strives to maintain as long as it is alive.

The Deweyan position I am proposing is that once we establish reliable correlations between certain regions of perceptual space and certain regions of behavioral space, experience emerges. An essential corollary of this position, which hopefully is clear from my extrapolation from the thermometer example, is that perceptual systems work only by positing a range of possibilities, and then receiving information from the world that tells us which of these possibilities are actual.[2] The advantage that we have over other creatures is that we have the greatest flexibility in changing the posits that define the range of those possibilities, partly (although not entirely) because of our ability to use language. Because we have posited the existence of certain useful theoretical entities (such as three-dimensional objects, or diseases, or quarks), we are able to make success-ful predictions about our worlds. *But it is the long-range success of these theoretical posits that prompts us to declare the entities they refer to as real, not contact with some sort of nonillusory reality that is different in kind from the rest of our experience.* Descartes was wrong when he claimed that we can tell how effectively a theoretical posit will be at helping us to avoid errors by simply contemplating it. We have to make an ontological leap of faith, accept that posit as true, and perform activities based on the assumption that it is true. When we do this wisely, when we make a good choice, we end up making fewer errors than if we make a bad choice. But no choice has ever produced a theory that enabled those who accepted it to make no errors whatsoever. If that ever happens, such a theory would be The Truth, and all other theories would be illusions. But in the real world, the only choice we have is between theories whose acceptance leads to varying amounts of errors, which means that the truth of a theoretical system is a matter of degree.

This is precisely what one would expect if the self arises from the inter-actions of the brain–body–world, rather than residing entirely in the brain.

Cartesian materialism draws a sharp line between illusions, which exist only in the mind–brain, and those perceptions and conceptions that directly relate to the world. In the view I am advocating, there can be no such line, because the human activities that constitute experience always fall short of their goals at least occasionally. Some of the posits that are the basis for certain activities lead their believers into so many errors that only a fool would continue to cling to them. Others are so effective that the few errors they produce can be easily ignored. But most theories lie between these two extremes, and there is thus no principled way of drawing a sharp line between illusions and reality. If the Cartesian materialist theory of illusions was true, the entities described by a theory would have to be either in the head or in the world, with no room for anything in between. This means that there would have to be a place on this continuum where a theory would lose its grip on the world, and snap back into the head like a broken rubber band. But if the self is already in the world, a theory's weakness would not spring from its inability to reach outside of the head. It would spring from the fact that the theory refers to the world in an equivocal and confused way, not from the fact that it doesn't refer to the world at all. And all theories would be equivocal and confused to some degree, even our best ones.

The most common objection to this kind of pragmatism is to ask "Are you claiming that pragmatism is true, and realism is false? If so, then your theory is self-contradictory." I will freely admit that I cannot prove that the One True Theory isn't out there. But even if it is, we still need a way of telling the difference between our good theories and our bad theories until the One True Theory is discovered. A pragmatist epistemology of the sort I am describing here will be useful for this purpose until the "scientific millennium" arrives. I personally am willing to make the leap of ontological faith and say I believe that such a millennium will never arrive, and we will never have the One True Theory. But I can't prove this, even with the following facts that are my main reasons for believing it.

Bridge Laws versus New Wave Reductionism

When Ernst Nagel wrote *The Structure of Science*, the view of science that I caricatured in chapter 6 was alive, and appeared to be reasonably well. Nagel was one of the first logical empiricists, which meant that to some degree he accepted epistemology as a legitimate enterprise as long as it was firmly grounded in an exegesis of scientific facts and procedures. However, Nagel's epistemology still accepted the logical positivist view that knowledge grew cumulatively by building on a foundation of directly given observations. This meant that Nagel had to account for the widely accepted "fact" that new scientific theories were conceptually compatible with old ones. This is why he came up with the concept of "bridge laws," which supposedly established logical identities between the entities referred to in old and new theories. However, as philosophers of science did more history of science, they discovered that establishing such identities was usually impossible. Paul Feyerabend's "Explanation, Reduction, and Empiricism," and Thomas Kuhn's *The Structure of Scientific Revolutions* provided detailed historical evidence that when a new theory replaced an old one, it was almost always impossible to establish bridge laws between the old and the new.

What then was the alternative? The most obvious conclusion was that old theories were simply falsified by new theories, the way science falsified claims for the existence of demons and witches. This seemed to follow from Kuhn's claim that the new theory and the old theory were what he called "incommensurable." If the old theory had no essential relationship to the new one, where else could it go but the ontological trash heap? This view, called eliminative materialism or eliminativism, became the basis for a program in philosophy of mind as well, thanks especially to Paul and Patricia Churchland. But there was a serious problem with eliminativism, in both philosophy of science and philosophy of mind. If each theory is falsified by whatever theory replaces it, that next new theory would also be proven false by whatever theory replaces it, and so on ad infinitum. This process can only produce a unified true science if it eventually ends with the discovery of the one true theory. Given how science has operated in the past, this seems very unlikely. As Paul Churchland puts it:

So many past theories, rightly judged excellent in their time, have since proved to be false. And their current successors, though even better founded, seem but the next step in a probably endless and not obviously convergent journey. (Churchland 1989, p. 140)

It is expected that existing conceptual frameworks will eventually be replaced by new and better ones, and those in turn by frameworks better still, for who will be so brash as to assert that the feeble conceptual achievements of our adolescent species comprise an exhaustive account of anything at all? (Ibid., p. 52)

So, if each theory is falsified by its successor, and every theory is succeeded by some other theory, therefore all scientific theories that ever existed or will exist are false. I think that Feyerabend succumbed to these skeptical implications of eliminative materialism, which is why he ended up writing books with titles like *Farewell to Reason,* and *Against Method.* The Churchlands, however, tempered this skepticism with a variety of evocative metaphors that for our purposes boil down to one point: the line between a true theory and a false one is not as sharp as is commonly supposed.

The Pragmatic Answer to Eliminative Skepticism

Given that the connection between old theories and new ones cannot be accomplished with identity statements, is there any other connective that can do the job? Unlike the logical empiricist's answer, which was straight-forward and false, Paul Churchland's answer is every bit as ambiguous as the phenomenon he is attempting to explain. Building on ideas first stated in Hooker 1979 and 1981, Churchland says that the two theories are "relevantly isomorphic," that the new theory has a "roughly equipotent image" of the old, and that the older theory "is just the target of a relevantly adequate mimicry" (all from Churchland 1989, p. 49). Yet despite all of this similarity it is still possible for the new theory to be true and the old theory to have "no extension whatsoever" (ibid.). How then do we get identities between two theories? Churchland's answer is somewhat equivocal: "[F]ull fledged identity statements are licensed by the comparative smoothness of the relevant reduction (i.e., the limiting assumptions are not wildly counterfactual, all or most of [the old theory's] principles find close analogs in [the new theory] etc.) . . . and thus allows the old theory to retain all or most of its ontological integrity" (Ibid., p. 50).

Note the modest criteria for determining smoothness. Limiting assumptions can be counterfactual as long as they are not wildly so, the principles of the two theories can be different as long as they are close analogs, the old theory need not retain all of its ontological integrity as long as it retains most of it. Yet all of this similarity gets accepted as identity, for all practical purposes. Apparently the binary distinction between real and unreal, true and false, cannot be preserved if we are to avoid skepticism in a post-Kuhnian World. We cannot say, for example, that the "smoothness quotient" for the light–electromagnetic energy relationship is 0.87 and therefore light is electromagnetic energy, whereas the relationship between caloric and molecular motion has an "S.Q." of only 0.34 and therefore there is no such thing as caloric.

This continuum between true and false theories is also implied by Patricia Churchland's description of how one theory succeeds another in a post-Kuhnian view of scientific history. In this passage she expands on Paul Churchland's claim that "Reduction may be smooth or bumpy, or anywhere in between" (Churchland 1979, p. 84).

Theories range themselves on a spectrum. . . . some require relatively little correction in order to be reduced. . . . but in other cases so much correction is needed that almost nothing save a few low-level homey generalizations can be retained. The spectrum . . . has at one end reduced theories that have been largely retained after the reduction and at the other end theories that have been largely displaced, with sundry cases falling in between. (1986, p. 281)

When the smoke clears after the reduction–elimination process, how few "low-level homey generalizations" about X must we have left before we are required to say "there are no Xs"? Apparently there is no straightforward answer to this question, which implies that falsifying an old theory is a somewhat ambiguous process.

Several years later, John Bickle's "Psychoneural Reduction: the New Wave" (1998) attempted to quantify this relationship between old and new theories. He developed Cliff Hooker's insight that even if one could not find logical identities that connected new and old theories, the relationship between them could be seen as an *analog* relationship (Hooker 1981). On page 30 of Bickle 1998, he creates a map that places several important reductions in the history of science on a continuum between reduction and elimination. This map, and the arguments that justify where certain reductions should be placed on it, provide good evidence for Bickle's claim that "ontological consequences depend on the nature of the reduction relation in a non-arbitrary, non–*ad hoc* fashion" (ibid., p. 31). But although Bickle's interpretations of Churchland and Hooker do manage to salvage the concept of reduction, in some sense of that word, they have disastrous implications for Cartesian materialism.

For illusions to exist only in the brain, there has to be not a continuum, but a sharp line between reality and illusion, a place where the theory loses its grip on the outside world and collapses back into the head. The history of science reveals that if any theory is that isolated from reality, then all of them are. Fortunately, no widely accepted theory is that far off the mark.

Astrology is widely discredited today, but Kepler and Brahe were both astrologers, and despite the numerous errors arising from their beliefs, their observations of the heavens provided the basis for the modern heliocentric theory of the solar system. Even the belief in Santa Claus enables one to predict effectively that Christmas presents will appear under a tree in December rather than April. An epistemology that places illusions in the brain, and says that there is a sharp distinction between what is in the brain and what is in the world, cannot make a principled distinction between astrology and quantum physics, given what we now know about the history of science. It would have to say that all of our theories are false, because they cannot measure up to a theory we will almost certainly never discover. This is a good reason for preferring a theory of truth that acknowledges that all thoughts and experiences arise from brain–body–world interactions. Such a theory can evaluate thoughts and experiences by placing them on a continuum that objectively measures how they enable the believer to interact with the world.

Some may say that any argument that leads one to grant ontological status to all theories should be taken as a reductio ad absurdum. After all, we have to draw the line somewhere. Surely we don't want to say that truth always admits of degrees. After all, statements like "Paris is the capital of France" and "2 plus 2 equals 4" are 100 percent grade A true; there are no degrees of truth there.

This objection, however, blurs a subtle but important distinction. The claim that an entire theory cannot be false in a binary true-or-false sense does not apply to statements made within the context of a theory. Suppose that a medieval merchant and his customers sincerely believed that various exotic items for sale in the merchant's shop (such as narwhal horns and kudu antlers) were unicorn horns. A customer asks, "Are there any unicorn horns in this shop?" The clerk goes back to the stockroom, and after a casual search that fails to reveal a small box with a few of these items on the third shelf from the left, comes back and tells the customer, "No, there aren't." The clerk's statement is false, in the traditional binary sense of true or false. Within the context of discourse for that statement, there are unicorn horns in the shop, and the clerk has made an error. But to conflate the observation statement "There are no unicorn horns in the stockroom" with the ontological assertion "There are no unicorn horns" is to make a serious category mistake. After all, the discovery of narwhals would not have justified the clerk's saying to the customer, "See, I told you we didn't have any unicorn horns."

A continuum theory of truth does not require us to refrain from criticizing or comparing theories. But just because a theory is muddle-headed, or prone to errors, or in need of replacement, does not mean that what it is talking about exists only in the head. Astrology is an illegitimate and useless conceptual system, but it is still a real objective fact that there are a certain number of Sagittarians in Kansas, and this is a fact about Kansas and Sagittarians, not a fact about our mind–brains. Even if almost everything that astrology says about Sagittarians is false, it still provides us with an observation language that divides up the world in a distinctive way, however crude and misleading. Once we have divided up the world with such an observation language, it becomes possible to make binary judgments. This is a good thing, for it is impossible to act in the world without making binary judgments. Every activity presupposes judgments like "Is this cake done or not?" or "Is this a predator or not?" The brittle silicon-inspired metaphors that are the basis for cognitive science models of mind are surely right about this, whatever their other limitations. (If the cake is done, take it out. Otherwise leave it in and repeat step one at a later time.) But before we can act, we must first embrace an ontology. The choices between ontologies, unlike the choices made within any given ontology, are not binary. No ontology is perfect, and which ontology is preferable varies depending on one's goals and purposes.

This claim is similar to the internal realism of Hilary Putnam, who denies "that 'which are the real objects' is a question that makes sense independently of our choice of concepts" (Putnam 1987, p. 20). Putnam also gives a brief overview of several other contemporary philosophers who argue that the best choice of concepts is determined, not just by the world itself, but by our relationship to the world as thinkers and doers.

Many thinkers have argued that the traditional dichotomy between the world "in itself" and the concepts we use to think and talk about it must be given up. To mention only the most recent examples, Davidson has argued that the distinction between "scheme" and "content" cannot be drawn; Goodman has argued that the distinction between "world" and "versions" is untenable; and Quine has defended "ontological relativity." . . . Quine has urged us to accept the existence of abstract entities on the ground that these are indispensable in mathematics, and of microparticles and space-time points on the ground that these are indispensable in physics; and what better justification is there for accepting an ontology than its indispensability in our scientific practice? he asks. Goodman has urged us to take seriously the metaphors that artists use to restructure our worlds, on the ground that these are an indispensable way of understanding our experience. Davidson has rejected the idea that talk of propositional attitudes is "second class," on similar grounds. (Putnam 1987, pp. 20–21)

Although it's nice to be in such distinguished company, I need to distance myself from them somewhat, for my position is actually more radical than any of theirs. As far as I can tell, we all agree that accepting an ontology involves something like a leap of faith, and that such a leap is evaluated on purely pragmatic grounds. This leap is necessary because there is no single best ontology that is true of the world independently of the projects and activities that constitute our experience. Consequently, if an ontology enables us to do science (Quine), or understand our aesthetic experience (Goodman), or make sense out of our use of language (Davidson), that is the only justification we need to accept it as true. But I am not just claiming that there are a variety of ontologies that can be justified on pragmatic grounds. I am saying that *all* ontologies can be justified on pragmatic grounds to some degree. No ontology is false in the sense of referring to entities that exist only in the head, not even ontologies that don't work very well. This does not mean that it would be impossible for a philosopher to construct a set of sentences that don't refer to anything and call it an ontology. Such an "ontology" would really be only a work of fiction,[3] because it would not have the proper relationship to a set of lived experiences that would enable it to function as an ontology in a world. But any ontology formulated by a community of living organisms fighting their way through the thick of things, who spent many lifetimes tuning it so as to minimize errors, will inevitably possess some epistemic virtue, along with numerous epistemic vices. But no matter how vice-ridden, an ontology that evolved in the world will always have some relationship to that world, not just to illusions that exist only in the head.

None of this implies that all ontologies that were ever in active use should be taken seriously. Every ontology needs improvement, and most of those that have been abandoned richly deserved their fate. There are also many ontologies that ought to be abandoned, even though they haven't been. But the lack of epistemic virtue of these ontologies does not spring from the fact that they accept the existence of entities that only exist in the head. It springs from the fact that their terms refer to entities in the world in a confused and equivocal manner. The problem is not that those terms refer to nothing. The problem is that, when compared to more effective ontologies, they sometimes refer to the same thing with several different terms, and other times refer to several different things with the same terms.

If true and false theories are on a continuum with each other, they are thus more like members of the same species, rather than opposites. We are always in the truth of the world, but see it with varying degrees of clarity. Reality is always present to us in some sense, but in varying kinds of focus depending on our goals and projects, and how skillfully we are striving toward them. No experience is veridical in the robust sense beloved by atomistic empiricism, and no experience is an illusion in the sense of being totally out of touch with reality. We are always right in the middle of reality. Where else could we be, seeing as nothing else exists? But this fact does not, alas, protect us from errors.

The concept of illusion is the shadow side of the wish that it must be possible to be in the presence of reality in such a way as to eliminate all possibility of error; to be in the presence of the given. This would be nice, but there is no reason to assume it's ever going to happen, and plenty of inductive evidence that it isn't. Fortunately, however, once we give up the hope of being in the presence of the given, we are no longer forced to see everything else as an illusion. We can instead agree with Ruth Millikan that "Knowing must have been something that man has been doing all along" (1984, p. 7), which saves us from having to accept that knowing is something we will probably never get to do.

Connectionist Support for Pragmatism

It is always gratifying to discover independent confirmation for the same theory in two separate fields of research. Perhaps this thought occurred to Paul Churchland when he worked out some of the implications of the idea that knowledge is embodied by neural networks. It is widely believed (I think correctly), that the connectionist architecture of neural networks is a more accurate depiction of how our minds work than the computer-based metaphors that dominated early cognitive science. Articulating the differences between these two models of mind is one of the dominant projects of contemporary philosophy, and a recurring theme throughout this book. Those of us who take the connectionist view seriously cannot ignore the fact that it provides further evidence for a continuum theory of truth.

According to connectionist theory, a knowledgeable neural network is one that makes few errors. When a network is learning, its response to its inputs is changing "in a fashion that systematically reduces the error messages to a trickle" (Churchland 1989, p. 177).

[N]othing guarantees that there exists a possible configuration of weights that would reduce the error message to zero. . . . nothing guarantees that there is only one global minimum. . . . perhaps there will in general be many quite different minima, all of them equally low in error, all of them carving up the world in quite different ways. . . . these considerations seem to remove the goal itself—a unique truth—as well as any sure means of getting there. (Ibid., p. 194)

Thus, Churchland claims that although there is no such thing as "the truth" from a neurocomputational point of view, there is such a thing as learning. Learning in a neural network is defined not as eliminating error, but as decreasing it. It is thus not surprising that human knowledge undergoes a growth process that might be fancifully described as becoming truer and truer without ever reaching "true," just as we can travel further and further without ever reaching "far." As the growth of science has made it possible for us to do more and more things with less and less error, we are obviously learning a great deal. At any point in the history of knowledge, another theory may be developed that has a much smaller error minimum than its predecessor, and we may decide to stop using the old theory and go with the new one. But this does not mean that the old theory never had any contact with reality, and is now revealed to have resided only between the ears of the poor dupe who once believed it.

Yet it seems odd, to say the least, to use brain research as the basis for criticizing Cartesian materialism. Doesn't connectionist theory operate on the assumption that all cognitive activity takes place in the brain? By and large it does at least for the moment. But it contains the conceptual tools for uniting brain, body, and world into a single cognitive system. The thing that distinguishes a connectionist system is that it operates by vector transformations, rather than by logic-based symbol manipulations. Simply put, this means that it transforms one set of values (a vector) into another set or sets of values. In a connectionist system, these values describe the input and output signals of natural or artifical neurons. Because these signals are analog values, they can measure continua much more flexibly than can logic-based systems. This is why they are better at dealing with the mushy nuances of the real world. However, the basic mathematics that makes connectionism possible does not require those values to be only neuronal signals. Any biological parameter, including those outside the brain, or even outside the body, can have a value describable as part of a vector. And the transformations between these nonneuronal parameters are in principle capable of performing the same kind of cognitive functions as the transformations that are performed in brain networks. There is now an emerging paradigm of cognitive science that studies these kinds of transformations, and it is called dynamic systems theory (DST). In the next chapter, I will explain why it seems likely that Cartesian materialism's weaknesses will most likely be overcome by DST, because of its commitment to the principle that "the cognitive system cannot be simply the encapsulated brain; rather it is a single unified system embracing the . . . nervous system, body, and environment" (Port and Van Gelder 1995, p. 13).

10   Dewey and the Dynamic Alternative

If Dewey had been your ordinary run-of-the-mill prophetic genius, he would have used his classic 1896 article "The Reflex Arc Concept in Psychology" to predict the downfall of behaviorism and the rise of cognitive psychology almost a century later. Instead he leapfrogged over both behaviorism and cognitive psychology, and articulated the basic principles of dynamic systems theory. Admittedly, Dewey's contribution was more like Democritus' than Newton's, for he didn't provide any of the mathematical details that could have turned his philosophical critique into a scientific alternative. But he was aware of presuppositions that would be shared by both behaviorism and cognitivism when one was barely born, and the other was not even a gleam in anyone's eye. And not only was he aware of the limitations of these presuppositions, he was able to conceive of the bare outlines of an alternative.

Dewey claimed that the distinction between stimulus and response does not replace the Cartesian distinction between mind and body, but merely repackages it. It was, in other words, a form of Cartesian materialism:[1] "The older dualism between sensation and idea is repeated in the current dualism of peripheral and central structures and functions; the older dualism of body and soul finds a distinct echo in the current dualism of stimulus and response" (Dewey 1896, p. 1).

This criticism is quite similar to the criticism that Chomsky made of Skinner's application of the stimulus–response connection to verbal behavior.

If we look at a red chair and say *red*, the response is under the control of the stimulus redness, if we say *chair* it is under the control of . . . chairness. . . . But the word stimulus has lost all objectivity in this usage. Stimuli are no longer part of the outside physical world, they are driven back into the organism. . . . The talk of stimulus control simply disguises a complete return to mentalistic psychology. (Chomsky 1959, p. 553, italics in original)

Dewey claims that the stimulus is really the physical and the response is the mental, so the distinction between the two is really only dualism under a slightly different label. Chomsky points out that, in the behaviorist concept of stimulus–response, even the stimulus is defined only by its relationship to the response, so both are equally mental. But both Chomsky and Dewey criticize the stimulus–response theory because it is a mental concept masquerading as a physical concept.

Chomsky's alternative to Skinner was part of what gave birth to modern cognitive psychology. His critiques of Skinner's theory of verbal behavior were aimed primarily at Skinner's atomism, that is, Skinner's belief that there was no need to posit any underlying structure to interrelate the individual S–R connections. But Chomsky's own theory of language was not as radical a break from atomism as was Dewey's. Chomsky's theory could be seen as "atomism-plus." He did claim that language learning could not be seen as learning how to respond to particular stimuli with particular responses, because there are many different appropriate ways to respond to any given stimulus, and many different stimuli that can produce the same response. He therefore concluded that the only way to account for this disparity is to posit some kind of structure more complicated than the stimulus–response chain, which could weigh and compare a huge variety of factors and make appropriate decisions based on those comparisons (see Rockwell 1999). But Chomsky still sees the job of this structure as working with and manipulating a set of fundamentally independent items, and consequently he is really only supplementing the behavorist's ontology, not replacing it. George Lakoff lists three presuppositions that he claims, I think correctly, are part of the Chomskian paradigm for linguistics:

(A) Every concept is either a primitive or built up out of primitives by fully productive principles of semantic composition.
(B) All internal conceptual structure is the result of the application of fully productive principles of semantic composition.
(C) The concepts with no internal structure are directly meaningful, and only those are. (Lakoff 1987, p. 279)

Lakoff thus interprets Chomskyian atomism as analogous to the atomism that is the governing principle of digital computers, for every computer program and data set is made up of primitive digital bits by fully productive principles of composition.[2]

Dewey's critique of the stimulus–response connection was far more radical than Chomsky's. He saw the reflex arc as ultimately not being divisible into parts at all, and having existence only insofar as it was a temporary outstanding moment in the flux of experience.

[T]he reflex arc idea, as commonly employed, is defective in that it assumes sensory stimulus and motor response as distinct psychical existences, while in reality they are always inside a coördination and have their significance purely from the part played in maintaining or reconstituting the coördination. (Dewey 1896, par. 9)

It is a question of finding out what stimulus or sensation, what movement and response mean; a question of seeing that they mean distinctions of flexible function only, not of fixed existence; that one and the same occurrence plays either or both parts, according to the shift of interest. (Ibid., par. 15)

Dewey is saying that rather than dividing experience up into a stimulus and a response, we should think of the reflex arc as being a continuous circle. It becomes divided into stimulus and response only when we are thinking about it, not when we are experiencing it. Here Dewey is making a distinction very similar to the distinction Heidegger made between Readiness-to-hand and Present-at-hand in *Being and Time* (Heidegger 1926, pp. 70–75)—and Dewey is making that distinction thirty years earlier. "The circle is a coördination, some of whose members have come into conflict with each other. It is the temporary disintegration and need of reconstitution which occasions, which affords the genesis of the conscious distinction into sensory stimulus on one side and motor response on the other" (Dewey 1896, par. 33).

When we study an organism, or reflect on our own organic life, it is the act of studying that brings into focus the distinction between stimulus and response in the first case, or between the self and the Present-at-hand object on the other. In *Democracy and Education*, Dewey's analysis of the relationship between subject matter and method makes three noticeably Heideggerian points. (1) First there is a description of what Heidegger would describe ten years later as Being-ready-to-hand. "In well-formed, smooth running functions of any sort—skating, conversing, hearing music, enjoying a landscape—there is no consciousness of separation of the method of the person and of the subject matter" (Dewey 1916, p. 166).

(2) He then describes how our Readiness-to-hand breaks down when we encounter the world as Present-at-hand. "When we reflect upon experience instead of just having it, we inevitably distinguish between our own attitude and the objects towards which we sustain that attitude. . . . such reflection upon experience gives rise to a distinction of what we experience (the experienced) and the experiencing—the how" (ibid.). (3) Dewey then makes a point that can now be translated into Heideggerian terminology thus: once we assume that Being-present-at-hand is the only reality, we conclude that it is possible to have Dasein without a world, and this conclusion gives rise to dualism. "This distinction is so natural and so important for certain purposes, that we are only too apt to regard it as a separation in existence and not as a distinction in thought. Then we make a division between a self and the environment or world" (ibid., p. 167).

Throughout this book, I have used Heideggerian terms for many of these concepts because they are now widely known in the cognitive science community, thanks to Dreyfus. I also first encountered these concepts in Heidegger myself, for although Heidegger was controversial when I was in school, Dewey was simply invisible. But most of the Heideggerian points that are of interest to AI, and to this book, were made first by Dewey, and I think it is important to give credit where it is due. It was Dewey, not Heidegger, who first said that the problems of modern epistemology arise from assuming that one can have Dasein without Being-in-the-world, although he said it in less technical language by saying that it is impossible to have experience without a body that interacts with an environment.[3] Because Dewey did not have Heidegger's suspicion of metaphysics, he was willing to draw a metaphysical conclusion from this phenomenological fact. Reality, Dewey claimed, was fundamentally a continuity, and most philosophical problems arise from artificially dividing this continuity into absolute dualisms (ibid., p. 333). Stimulus and response, mind and matter, subject matter and method, are but moments in a flux that we define only by their relationship to each other within that flux.

Some may object that stressing the primacy of continuity and process over discreteness appears to make science impossible, or at best needlessly difficult. If we're going to think clearly, this line of reasoning goes, we have to talk as if A and B are different from each other. So what's the point of repeatedly asserting that A and B are not ontologically independent? What does this annoying litany accomplish other than to sap our confidence?

What this criticism ignores is that it *is* possible to talk scientifically about the world in terms of process. Physics, the widely accepted exemplar of science at its best, talks at least as much about process as it does about particles. The physics of gravity, electromagnetism, and the traveling of waves through media, are all ways of quantifying physical phenomena in terms of process. Many physics equations measure patterns that arise when forces create an equilibrium. These equations are providing us with scientific explanations based on process, not particles. This fact is usually ignored because if you ask a physicist studying these phenomena, he may tell you that these processes are traveling through a medium that is made up of particles. But there are many explanations in physics in which this fact makes no significant difference. Those who have a metaphysical commitment to the nonexistence of emergent properties may claim on faith that processes are only epiphenomenal manifestations of what is fundamentally particle behavior. But the fact that physics can talk about processes in as precise a manner as it talks about particles shows that a process ontology is not a mere excuse to slip into mushy metaphors. Kelso 1995 and Port and Van Gelder 1995 are filled with physics equations, most of which make no reference to particles at all. They are measuring only the processes that emerge from the flow and interaction of forces. The fact that research described in those books and elsewhere is now using a new paradigm for studying mind called dynamic systems theory (DST), which studies cognitive systems in process terms rather than atomistic terms, shows that philosophy of mind can be done using a process ontology as well.

The key question here is not whether physics sees the world as fundamentally particulate. The important point is that the particles that are essential to any physical study of the world are almost certainly going to be epiphenomenal with regard to the biological functions that produce consciousness. We don't perceive the atoms and quarks that the physicists tell us make up the world, and it is highly unlikely that our brains do information processing using quarks as fundamental computational units. It follows from the postulates I outlined in chapter 1 that if consciousness is fundamentally particulate, it would have particles that are essential to its function, and epiphenomenal with respect to physics. This is why computers operate by manipulating fundamental particles called bits, but those bits are not discrete particles from the physicist's point of view. They are simply moments in the flow of electricity. Some have even cited this fact as proof that computers are really dynamic systems in a sense, and argue correctly that, with regard to the computer, this sense is trivial. The computer defines certain moments of that flow as bits, because they function as bits within the context of its system. From the computer's point of view the process attributes of electrical flow are epiphenomenal. One of the key questions that will decide the relative accuracy of DST versus digital computationalism is this: Does the system that is responsible for the emergence of our consciousness work by creating a single kind of fundamental particle, and then manipulating it by a variety of different computational principles? Or is that system fundamentally a process, whose parts are constituted solely by the function they are performing at any given time? A computer interrelates its bits, but never blends them together. Those bits remain fundamentally present in all of its operations, performing an essential function in the system. But a dynamic system is fundamentally analog, not digital. Its parts are merely moments in a flux or flow, which is why Port and Van Gelder title their 1995 anthology on DST *Mind as Motion*.

The symbolic system theory of mind is committed to the claim that the mind is fundamentally digital, manipulating independent atoms of meaning and/or experience by logical algorithms (Haugeland 1997, p. 16). Classical sense-datum theory, and the linguistic atomism of Wittgenstein's *Tractatus* are also committed to this position. Dreyfus offers compelling evidence against this claim by documenting the failures of computational AI, and describing the phenomenological evidence that we experience the world not as discrete bits of information, but as moments surrounded by fringes and horizons. Dewey presents similar evidence and arguments against the atomism that would eventually dominate behaviorist psychology, and offered an evocative description of an alternative that contains in embryo the principles of modern DST. "In the physical process, as physical, there is nothing which can be set off as stimulus, nothing which reacts, nothing which is response. *There is just a change in the system of tensions*" (Dewey 1896, par. 15, italics added).

DST sees a cognitive system as fundamentally a set of forces that are interacting in such a way as to create a system of tensions. This aspect of cognitive systems is not that obvious, however, in the most widely discussed form of cognitive dynamic system: the connectionist neural net. For that reason, it will be necessary for me to start with the standard description of neural nets, then reinterpret that description to show why neural nets are best seen as a particular species of dynamic system. I believe that the main reason the initial enthusiasm for neural nets has decreased is that much of the current research is still trapped in the presuppositions of Cartesian materialism. The best way to free connectionist research from those presuppositions is to confront them head on, and then show how they can be bypassed if we see connectionist systems as only one kind of cognitive dynamic system. Once we understand the basic principles of connectionism, it can be shown that it is possible to separate those principles from Cartesian materialism, because many researchers in cognitive dynamic systems theory have already done so.

The Traditional View of Neural Nets

The basic principles of connectionist cognitive systems have been paraphrased many times in the books and journals of the cognitive philosophy community (P. M. Churchland 1989, 1995; P. S. Churchland 1992; Clark 1993; Bechtel and Abrahamsen 1991; Bickle 1998; Haugeland 1997 and on and on). No one who tells this story emphasizes exactly the same points, for the full philosophical implications of these discoveries are still being explored. My version of the story will, of course, help to grind my particular philosophical ax, and will therefore ignore many other points of philosophical and scientific interest. Those who find my version too lacking in detail are encouraged to read any and all of the other sources cited above.

Most of these other paraphrases have (with good reason) stressed the differences between connectionist and classical, logic-based, artificial intelligence. I still believe that these differences are the most important characteristics of connectionist systems. But the main point of this section is that the first artificial neural nets were designed to solve the problems that arose out of logic based AI, and consequently they *shared* many of the same presuppositions about the nature of perception and intelligence. Perception was assumed to be the gathering of bits of information about the outside world, which could then be used and manipulated by a disembodied language-based system. But as long as we see this as the only way of utilizing connectionism, the relationship between connectionist and other dynamic systems becomes obscured, and connectionism loses almost all of its original revolutionary force. A connectionist net becomes rather like an AI "toy world" version of a dynamic system, and is still subject to many of the objections raised by Dreyfus against logic and language-based systems. (See Dreyfus 1994, pp. xxxiii–xxxviii.) I am tempted to think of the connectionist modules used in contemporary AI as little dynamic systems imprisoned like birds in cages, so that they can communicate with other modules only by means of input-and-output devices. There are good reasons for accepting this way of thinking, at least for the short term. It enables engineers to utilize connectionist modules as one more trick in an AI toolbox that is still running on fundamentally logic-based principles, and thus continue to build on the engineering triumphs of the past. Even operating within these limitations, connectionism's accomplishments are undeniably impressive. As long as one remains committed to Cartesian materialism, connectionism seems the only possible way to create a system that is both cognitive and dynamic. To understand the limitations of the traditional view of connectionism, we must therefore first describe its principles so as to stress their affinity with logic based AI, and then show how and why those principles are better described in terms of dynamic systems theory.

Figure 10.1 is a highly simplified diagram of the sort of connectionist system that can recognize different typefaces of the same letter. The row

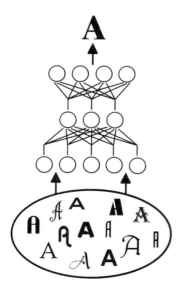

Figure 10.1

of nodes at the bottom of the diagram are functionally similar to the rods and cones in animal retinas. They respond to light reflecting off any one of the letters in the adjacent oval by sending a set of electrical signals into a second row of nodes. The nodes in the second row "weight" this array of signals (i.e., stimulate or inhibit the signal in accordance with a variety of mathematical functions), then send the weighted signal on to another row of nodes, which weights the signal again. Eventually, when the right number of rows is chosen, with the right number of nodes in each row, and each row weights the signal in exactly the right way, an output signal is generated that acquires a genuinely cognitive ability. When all of these factors are correctly balanced, this system gives the same output for a variety of inputs of the same type. In this case, that means it sends the same output signal when it receives inputs from any of those different type faces of the letter A. (This is symbolized in the diagram by the one letter at the top, and the several different typefaces of that same letter at the bottom.) When this output signal is sent to another system that is designed to respond appropriately (such as make the sound "A," or store the ASCII code for "A" at a computer address) the result is a device that performs the cognitive task known as pattern recognition.

The science required to make a system of this sort perform successfully is subtle and complex. But the main thing we need to concern ourselves with is this: it really does work, and it makes possible all sorts of cognitive abilities that were difficult and/or impossible to duplicate using logic-based computer science. There are systems like this one that can send a different signal for each of the twenty-six letters of the alphabet, and thus translate hand-written text into either spoken word or ASCII code. (The former requires learning the highly irregular rules that govern the relationship between pronunciation and spelling, which certain connectionist nets have mastered quite well.) There are connectionist systems that can analyze sonar signals received by submarines, and determine which signals have located landmines and which have located rocks. There are systems that can recognize and classify fingerprints, and there are systems that can recognize faces, and tell which faces belong to men and which to women, *even with people they are seeing for the first time.*

This last property is an example of one of the most amazing powers possessed by connectionist nets of all sorts. Most connectionist nets acquire their powers through a complicated (and very unbiological) training process, in which they are exposed to prototypical members of the category they must learn to recognize. After the training process, they are able to recognize other members of that category that they have never seen before. For example, a system trained to recognize a letter using fonts like Helvetica and Times would be able to recognize the same letter in Palatino and Zapf Chancery, even if those fonts were not part of the training set. There is, however, an explanation for this apparently amazing fact.

Recall that in chapter 8, I mentioned that we can think of a single neuronal node in a net as representing a dimension in a Cartesian coordinate space, and think of the nodes' possible inputs or outputs as describing points along that dimension. If we have ten possible values that are significant to the network for each node, then three nodes could describe 10^3 different points in what is called computational space. Figure 10.2 is a picture of a very simple computational space of this sort, which is divided up into two distinct regions. Every possible signal the net can receive is a

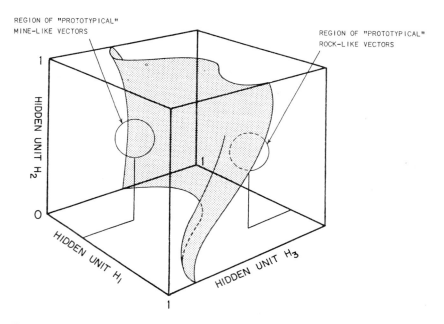

Figure 10.2
Learned partition on hidden-unit activation-vector space. Axes are shown for only three of seven hidden-unit activation levels. From Paul M. Churchland, *A Neurocomputational Perspective: The Nature of Mind and the Structure of Science* (Cambridge, Mass.: The MIT Press, 1989).

point in this computational space. Due to the limitations of our visual system only the values of three input nodes are pictured. But essentially all connectionist systems are actually using spaces with dozens or even hundreds or thousands, of different dimensions. What this particular connectionist net learned to do was respond to any signals it received with one of two possible outputs, depending upon which of these two regions contains the point described by value of the signal. It has two output nodes; if the first sent out a signal and the second did not, the system was recognizing that the input belonged in one category, and if the second node sent out a signal and the first did not, that meant that the input belonged in the other category. Every possible input the system could receive is mapped by a multidimensional space of this sort, and the borders that divide the space show which signals would produce the first output, and which would produce the second. A net trained to recognize the letters of the alphabet would send its output to a system that could distinguish twenty-six different outputs, each of which was designated to symbolize one of the letters. In such a system, the computational space would be divided into twenty-six regions.

During the training process, the net is exposed to members of the categories it is learning to recognize, and then the boundary lines of these computational regions are readjusted so that the net gives the correct response in each case. Once this training process has been completed, the net will respond correctly to other members of the same category, because the signals they produce are within the borders of the newly adjusted computational spaces. Thus, a network trained to recognize the letter "A" will see a new typeface that was not part of its original training set, but the net will recognize it because its input vector describes a point within the boundaries marked off during the training process. Because there could be literally trillions of points within a region that was outlined by relatively few training examples, a properly trained network can make accurate judgments about many things it has never seen before.

Again recall from chapter 8 that because these systems transform an array of input signals, called a *vector*, into a different array of output signals, this cognitive process is referred to as *vector transformation*. The main point of this section is that most creations of connectionist AI (particularly those cited in the philosophical literature) use vector transformations to solve problems and perform tasks that are fundamentally linguistic. The rules of the game were basically set by AI research that began with computer-language-based systems, and connectionist systems downplayed or ignored many of their greatest strengths so that they could play by those rules. Even within these constraints, connectionist systems did remarkably well. In fact, because of the cognitive powers of vector transformation, it seems plausible that such a system could actually function the way philosophers like Locke and Hume said a visual system functions. Given the vast amount of resources that our nervous system has to work with, perhaps a connectionist system might be able to use the same basic architecture to establish a similar relationship between (A) the computational space described by the input received from our retinas, and (B) an appropriate linguistic response, such as "there is a pink ice cube in front of me." A point or set of points in the first computational space could embody a sense datum, and a corresponding set of points in the second space could embody the possible linguistic responses, such as "there is a pink ice cube," "there is a red apple," and so on. Learning about the world would consist of correlating the right retinal input with the right sentences. The fact that the computational space is so vast seems to explain how we are able to store so many of them, and correlate them with sentences.

However, this description between the relationship between language and experience would not have satisfied Dewey. He saw experience not as discrete moments that could be correlated with discrete observation sentences, but rather divided into activities that blurred into each other, which took amounts of time varying from seconds to hours. More important, he saw experiences not as detached observations of a world, but rather constituted by the emotions, goals, and activities of the experiencer. This Deweyan view is a much more accurate description of experience as understood by modern neuroscience, although sometimes certain AI experiments make it difficult to see this. To some degree, the AI experiments described above are shaped by the presuppositions of logical positivism, and research has a tendency to find what it is looking for.

For one thing, these experiments superimpose the law of the excluded middle on top of a system that doesn't really support it. The outputs of the net are not actually identical for every single response that the experimenters label as identical. Even in the simple two-node output of the first example, the system would label an output like "0.8 or 0.6" as a "1 and 0," simplifying a measurement of similarity into an either/or distinction.

In an alphabet recognition system, a certain range of responses is labeled as the "A" response, another range of responses is considered to be the "B" response and so on. When the experimenters are training the net, they are only trying to get every single "A" to produce an output within the "A" range. For the purposes of the experimental protocol, these responses can be interpreted as one of twenty-six different and discrete responses, which can be correlated with observation sentences like "That's an A," "That's a B," and so forth. This is an essential interpretation if we start with the assumption that a knowledgeable person is one who can emit the correct sentence when in the presence of the object that the sentence refers to. The fact that no two responses are exactly alike can be dismissed as harmless noise that doesn't really detract from the signal.

When a neural net is in an actual biological brain, however, this "noise" is not a bug, it's a feature. This is because the perceptual inputs received by real biological organisms are rarely used for the purpose of generating observation sentences. They are never used for that purpose in other animals, for obvious reasons. Instead they are used to control complicated pieces of skillful motor movements—tracking prey with the eyes as it runs through tall grass, monitoring the sound of a violin to make sure the finger muscles keep the music in tune, or stripping leaves off branches in such a way as to make sure that the edible parts come off in your prehensile paws or trunk. To control a process as complicated as any of these, the neural net needs to set up a relationship with more than just a single output vector that can be assigned a single linguistic value. It needs to have a relationship with another whole region of multidimensional computational space, and that means that the output must vary depending on the variations in the stimulus. Thus the analog nature of the net's responses, which is deliberately ignored when pattern recognition means making a particular linguistic response, becomes essential to the functioning of those nets that are designed to control "knowing-how" abilities like the examples listed above. We would thus need to redescribe the basic architectural principle of connectionist nets to capture their ability to embody know-how.

Instead of correlating a cube with a set of observation sentences, we would need to think of two cubes A and B, each like the one in figure 10.2, except that each cube is divided into several different regions instead of only two. (figure 10.3). No two regions in either cube are the same shape or cover exactly the same territory. In a skillful cognitive system,

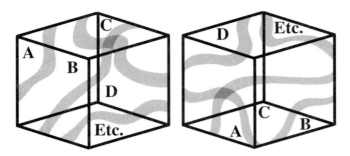

Figure 10.3

correlations are established between region "A" in one cube and region "A" in the other cube, and so on for the ordered pairs of regions "B," "C," and so on. This illustrates the relationship between ordered pairs of computational spaces that empowers any dynamic system, connectionist or otherwise. Whenever such a system receives input that describes a set of points within the "A" region of the first cube, it outputs a set of points described by the "A" region of the second cube, and so on for all the ordered pairs interacting computational spaces in the two cubes. Imagine, for example, that the "A" region of the first cube contains all the different points that describe a particular kind of perceptual input, such as all the different angles and speeds of an oncoming fast ball, and the "A" region of the second cube contains all of the different ways that one could stand, hold the bat, time one's swing, and so forth. If the relationship between the two cubes is tuned properly, the muscles' movement will change as the perceptual inputs change, and the result will be a home run for most of the different ways that the ball could travel over the plate. In principle the same kind of relationship could be established between an organism and its environment for a variety of other skills: painting a picture, closing a business deal, comforting a child.

Of course skills of this level of complexity could not be modeled by only two connected computational spaces. To get a sense of the architecture for these more sophisticated skills, we would have to imagine even more multidimensional spaces that are linked together in a variety of complex ways, including links that feed back to previous links (figure 10.4). This way of picturing connectionist systems is complicated and confusing, but it is in principle far more accurate than the simple input and output diagrams

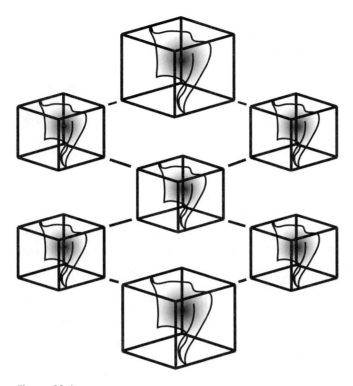

Figure 10.4

exemplified by figure 10.1. It reveals connectionism's potential for modeling cognitive abilities that have little or nothing to do with language. And more important for the purposes of this book, it underscores the fact that *there is no need to limit this kind of vector–transformational computation to neural activity.* An array of neural voltages is not the only set of values that can define a multidimensional space. Several scientists have, in fact, recently concluded that this assumption can be seriously misleading for their research. Instead they account for cognitive abilities by describing vector transformations between vectors that contain other interrelated factors: biological factors outside the brain, and sometimes even factors that interrelate the brain and body with the surrounding environment. Before I discuss their work, however, I am going to redescribe the principles of cognitive vector transformation in a way that makes no specific reference to neurons. These principles are equally applicable to that system of tensions we call a connectionist neural network. But neural networks are only one species of dynamic system that can be described by these generic principles when they are formulated at the appropriate level of abstraction. At this level of abstraction, a host of new mathematical factors become cognitively relevant, in ways that we are now only beginning to fully understand.

A Brief Introduction to DST

A dynamic system is created when conflicting forces of various kinds interact, then resolve into some kind of partly stable, partly unstable, equilibrium. The relationships between these forces and substances create a range of possible states that the system can be in. This set of possibilities is called the *state space* of the system. The dimensions of the state space are the variables of the system. Every newspaper contains graphs that plot the relationship between two variables, such as inflation and unemployment, or wages and price increases, or crop yield and rainfall, and so forth. A graph of this sort is a representation of a set of points in a two-dimensional space. Newspapers and journals will also sometimes contain graphs that add a third variable, and thus represent a three-dimensional space, using the tricks of perspective drawing. The state space of the sort of dynamic system studied by cognitive scientists will have many more dimensions than this, each of which measures variations in a different biologically and/or cognitively relevant variable: air pressure, temperature, concentration of a certain chemical, even (surprise!) a position in physical space. But the mathematics is the same regardless of how many variables the space contains, or the physical or biological process that each dimension is tracking.

However, although these variables define the range of possibilities for the system, only a few of these possibilities actually occur. To study a dynamic system is to look for mathematically describable patterns in the way the values of the variables change and fluctuate within the borders of its state space. The patterns that a system tends to settle into are called *invariant sets*, and these sets contain regions called *attractors* or *basins of attraction*. In Port and Van Gelder 1995, an invariant set is defined as "a subset of the state space that contains the whole orbit of each of its points. Often one restricts attention to a given invariant set, such as an attractor, and considers that to be a dynamical system in its own right" (p. 574). In other words, an invariant set is not just any set of points within the state space of the system. When several interrelated variables fluctuate in a predictable and lawlike way, the point that describes the relationship between those variables travels through state space in a path that is called an *orbit*. The set of points that contains that orbit is called an invariant set because the variations in that part of the system repeat themselves within a permanent set of boundaries.

Port and Van Gelder define "attractor" as "the regions of the state space of a dynamical system toward which trajectories tend as time passes. As long as the parameters are unchanged, if the system passes close enough to the attractor, then it will never leave that region" (p. 573). The simplest example of an attractor is an attractor point, such as the lowest point in the middle of a pendulum swing. The flow of this simple dynamic system is continually drawn to this central attractor point, and after a time period determined by a variety of factors (the force of the push, the length of the string, the friction of the air, etc.), eventually settles there. A slightly more complex system would settle into not just an attractor *point* but an attractor *basin*, that is, a set of points that describes a region of that space. The reason that these attractors are called basins of attraction is because the system "settles" into one of these patterns as its parameters shift, not unlike the way a rolling ball will settle into a basin on a shifting irregular surface. A soap bubble[4] is the result of a single fairly stable attractor basin, caused by the interaction of the surface tension of the soap molecules with the pressure of the air on its inside and outside. Because a spherical shape has the smallest surface area for a given volume, uniform pressure on all sides makes the bubble spherical. But when the air pressure around the soap bubble changes, for example, when the wind blows, the shape of the bubble also changes. The bubble then becomes a simple easily visible dynamic system of a sort, marking out a region in space that changes as the tensions that define its boundaries change. To see how these same principles can eventually reach a level of complexity that makes them a plausible embodiment of thought and consciousness, imagine the following developments.

(1) The soap bubble could get caught up in an air current that flows regularly so that, even though the soap bubble is not staying the same shape, it changes shape in a repeating pattern. As I mentioned earlier, this pattern

is often called an orbit, because the trajectory that describes this repeating change forms something like a loop traveling through the state space of the system. Systems that settle into orbits are usually more complicated than those that settle only into attractor basins that are temporally static, particularly when those orbits follow patterns that are more complicated than mere loops.

(2) Instead of having the soap bubble fluctuate in three-dimensional space, imagine that it is fluctuating in a multidimensional computational state space. As I mentioned earlier, state space is not limited to the three dimensions of physical space, for it can have a separate dimension for every changeable parameter in the system. The most popular example in cognitive science of a system that operates within a multidimensional state space is a connectionist neural network. Connectionist nets consist of arrays of neurons, and each neuron in a given array has a different input or output voltage. Each of those voltages is seen as a point along a dimension of a Cartesian coordinate system, so that an array of ten neurons, for example, would describe a ten-dimensional space. But in other kinds of dynamic systems analyses, any variable parameter can be a dimension in a Cartesian computational space. Our friend the soap bubble can be interpreted as a visual representation of the air pressure coming from every possible angle within the three dimensions in physical space, if all other background conditions remain stable. When the various interacting forces and variables in a dynamic system are designated as dimensions in a multidimensional space, it becomes possible to predict and describe the relationships between different attractor basins in that system. This is the most relevant disanalogy between a soap bubble and the more complicated dynamic systems studied by cognitive scientists. Because:

(3) A soap bubble has really only one stable attractor basin. Although the attractor space that produces a soap bubble is fairly flexible, the bubble pops and dissolves if too much pressure is put on it from any one side. But in certain systems, there are fluctuations of the variables that can cause the system to settle into a completely different attractor space. These systems thus consist of several different basins of attraction, which are connected to each other by means of what are called *bifurcations*. This makes it possible for the system to change from one attractor basin to another by varying one parameter or group of parameters, and thus initiate a different complex pattern of behavior in response to that change.

This propensity to bifurcate between different attractor basins is what differentiates relatively stable systems (like soap bubbles) from unstable systems (like living organisms or ecosystems). In this sense, all living systems are unstable, because they don't settle into an equilibrium state that isolates them from their surroundings. Organisms are constantly taking in food, breathing in air, and excreting waste products back into the environment they are interacting with. We usually think of unstable processes as formless and incomprehensible, but this is often not the case. Certain unstable systems have a tendency to settle into patterns that still fluctuate, but fluctuate within parameters that are comprehensible enough to produce an illusion of concreteness. When the various forces that constitute the processes shift in interactive tension with each other, a basin of attraction destabilizes in a way that makes the system bifurcate, that is, shift to another basin of attraction. This kind of system is sometimes called *multistable*, because its changes between various basins of attraction are predictable and (to some degree) comprehensible. A complete pictorial graph of a dynamic system of this sort would resemble figure 10.4. It would show interlocking computational spaces whose transitions were governed by the relationships between the constituting forces of the system.

This process of bifurcation bears a significant resemblance to the switching between possible branches of decision trees, which is the fundamental cognitive process performed by computer languages. Skillful sensory-motor activity utilizes these same decision trees in processes that take place outside the brain. This fact plays havoc with Descartes's distinction between the so-called automatic functions of the body and the rational decision making of the mind. One of the reasons that Descartes believed that mind and body were fundamentally distinct was that he believed it was impossible for a physical device to make rational decisions that would vary so as to be equally appropriate in different contexts. This was understandable, because the most sophisticated machinery of his time was clockwork. The humanoid automata that he had seen could do relatively complicated things, but they were all stored in the machine in advance and would always be the same regardless of what the outside world did (see Dreyfus 1972, pp. 235–236). Once you wound up a clockwork dummy, it would continue to do the same actions every time you flipped the switch, even if that meant piling into a wall or plunging into a fountain.

It was only after the computer was invented that it was possible for a machine to have some of the flexibility that we associate with rational thought. One of the reasons that Cartesian materialism has continued to thrive is the assumption that the computer metaphor is applicable only to the brain. It is often assumed that motor control does not involve decision making, but is rather a matter of the brain flipping the switches of a variety of preset muscular clockwork systems. However, the following examples will illustrate that many scientific discoveries cannot be accounted for with this simplistic scenario.

Thelen and Smith on Infant Locomotor Development

Scientists who study animal locomotion once believed that motor control develops to maturity by the gradual unfolding of what is called a central pattern generator (or CPG), that is, a self-contained program that controls the motor processes from a central location in the nervous system. Because Cartesian materialism had been assumed to be a scientific fact, it seemed inevitable that a complete explanation would involve merely a more detailed account of this CPG.

Consequently, when Esther Thelen and Linda B. Smith (T&S) began researching the development of infant motor skills, they assumed that they could account for them by measuring the neural voltages that were being sent from the infant's nervous system to its muscles. Unfortunately, there was no repeating pattern that could be found. It was not even possible to find a constant relationship between the voltages sent to the flexor and extensor muscles. In theory, there had to be a precise alternation between signals sent to the flexor and extensor muscles in order for the infant to move its legs. In practice it didn't always work out that way. However, T&S were able to account for these variations with greater accuracy when they saw the infant's locomotor skills as emerging from the interaction of several different factors, including the elasticity of the muscles and tendons, the excess body weight produced by subcutaneous fat, the length of the bones, and so forth. When all of these factors were combined into what T&S called a *collective variable*, it was possible to make sense of how the infant was learning to move its legs.

The infant learned to walk because this collective variable gradually settled into "evolving and dissolving attractors" (p. 85). When the skill was fully developed, the attractor was a deep basin in the state space, that is, only radical changes in the variables that defined the space would throw the system out of equilibrium. But the times in which the infant was still learning to walk would be mathematically described by saying that the collective variables formed a system with shallow attractors, that is, a slight change in any variable could cause the infant to topple over. To say that the infant was learning to walk was to say that these basins of attraction were adjusting themselves so that they gradually became deeper and more stable. Any attempt to describe this process by referring to changes in only one of these variables, such as the nervous system, would be essentially incomplete. The only thing that you could identify as being the embodiment of the walking skill was the system of attractor basins that existed when all of these factors interacted in a single dynamic system. Consequently, it is these attractor spaces that must be identified as the "walking module." T&S claim, I think correctly, that a complete living organism is best understood by identifying all the significant variables that constitute its behavior, both inside and outside the head, then measuring the patterns that emerge as the resulting system fluctuates from one attractor space to another.

Of course everyone acknowledges that the biological processes in the nervous system cannot be completely responsible for locomotion. We can't walk on our nerves. But T&S claim that traditionally researchers have privileged those aspects of locomotion skills that occur in the nervous system as being "a fundamental neural structure that encodes the pattern of movement" (p. 8) and consider everything else necessary for locomotion as being somehow less important. They even quote one researcher who claims that the pattern must be stored in the genes (p. 6). They are quite right to consider this distinction as ad hoc and misleading, and to insist that the parts of the locomotion process that take place outside the brain or genes are every bit as important as the so-called neurological or genetic "encoder."

To some degree, the question of whether locomotor development is controlled by a module in the brain is obviously an empirical one. But although data and research are clearly necessary for answering this question, they are not sufficient. There are significant disanalogies between computers and biological systems that the computer metaphor tempts us to ignore, and that can render the centralized control theory dangerously unfalsifiable. After all, no computer program completely controls anything from a central point. If it did, it would be, as MacKay (1980) points out, more like a tape or phonograph record. MacKay argues that because "the true concept of programming transcends the centralist–peripheralist arguments . . . the term 'central program' is an oxymoron, and the concept unviable in the real world" (pp. 97, 100). The cognitive power of a program comes from its ability to respond in different ways to different inputs. The instructions in the program "detail the operations to be performed on receipt of specific inputs" (ibid., p. 97), and without those inputs it would not be a program at all. One could use these facts about computer programs to respond to all of the objections that T&S raise against the CPG. One need only say that what happens in the brain and/or genes is not a *complete* central pattern generator. CPGs should instead be seen as "generalized motor 'schemata,'" which encode only general movement plans but not specific kinematic details" (Thelen and Smith 1994). The problem with this answer is that it can deal not only with all of T&S's objections, but with every possible objection that anyone could ever make. Whenever an organism makes a motion, there will always be something happening in the nervous system. This version of the CPG theory enables you to call that neural activity the CPG, and everything else in the body or environment mere "kinematic details." There would be no reason you couldn't do this regardless of the empirical results. Clearly it is not acceptable to use a scientific theory that predetermines your answer before the data are in.

Why then does the distinction between program and hardware work so well when we are talking about computers? In a computer, what is going on inside the CPU is the program, and what is going outside the CPU is obviously "peripheral" in some significant sense. Why doesn't this distinction carry over to biology? I believe that this is only because of the way computers are made and used in our society, and that there is no comparable set of criteria that would enable us to make the distinction for biological systems. Computers of a given brand are all engineered the same, which makes it possible for the programmers to ignore the hardware and create a control structure that resides in a central location. MacKay's description (mentioned above) says that a computer program must "detail the operations to be performed on receipt of specific inputs." To specify these operations, however, the program must have a taxonomy of possible input it will receive, so it can specify responses to each of them. With a computer, we can tell ourselves that if we know the central program we know how it works. The hardware never changes so it can be safely ignored. T&S point out, however, that neural activity, unlike computer programs, does not have the advantage of knowing precisely what kind of input it will receive. No two human infant bodies are alike, and the bodily structure of the infant changes radically as the infant matures. Because of these differences, radically different neurological development is needed in order to produce the same behavior in two different people, or even in the same person at different times. Although there are obviously things going on in the nervous system that are necessary for developing locomotor skills, studying the nervous system isn't going to tell us the essential story if we don't also know the peripheral inputs that the nervous systems must interact with. "There is . . . no essence of locomotion either in the motor cortex or in the spinal cord. Indeed it would be equally credible to assign the essence of walking to the treadmill than to a neural structure, because it is the action of the treadmill that elicits the most locomotor-like behavior" (Thelen and Smith 1994, p. 17).

Freeman and the Attractor Landscape of the Olfactory Brain

Unlike T&S, neurobiologist Walter Freeman is willing to study cognitive functions by focusing entirely on the brain. Nevertheless, their similarities are more important than their differences, for Freeman believes that the brain itself is a dynamic system and not a system made up of mechanical modules. Furthermore, Freeman was able to use dynamic systems theory to account for a mental process that would be considered cognitive by even the most orthodox devotee of computer-based AI. After training rabbits to recognize different kinds of odors, and measuring the neurological signals on their olfactory bulbs, he decided that the best way to account for their discriminative abilities was with the concepts of DST. His description of the olfactory system of the rabbit is similar to the picture of a dynamic system shown in figure 10.4.

To use the language of dynamics . . . there is a single large attractor for the olfactory system, which has multiple wings that form an "attractor landscape." . . . This attractor landscape contains all the learned states as wings of the olfactory attractor, each of which is accessed when the appropriate stimulus is presented. Each attractor has its own basin of attraction, which was shaped by the class of stimuli the animals received during training. No matter where in each basin the stimulus puts the bulb, the bulb goes to the attractor of that basin, accomplishing generalization to the class. (Freeman 2000, p. 80).

Freeman has thus come very close to articulating the thesis of this chapter: that cognition is best explained by identifying mental functions, not with organs or modules in the brain, but rather with attractor basins. I, however, agree with Thelen and Smith that neurological activity is not sufficient to explain cognitive functions, and therefore we need to analyze the attractor basins created by interacting variables throughout the brain–body–world nexus.

This is not a criticism of Freeman's scientific work. Every DST analysis has to focus on some variables and ignore others. Focusing on the brain is as good a choice as any, as long as one remembers that it is not the only possible choice. But I am saying that there is no essential difference between T&S's use of these principles and Freeman's. T&S are, I believe, correct in saying that locomotion cannot be effectively understood with a modularity theory that assumes that each locomotive module must be located in a particular spot in the brain. Their data indicate that the most effective explanation for animal locomotion identifies and/or replaces these modules with attractor basins in state space. When we compare T&S's work to Freeman's, there appears to be no essential difference between the attractor basins that govern the interactions between neural activity, and those that govern the interaction between other biological and environmental factors.

Recent discoveries have, in fact, revealed that certain dynamic principles operate the same way for both cell-to-cell connections within the brain, and an organism's connections to the world. J. A. Scott Kelso claims that there is evidence that neurons within the brain can communicate with each other by means of a physical process known as *coupling*, even when they are not connected by axons and dendrites (Kelso 1995, p. 244). Rather than being part of a neural network, these neurons are described as *neural oscillators*. They are connected by the same coupling process that prompts the pendulums of two clocks on the same wall to eventually end up swinging in a synchronized motion. Kelso claims, along with J. J. Gibson, that coupling also explains how a perceiver interrelates to her environment (ibid., pp. 187–192). If the same process that connects neurons together also connects an organism to the world, how can we make a principled distinction between the neural network and the organism–environment network?

When we are still in the grips of Cartesian materialism, it seems natural to assume that the computer metaphor is applicable only to the brain. Motor control is seen as the brain flipping the switches on preset muscular clockwork systems. The brain is seen as "the machine in the machine," which must decide which switches to flip because it alone possesses computerlike circuitry. However, modern biology seriously weakens this distinction between brain as computer and body as clockwork. We now know that every step we take requires a constant flow of information between an organism and its environment, and a variety of adjustments and "decisions" made in response to that information. Locomotion is "not controlled by an abstraction, but in a continual dialogue with the periphery" (Thelen and Smith 1994, p. 9) The following examples show that, the walking organism must make "decisions" that can be seen as functionally equivalent to the conditional branching that is expressed in computer languages. There is good reason to believe that these examples could be the first of many more.

How Animals Move

The ambulatory system of a horse divides into four distinct attractor spaces, colloquially referred to as walk, trot, canter, and gallop. Each of these consists of a set of motions governed by complex input from both the environment and the horse's nervous and muscular system. Careful laboratory study has made it possible to map the dynamics of each gait (see Kelso 1995, p. 70), and each map reveals a multidimensional state space that contains a great enough variety of possible states to respond to variations in the terrain, the horse's heart and breathing rate, and so forth, and yet regular enough to be recognizable as only one of these four types of locomotion. There are no hybrid ways for a horse to move that are part trot and part walk; the horse is always definitely doing one or the other. If all other factors remain stable, the primary parameter that determines the horse's utilization of each gait is usually how fast the horse is moving. From speed A to B the horse walks, from speed B to C it trots, and so on. There is not an exact speed at which the transition always occurs. If there were, a horse would wobble erratically between the two gaits whenever it ran anywhere near those speeds. What usually happens, however, is that the horse rarely travels at these borderline speeds (unless it is being used as a laboratory subject). Instead, it travels at certain speeds around the middle of each range for each gait, because those are the ones that require the minimum oxygen and/or metabolic energy consumption per unit of distance traveled. This means that a graph correlating the horse's choice of gait with its speed usually consists of bunches of dots, rather than a straight line, because certain speeds are not efficient with any of the four possible gaits.

We can make a computer model of the horse's ability to adapt its gait to its speed using LISP, which is one of the most popular AI computer languages. LISP models cognitive processes by means of commands that tell the program how to behave when it comes to a branch in the flow of information, which seems isomorphic to a bifurcation in the flow of a dynamic system from state space to state space. We'll start by positing four subroutines we'll call WALK, TROT, CANTER, and GALLOP, as well as a fifth subroutine we'll call "CURRENT SPEED," which measures how fast the horse is moving. Because we are only modeling the decision-making process, rather than the entire dynamic system, we will accept those subroutines as unexplained primitives. To these five subroutines, we will add some basic subroutines from LISP:

(1) "defun," which defines a new subroutine;

(2) "equal," which compares two numbers and checks whether they are equal;

(3) "<," which compares two numbers and checks whether the first is less than the second; and

(4) "if . . . else," the conditional that performs the decision-making process

We can now describe a possible program that essentially duplicates the decision function of the horse's dynamic ambulatory system. We will posit convenient speeds for each gait of 5, 10, 15, and 25. The LISP term "defun" will establish the word "GO" as the name of this program.

```
(defun GO (CURRENT-SPEED)
     (if    (equal CURRENT-SPEED 0)  0
     (if    ( <   CURRENT-SPEED 5)  (WALK)
     (if    ( <   CURRENT-SPEED 10) (TROT)
```

```
(if    ( <   CURRENT-SPEED  15)  (CANTER)
(if    ( <   CURRENT-SPEED  25)  (GALLOP)
(else  (GO) ) ) ) ) )

)
```

The complete program would have to contain four definitions that looked something like this: (defun WALK (make the horse walk)), and so on for the subroutines trot, canter, and gallop. The phrase "make the horse walk" is of course deliberately empty hand waving, because the details of the four gait programs are of no significance for the point I am making with these examples,[5] which is this: the ambulatory system of a horse regularly performs the same function as the if-then-else command in LISP. The paradigm cognitive ability in computer science is often considered to be choosing between alternatives. This was the main point expressed by the definition of intelligence formulated by AI pioneers Newell and Simon.

... [We] measure the intelligence of a system by its ability to achieve stated ends in the face of variations, difficulties, and complexities posed by the task environment. (Quoted in Haugeland 1997, p. 83)

By this definition, the ambulatory system of a horse can legitimately be seen as a genuinely cognitive system, not as a piece of clockwork, because it makes decisions in the face of complexities posed by the horse's environment.

There is also other research that finds similar kinds of conditional decision making within the distinctive gaits used by other animals. Taylor (1978), for example, describes research done with birds, lions, and kangaroos, showing how changes in gait require "recruitment" of different muscles and tendons. When any of these animals is walking, a certain set of muscles and tendons are brought into play, and it is possible to measure how much energy is being used by each muscle by measuring glycogen depletion. When an animal increases its speed, however, it must run another "program" that decreases the reliance on those muscles, and simultaneously recruits a different set of muscles. Taylor also discovered that the relationship between speed and glycogen depletion turned out to be dependent on several other factors as well. Gravitational energy is stored by means of the stretch and recovery of muscles and tendons in the faster gaits, making it possible for certain animals to actually use less muscle energy when traveling at faster speeds. These relationships can only be described accurately by means of complex conditional relationships very much like computer subroutines. And just as Thelen and Smith discovered, these relationships involve not just neurological factors, but environmental and other biological factors as well.

The balance between flexibility and stability is achieved because all of the forces in these systems of tensions are interacting in a fluctuating equilibrium, rather like a soap bubble in the wind, but a bubble that is suspended in several dimensions instead of only three. As the terrain shifts from smooth to rocky to muddy, or the horse becomes more winded, the system of tensions that determines the shape of this multidimensional soap bubble shifts accordingly. This enables the gallop or trot to be flexible enough for the horse to respond to the changes in the terrain and its own physiological state, yet stable enough to still be a gallop or trot. If all other relevant factors remain the same (say if the horse is running on a treadmill in a laboratory), the decision of when to switch to which gait will be made almost entirely by the speed parameter. But when a horse is out traveling through the real world, all of these factors interact to maintain that system of tensions, which is a particular gait. The switch from one gait to the next is decided by a "consensus vote" among these various forces, which shifts the entire system of interacting parameters so as to form another kind of multidimensional bubble (i.e., produce a bifurcation to another basin of attraction, such as from walk to trot.) This is truly what Port and Van Gelder call *Mind as Motion*, and this undeniably cognitive flexibility cannot be achieved by a brain that is isolated from a body and a world.

Dynamic Systems as Behavioral Fields

When one measures the dynamics of a complete dynamic organism interacting with a world, there is no reason to doubt, as Kelso puts it, "that both overt behavior and brain behavior, properly construed, obey the same principles" (Kelso 1995, p. 28, quoted in Clark 1997 p. 116). Of course, there are too many factors at work in an embodied living system to delineate the state space with the same level of precision that can be done when we are measuring or building a single connectionist network. Consequently, every dynamic systems analysis will necessarily be incomplete, and must focus on different parameters depending on the goals of the experiment. For some research, it would obviously be fruitful to deal only with processes that happened to be in the brain. Freeman refers to his research as dynamic neuroscience, and he goes beyond traditional connectionist assumptions by relying on bifurcation between basins of attraction to understand the brain. There is no question that important and revolutionary work has been (and will be) done by studying the brain as a dynamic system. But we must not forget that every dynamic system is itself part of a bigger system ad infinitum. The fact that many fruitful experiments can focus on the brain should not be seen as proof that the brain is the sole embodiment of consciousness. It is merely a reflection of the fact that all DST models have to measure certain parameters and ignore others when defining a computational space. You must draw the line somewhere, and for certain experiments, the brain is the right place to draw it.

When the borders of possible mental embodiment expand like this, cognitive science becomes much more difficult. It is very difficult, and often impossible, to measure the countless other cognitive parameters that extend out into the world. It is relatively easy (in comparison) to measure neural activity. But the fact that it is harder to measure the state space parameters of an embodied dynamic system in a world does not make any difference to the fundamental nature of the cognitive process. To achieve the fullest possible understanding of human cognition and experience, we must study what is called an "invariant set" of state space transformations, which arise from the interaction of forces and tensions that determine the relationships between an embodied organism and a lived world. Because "invariant" sets are only relatively enduring moments in a flux that is always subject to pressures from forces outside of that invariant set, we can never formulate completely deterministic laws about such a system. But we can still know a great deal about what it will probably do, and we have good reason for believing that this is probably as good as a science of mind can get.

Because there is no principled way to differentiate between the state space transformations that take place in the skull and those that take place in the interactions of the organism and its world, there is no reason to privilege the transformations of neural voltage values by labeling them as the embodiments of mind. As I pointed out in chapter 3, many of the parameters that are arguably responsible for embodying consciousness are hormonal, rather than neural. Furthermore, as I pointed out in chapter 5, when we consider the organism's relationship to its environment, there are only pragmatic and ad hoc answers to the question of which parts of the causal nexus responsible for conscious experience are intrinsic powers of the mind and which are extrinsic relations to the outside world. Only prejudice compels us to assume that we can automatically draw that line at the borders of the skull. We have no evidence whatsoever that what happens in the brain can create conscious experiences all by itself. Consequently, it seems sensible to conclude that the supervenience base for all mental events, including subjective experiences, includes not only brain events, but events in the rest of the body and in those parts of the environment with which the conscious organism maintains a synergetic relationship. At any given moment, there will be a distinction between those processes that constitute the subject and those that constitute the environment. But there is good reason to think that this distinction does not have a constant and enduring borderline.

Without DST, these various biological and environmental factors cannot be seen as a comprehensible system. With DST, we can in principle create a map that describes a field of forces interacting in a multidimensional state space, using the same kinds of mathematical principles that science uses to study gravitational or electromagnetic fields. This map would be outlining what I referred to as a behavioral field in chapter 1, and would enable us to attempt to measure the fluctuating borders between self and environment. "Behavioral field" is not a mere metaphorical extrapolation from other kinds of field theories. The interacting basins of attraction that constitute such a field are every bit as physically real as gravity, capacitance, voltage, or any other theoretical scientific entity that we cannot see, feel, hear, or trip over. If the science were in place to quantifiably study how such a field radiates out from the organism into its environment, there would be no reason to dismiss such studies as mere mystical claims that we are "one with everything." On the contrary, this behavioral field would be our best scientific approximation of what the mind is identical with.

There is nothing I can say, however, which can compel scientists to do research based on this assumption, or to abandon Cartesian materialism. As Quine pointed out, any theory can be held true come what may if you are willing to make enough other adjustments in your beliefs. For centuries we have lived with the paradoxes created by the polarities of Cartesian materialism: physical and mental, brain and behavior, reality and illusion, sense and reference. Many people are more comfortable with old para-doxes, because a familiar metaphysical assumption seems less speculative and better justified than a new counterintuitive one. But this new alternative to Cartesian materialism has already been in the air for sometime, as I have tried to show with many quotations from other sources, and perhaps its time has come. The purpose of this book is to state this alternative in the boldest manner possible, so that it will receive either the criticism or the respect that it deserves.

Notes

Introduction

1. In *Consciousness Explained*, Dennett uses this term to mean something slightly but significantly different. Dennett defines Cartesian materialism as the belief that the self resides in a part of the brain, rather than the whole brain. In my 1995 (pp. 113–116, and in ch. 2 of this book), I argue that most of the problems with assuming that part of the brain contains the self remain unsolved if we accept Dennett's claim that "the head is headquarters." (Dennett admits to many of these problems a few years later in Dennett 1996.) For this reason, I use the term "Cartesian materialism" the way I defined it in my 1995 article, which became the basis for this book: to refer to any position that tries to single out one part of the brain–body–world nexus as the only true "seat of the soul."

2. It seems strange that Descartes would say this, because he has also asserted that the mind was without spatial properties. But Descartes's thinking was somewhat muddled on this issue; the relationship between the mind and the body was the weakest link in his philosophy. He does say that "the soul is of such a nature that it has no relation to extension" (Cottingham et al. 1985, p. 339), but when he actually gets down to describing how the soul and the body act on each other he says "the soul has its *principal seat* in the small [pineal] gland located in the middle of the brain. *From there* it radiates through the rest of the body . . ." (ibid., p. 341). The phrases I have put in italics clearly presuppose spatial location, regardless of Descartes's earlier claims to the contrary.

3. I am willing to take Rorty's word for Dewey's effect on other American philosophers during his time, but Dewey himself was not guilty of such provincialism. His collaboration with scientists, such as child psychologist Mrytle McGraw, and his detailed writings on a variety of other topics, showed his constant willingness to apply his ideas to specific situations. This was often interpreted as a sign of dilettantism when philosophers began to think of themselves as specialists. But this interpretation is wrong, for almost everything he wrote was designed to reveal a specific application of his radically new philosophical viewpoint. For example, his

writings about art reveal how his views about experience differ from classical empiricism, and his writings about education reveal the practical implications of his theory of knowledge. Because he agreed with Peirce and James that a theory's cash value came from its application to concrete problems, he took pains to show how his theories would cash out in as many different situations as possible.

4. See Putnam 1995 (p. 14) for a tracing of the ancestry of this formulation of the pragmatist position back to William James through Churchman and Singer.

Chapter 1

1. The parts, however, need not be distinct physical modules. For example, they could be (and I believe they probably are) moments of equilibrium in a dynamic system. Note also that even modules are ontologically constituted by the system that they are part of. They are distinct from the other parts of the system only because they derive their being from that system. If there were no differences between the functions performed by batters, pitchers, and catchers, there would be no game of baseball, only an unseemly free-for-all. But on the other hand, there were no batters or pitchers in existence before baseball was invented, waiting in the world for someone to get the idea to put them in game of some sort.

2. This is a quote from the British comedy revue "Beyond the Fringe."

3. For example, consider this passage: "to find that most people have minds . . . is simply to find that they are able to and prone to do certain sorts of things . . . We are familiar with such specific matters long before we can comprehend such general propositions that John Doe has a mind" (Ryle 1949, p. 61). This passage could be interpreted to mean that people do in fact have minds, and that specific behavior is epistemologically, but not ontologically, prior to the minds that cause it. This interpretation would imply that Ryle believed that minds existed, and was only denying that minds were ghosts or brain states. Consider also "It is perfectly proper to say in one logical tone of voice that there exist minds, and to say, in another logical tone of voice, that there exist bodies" (ibid., p. 23). There are, however, plenty of other passages that indicate that Ryle thought that minds were only dispositions to produce behavior, and as this was widely accepted to be his position, it was the one that Fodor and others devoted most of their energy to refuting. This purely dispositional theory of mind seems obviously false now, partly because of Skinner's unsuccesful attempt to base an autonomous psychology on it. Without the interpretation of (extrapolation from) Ryle I am outlining in this chapter, Cartesian materialism seems the only other alternative.

  We should also remember a point that Fodor largely ignored: Ryle's behaviorism is very different from Skinner's. Skinner's talk about stimulus–response connections was as tautologically dispositional as Moliere's talk about dormative powers, as Chomsky's review of Skinner's "Verbal Behavior" eloquently illustrated (Chomsky

1959). (See also "Skinner Skinned" in Dennett 1978.) But Ryle, unlike Skinner, was not an eliminativist, which is why Ryle made statements like the quotes above. Ryle believed that Skinner was mistaken in claiming that ordinary talk about mental processes could ever be replaced by mechanical talk that analyzes human behavior into discrete parts, whether those parts are the atoms of physics or stimulus–response connections. He saw mental processes as being real things, not illusions that science should dispense with.

Chapter 2

1. This expression was originated by Robert P. Pula.

2. There are also many widely accepted critiques in contemporary epistemology of the once hallowed dichotomy of sensing and thinking . Quine, for example, believes that we cannot make a precise distinction between knowledge caused by sensations and knowledge produced by cognitive activity. Because we never encounter experience directly (in the way that traditional empiricism assumed) "our statements about the external world face the tribunal of sense experience not individually, but only as a corporate body" (Quine 1963, p. 41). This is why there can be no such thing as a pure observation statement, because our sense organs can never function independently from our theories about the world. This would be hard to explain if science still told us our sense organs were independent modules connected to the brain by message cables. But now that we know that our perceptual and cognitive faculties are basically doing the same sorts of things, it is understandable that epistemology cannot separate them. One would expect that perception and cognition would not be functionally distinct, given that they are distributed throughout the entire nervous system, and not localized in the sense organs and brain respectively. I find this agreement between recent developments in neuroscience and epistemology to be encouraging for both.

3. There is some evidence that even the rods and cones might not be purely input neurons, because sometimes they are directly connected to each other and affect each other's voltage. Whether this effect is "noise" or "signal" has not yet been determined (Dowling 1988, p. 110). If it turns out to be a cognitively significant signal, the voltage change produced by light rays striking the rods and cones would not be solely a function of the light itself, but instead would be mediated and conditioned by signals from other neurons. This would mean that, strictly speaking, there would be no pure input neurons in the visual system at all.

Chapter 3

1. Chalmers makes such a distinction, but bases it on the assumption that we have a direct awareness of consciousness; an assumption I do not share (see ch. 7).

Chapter 4

1. Actually, even though Mill insisted that there was no genuine distinction between a cause and its conditions, he still kept the verbal distinction between the two. Mill always referred to what I call a pragmatic cause simply as "the cause." Furthermore, the scientific methods he said were designed to help find causes were actually only methods to find pragmatic causes. I see this as one more example of his inability to completely free himself from the atomism of his empiricist heritage.

2. I originally used the term "metaphysical cause," but Colin Allen objected to this term because he claimed that this term could be taken to imply that this cause was not physical in some sense. He suggested using the term "compleat cause" with this archaic spelling, to show both that this is a technical term, and to underscore the fact that there is a certain naïveté in assuming that it is possible for us to ever fully uncover this cause. There is a lot to be said for creating your own terminology when you don't want to take on the baggage of a word's previous history.

3. But not always, of course. We say that the hurricane caused the destruction of the house, even though we had no hope of saving the house from the hurricane. But identifying a single factor as *the* cause is always the first step in controlling that cause, even if human frailty makes further steps impossible.

4. But not always. There are many biological functions in which the brain participates that have no more relation to mental activity than the biological functions performed by the liver or the gall bladder. Even if all mental activity involves the brain, there is still plenty of brain activity that does not effect the mind any more (or less) than many other processes taking place in the rest of the body, or in the environment. This seems to me to be a potentially compelling argument against mind–brain identity, but I won't pursue it any further here.

5. Mill's other two methods of experimental inquiry, the methods of residue and concomitant variation, are not different from the two described here in ways that are relevant to the points under discussion.

6. We cannot assume, however, that just because the nexus of responsibility for any given event is finite, it would therefore be possible in principle to list every single cause for a given event. Just because a region does not contain everything does not mean that its characteristics are finite. A single line contains an infinite number of points, and there is no reason that there couldn't be an infinite variety of causal interactions within a causal nexus whose boundaries are finite. There are characteristics of language, described in the chapter on background, that appear to make it impossible to create a complete description of anything.

7. See Wilson 1995, p. 131. Wilson quotes McGinn as saying that causal factors can be divided into powers and parameters. "Powers drive nature's motor, parameters are just points on nature's map."

Chapter 5

1. In chapter 10 of Kim 1993, Kim frequently illustrates supervenience by considering molecule for molecule duplicates of a complete person rather than of just a brain. It is clear, however, that he does this only because it makes it easier to understand certain of his examples. It's hard to imagine a disembodied brain signing a check, for example. In footnote 13 on page 185 he specifically says that by "physical" he means "neurophysiological."

2. Professional philosophers will no doubt be able to think of counterexamples to this claim, such as this one suggested by Colin Allen. Suppose I were going to a ballet performance, which I had reason to believe might be cancelled. I might decide that I would come home early and take my children out to MacDonald's if I get there and discover that it was cancelled. I would therefore tell the babysitter that she should start boiling the water to make spaghetti for them only if I called her from the theater and told her to do so. In that case, one could say that once I made the phone call, the ballet performance caused the water to boil. The fact is, however, that this sort of thing doesn't happen enough to be part of what constitutes our concept of boiling. My point is that things are not classified into categories totally on the basis of their intrinsic qualities, but also by those relationships that they have regularly and characteristically with other kinds of things.

3. This description is, of course, exactly backwards because we designed computers to be mechanized versions of the Cartesian materialist view of the mind. But the basic point remains the same.

4. There are, of course, many differences between the sense data of empiricism and the stimuli of behaviorism. The most important of these (to the behaviorists, at any rate) is that sense data are subjective and stimuli are objective. But that difference is not relevant here, for both sense data and stimuli are atomistic, rather than holistic. Consequently, the transition from behaviorism to cognitivism, like the transition from Hume to Kant, is one from knowledge being gathered from the outside world to knowledge being constituted by internal processes.

Chapter 6

1. Except for Jerry Fodor and Ernest Lapore, who criticize most contemporary arguments for holism in their *Holism: A Shopper's Guide*. They do point out, however, that none of their criticisms can be construed as a full-fledged defense of atomism, and that they are meant to apply only to holistic semantics, not to epistemology or philosophy of mind.

2. See especially the first chapter of *Experience and Nature* and the third chapter of *Art as Experience*.

3. The same point is made about computers in Haugeland 1985.

4. Thanks to Jim Garson and Robert Atkins respectively for these two counterexamples.

5. Colin Allen objected to the word "symbiotic," because by definition it refers to a relationship between two organisms, rather than a relationship between an organism and its environment. For that reason, I probably should use the word "synergetic," as does Hermann Haken in his many books on cognitive dynamic systems. However, "symbiotic" is a widely understood word, rather than a technical term, so I decided to be precise only in this footnote, in hopes of being better understood in the main text. Also, part of what I am questioning here is the assumption that the biological and nonbiological are ontologically independent of each other, so this distinction may not be as important in my ontology (see chapter 8).

6. And there are billions of such people, a fact that is easy to forget if one spends too much time talking to no one but philosophers. If you are a nonphilosopher reading this book, this explanation's for you! Welcome to the world of possible worlds!

7. See also Dupré 1993 or chapter 13 of Churchland 1989.

8. Putnam also says in the same paragraph, "what I have said is that it has long been our *intention* that a liquid should *count* as 'water' only if it has the same composition as the paradigm examples of water (or as the majority of them). I claim that this was our intention even before we knew the ultimate composition of water. If I am right, then, *given those referential intentions*, it was always impossible for a liquid other than H_2O to be water, even if it took empirical investigation to find it out." This refinement and/or restatement of Putnam's position makes it basically the same as mine. The only thing that stops XYZ from fulfilling the referential intentions of "water" is the fact that it doesn't exist. If there were such a thing as XYZ, it would have as much right to be called water as does H_2O, because both fulfill the referential intentions of the term as it is used in the pre-Lavoisier community. Or in my terminology, because there is no difference between XYZ and H_2O in either Oscar's or Twin Oscar's umwelt, the word "water" refers with equal justification to both of them, the way "jade" refers to both jadeite and nephrite.

9. I say "Gibsonian," rather than simply attributing this position to Gibson himself, because, as I remarked earlier, Gibson sometimes appeared to have thought that the light was solely responsible for the experience and didn't need the brain activity.

10. What I mean by this somewhat hasty statement is that an animal would probably not hear music as music. This does not mean an animal or human could ever simply hear sound as sound. Animals would hear sounds in ways that would relate to their projects: they would hear sounds as being manifestations of food, predators, etc. And they would, in many cases, be able to respond in a more sophis-

ticated way to what they heard (or especially, what they smelled) than most humans could.

11. Or it may not. During a time when I was suffering from repetitive strain injuries, I tried to imagine myself practicing my musical instrument as a way of preserving my skills. I found that even if I sat perfectly still while imagining, my arms and neck would contract in the same sort of spasms that had forced me to quite playing. Apparently in my case, at least, even imagining myself playing involved muscle activity.

12. I doubt that anyone has ever actually believed this. But I think this is the position that people have in mind when they claim that panpsychism is preposterous and unthinkable. It does somewhat resemble a position that Skrbina attributes to several well-known panpsychist philosophers: the claim that reality consists of fundamental substances (atoms, monads, entelechies, etc.), each of which has something like "spirit" lurking within it. These positions are usually motivated by the belief that it is unthinkable that consciousness is an emergent property.

Chapter 7

1. This is a paraphrase of a distinction made on page 74 of Dennett 1991.

2. Not all philosophers are guilty of this kind of inbred specialization. Tom Polger (forthcoming) uses the zombie problem in a way that makes no attempt to evaluate any scientific theory of consciousness. He uses it as a way of analyzing the concept of possibility, distinguishing amongst logical, metaphysical, and physical impossibility. This is philosophically quite useful in ways that relate to all questions of science and knowledge, and not exclusively to questions about the nature of consciousness.

3. This is not to say that animals would be incapable of having something like higher-order thoughts. Creatures must have mechanisms that enable them to pick out from the range of experience those items that were worthy of attention. I think that Rosenthal's higher-order-thought theory, and Baars's (1988) global-workspace theory are primarily ways of explaining the mechanisms of attention that enable us to focus on certain aspects of our experience and ignore others. Language probably helps us with this function, which is why we are almost certainly better at it than animals are. But the mechanisms that enable us to do this are clearly different from those that enable us to have experiences in the first place. Yet another reason why it is so easy to imagine Rosenthal's and Baars's mechanisms not producing consciousness is that these mechanisms almost certainly couldn't produce consciousness if they didn't have a range of experiences to select from. I'm sure Baars doesn't believe that the sections of the brain that perform the global workspace function would be conscious if they were surgically removed and placed in a vat. See Rockwell 1996 for a further development of this distinction.

Chapter 8

1. See also *Why You Still Cannot Talk to Your Computer* (Kronfeld 2001). Ami Kronfeld, who worked on the NLI natural language program from 1989 to 1996, says "The NLI product was the most sophisticated natural language program I have ever seen, bar none . . . in the final analysis no one could make it work" (p. 3).

2. I first saw this point made in Campbell 1982.

3. Assuming for the moment that Sally's mind is identical to her brain, even though I'm sure that the reader is now well aware that I do not accept that assumption.

Chapter 9

1. For a more thorough development of the relationship between ideas and judgments in Descartes, see Rosenthal 1990.

2. This system also enables us to conceive of possibilities that are not actual, such as purple cows, and to know that certain other things are not even possible, such as triangular cows. Some would claim that such possibilities exist only in the head. But would we really want to claim that the other possible temperatures that are not actual at any given moment exist only in the thermometer? I see this point as largely derived from the work of Ruth Millikan, but whether she would recognize it in my translation is another very empirical question.

3. I don't intend to deal in any depth with the ontological status of fictional entities here. I am only claiming that the entities posited by ontologies are not fictional entities, because they have a relationship to lived experience that fictive entities do not possess. Consequently even if fictional entities do exist in the head, this does not imply that the entities posited by bad ontologies are in the head. However, I doubt very much that Sherlock Holmes exists in someone's head. Holmes exists in books, magazines, and probably by this time in cyberspace, given the number of classic literary works that are now available on the Web. Either that, or he exists in Plato's realm of the forms, in a slightly less upscale neighborhood than that of Justice and the number 6. If someone dreams up an imaginary character, and never speaks or writes about her, perhaps that character exists only in that person's head, in the same sense that Holmes exists in books. There may be numerous counterexamples to this explanation in the philosophical literature on fictive entities, but it looks convincing to me.

Chapter 10

1. Some might say that because behaviorist explanations have always downplayed the importance of the brain, they cannot be Cartesian materialist. But this incon-

sistency is behaviorism's, not mine. Pavlov always referred to S–R connections as neurological, and Skinner would usually admit under duress that eventually neurology would provide explanations for what behaviorism was studying. (see Rockwell 1994 for more historical details.) Dewey was writing during Pavlov's time, not Skinner's, so S–R connections were thought of as being neurological when the above quoted article was written.

2. This point is also documented in considerable detail in Devlin 1997, which describes how Chomsky transformed linguistics from a descriptive discipline closely related to anthropology into a mathematical science based on the same principles of logic that govern computer programs. He also shows how the rebirth of psycholinguistics and sociolinguistics required a soft-pedaling of this logic-based approach and a return to a more descriptive approach that does not sharply separate the elements it is working with. Natural languages, unlike logical languages, do not work by stringing together individual names and predicates, each of which has a meaning independent of the others. Even an apparently simple concept like "red," has very different meanings in the phrases "red hair," "red wine," "red potatoes," "red wood," etc. (ibid., p. 197).

3. There are, of course, numerous differences between Heidegger and Dewey in their descriptions of this distinction, which would require at least a whole paper to fully explicate. Heidegger's technical language produces a network of implicit references to other concepts in *Being and Time*. Because a grasp of this technical language is essential to understanding Heidegger, it is very difficult to find a single quote that clearly shows the parallels with Dewey when taken out of context. There is also a very important difference between the state of mind produced by Deweyan inquiry, and that produced by encountering Being-present-at-hand, although it may be only a difference in emphasis. Heidegger refers to the Present-at-hand with terms that stress our helplessness in the face of the world when things are not Ready-to-hand, such as "conspicuousness, obtrusiveness, and obstinacy" (Heidegger 1926, p. 74). For Dewey, the loss of the unity of self and world is the first step in a process of inquiry that will eventually restore that unity, at least temporarily. Heidegger makes no reference in the above cited pages to any process that corresponds to inquiry's ability to restore the Readiness-to-hand of the world. I think this reflects the fact that Dewey admired science, and Heidegger was suspicious of it.

4. Dreyfus 1996 paraphrases Merleau-Ponty's use of this same soap-bubble analogy to explain how we acquire what he calls maximum grip on our world. Maximum grip is repeatedly described using terms that have been incorporated into DST. "As an account of skillful action, maximum grip means that we always tend to reduce a sense of disequilibrium. . . . Thus the 'I can' that is central to Merleau-Ponty's account of embodiment is simply the body's ability to reduce tension. . . ." Dreyfus 1996, par. 42).

5. Thanks to Barry Smiler of Bardon Data Systems for my first advice on LISP programming, and for pointing out that this program did not need to have ways of dealing with negative numbers because "The horse isn't going to run backwards." The final version of this program was written by Jason Jenkins of Stanford Research International.

References

The citations for Web pages have no page numbers, since a Web page can contain the equivalent of dozens of pages of paper text. For this reason, I advise anyone who wishes to find the original context of any quote to simply type some portion of the quote into the Web browser's "find" command, which will automatically locate the quote in context.

Baars, B. J. 1988. *A Cognitive Theory of Consciousness*. London: Cambridge University Press.

Bailey, R. H. 1975. *The Role of the Brain*. New York: Time-Life.

Barlow, H. B. 1953. "Summation and Inhibition in the Frog's Retina." *Journal of Physiology*, 119:69–88.

Bechtel, W., and A. Abrahamsen. 1991. *Connectionism and the Mind: An Introduction to Parallel Processing in Networks*. Oxford: Blackwell.

Beckermann, A., H. Flor, and J. Kim, eds. 1992. *Emergence or Reduction?* Berlin: De Gruyter.

Bekoff, M., C. Allen, and C. Burghardt. 2002. *The Cognitive Animal*. Cambridge, Mass.: The MIT Press.

Bergland, R. 1985. *The Fabric of the Mind*. New York: Viking.

Bickle, J. 1998. *Psychoneural Reduction: The New Wave*. Cambridge, Mass.: The MIT Press.

Block, N. 1978. "Troubles with Functionalism." Pp. 261–325 in *Perception and Cognition: Issues in the Foundations of Psychology*, ed. C. W. Savage. *Minnesota Studies in the Philosophy of Science*, vol. 9. Minneapolis: University of Minnesota Press.

Bohm, David. 1957. *Causality and Chance in Modern Physics*. Philadelphia: University of Pennsylvania Press.

Borst, C. V., ed. 1970. *The Mind–Brain Identity Theory*. New York: St. Martin's Press.

Brothers, Leslie. 1997. *Friday's Footprints*. Oxford: Oxford University Press.

Campbell, J. 1982. *Grammatical Man: Information, Entropy, Language, and Life*. New York: Simon and Schuster.

Cannon, W. B. 1929. *Bodily Changes in Pain, Hunger, Fear, and Rage*. New York: Appleton.

Chalmers, David. 1990. *Consciousness and Cognition*. See http://ling.ucsc.edu/~chalmers/papers/c-and-c.html.

———. 1995. "Facing Up to the Problem of Consciousness." *Journal of Consciousness Studies*, 2, no. 3:200–219.

———. 1996. *The Conscious Mind*. Oxford: Oxford University Press.

———. 1997. Moving Forward on the Problem of Consciousness. *Journal of Consciousness Studies*, 4, no. 1:3–46.

Chomsky, N. 1959. "Review of Skinner's 'Verbal Behavior.'" *Language*, 35:26–58. Reprinted in *The Structure of Language*, ed. J. Fodor and J. Katz. Englewood Cliffs, N.J.: Prentice-Hall, 1964.

Churchland, P. M. 1979. *Scientific Reason and the Plasticity of Mind*. London: Cambridge University Press.

———. 1989. *A Neurocomputational Perspective*. Cambridge, Mass.: The MIT Press.

———. 1990. "A Deeper Unity: Some Feyerabendian Themes in Neurocomputational Form." Pp. 341–480 in *Minnesota Studies in the Philosophy of Science*, vol. 5, no. 15. Minneapolis: University of Minnesota Press.

———. 1995. *The Engine of Reason, The Seat of the Soul*. Cambridge, Mass.: The MIT Press.

Churchland, P. S. 1986. *Neurophilosophy*. Cambridge, Mass.: The MIT Press.

Clark, A. 1997. *Being There: Putting Brain, Body, and World Together Again*. Cambridge, Mass.: The MIT Press.

Cottingham, J., R. Stoothoff, and D. Murdoch. 1985. *The Philosophical Works of Descartes*. New York: Cambridge University Press.

Damasio, A. 1994. *Descartes' Error*. New York: Avon Books.

Dawkins, R. 1986. *The Blind Watchmaker*. London: Longmans.

Dennett, D. 1978. *Brainstorms*. Cambridge, Mass: The MIT Press.

———. 1982. "Where Am I?" Pp. 217–230 in *The Mind's I*, ed. D. Hofstader and D. Dennett. New York: Bantam New Age.

————. 1991. *Consciousness Explained.* New York: Little, Brown.

————. 1995. The Unimagined Preposterousness of Zombies. *Journal of Consciousness Studies,* 2, no. 4:322–326.

————. 1995a. *Darwin's Dangerous Idea.* New York: Simon and Schuster.

————. 1996a. "Facing Backwards on the Problem of Consciousness." *Journal of Consciousness Studies,* 3, no. 1:4–6.

————. 1996b. *Kinds of Minds.* New York: Basic Books, Harper Collins.

————. 2003. *Freedom Evolves.* New York: Viking.

Devlin, K. 1997. *Goodbye, Descartes.* New York: John Wiley and Sons.

Descartes, R. 1641/1911. *The Philosophical Works of Descartes.* Translated by Elizabeth S. Haldane. Cambridge: Cambridge University Press. See http://www.utm. edu/research/iep/text/descart/des-med.htm.

Dewey, John. 1896. "The Reflex Arc Concept in Psychology." *Psychological Review* 3. See http://psychclassics.yorku.ca/Dewey/reflex.htm.

————. 1910/1997. *The Influence of Darwin on Philosophy and Other Essays.* Amherst, N.Y.: Prometheus Press.

————. 1916. *Democracy and Education.* New York: Macmillan.

————. 1929. *Experience and Nature.* New York: Dover.

————. 1931. "Qualitative Thought." In *Philosophy and Civilization.* New York: Minton, Balch.

————. 1934. *Art as Experience.* New York: Perigee Books.

Dowling, John. 1987. *The Retina: An Approachable Part of the Brain.* Cambridge, Mass.: Belknap Press.

Dreyfus, H. L. 1994. *What Computers Still Can't Do.* Cambridge, Mass.: The MIT Press.

————. 1996. "The Current Relevance of Merleau-Ponty's Phenomenology of Embodiment." *Electronic Journal of Analytic Philosophy.* See http://www.phil.indiana. edu/ejap/1996.spring/dreyfus.1996.spring.html.

Eddington, A. 1978. *The Nature of the Physical World.* Ann Arbor: University of Michigan Press.

Einstein, Albert. 1916. *Relativity.* New York: Three Rivers Press.

Feyerabend, P. K. 1962. "Explanation, Reduction, and Empiricism." Pp. 28–97 in *Minnesota Studies in the Philosophy of Science,* vol. 3, ed. H. Feigl and G. Maxwell. Dordrecht D. Reidel.

Fodor, J. 1975. *The Language of Thought*. Scranton, Penn.: Crowell.

———. 1981. *Representations*. Cambridge, Mass.: The MIT Press.

———. 1983. *The Modularity of Mind*. Cambridge, Mass.: The MIT Press.

———. 1985. Précis of *The Modularity of Mind*. *Behavioral and Brain Sciences*, 8:1–5.

———. 1987. *Representations*. Cambridge, Mass.: The MIT Press.

———. 1994. *The Elm and the Expert*. Cambridge, Mass.: The MIT Press.

Fodor, J., and E. Lapore. 1992. *Holism: A Shopper's Guide*. Oxford: Basil Blackwell.

Freeman, Walter. 2000. *How Brains Make Up Their Minds*. New York: Columbia University Press.

Gibson, J. J. 1955. *Perception as a Function of Stimulation*. Lecture given at Institute of Experimental Psychology, Oxford, with glosses by U. T. Place. See www.california.com/~mcmf.

Guzeldere, G. 1995. "Varieties of Zombiehood." *Journal of Consciousness Studies*, 2, no. 4:326–333.

———. 1997. "The Many Faces of Consciousness: A Field Guide." In *The Nature of Consciousness*, ed. N. Block, O. Flanagan, and G. Guzeldere. Cambridge, Mass.: The MIT Press.

Haugeland, J., ed. 1981. *Mind Design*. Cambridge, Mass.: The MIT Press.

Haugeland, J. 1985. *Artificial Intelligence: The Very Idea*. Cambridge, Mass.: The MIT Press.

———. 1995. "Mind Embodied and Embedded." In *Mind and Cognition*, ed. Y. Houng and J. Ho. Taipei: Academia Sinica.

Haugeland, J., ed. 1997. *Mind Design II*. Cambridge, Mass.: The MIT Press.

Heidegger, M. 1926. *Being and Time*. New York: Harper and Row.

Hooker, C. A. 1981. "Towards a General Theory of Reduction." *Dialogue*, 20:30–59, 201–236, 496–529.

Horgan, T., and J. Tienson. 1996. *Connectionism and the Philosophy of Psychology*. Cambridge, Mass.: The MIT Press.

Jackendoff, R. 1987. *Consciousness and the Computational Mind*. Cambridge, Mass.: Yhe MIT Press.

James, William. 1884. "What Is an Emotion?" *Mind*, 9:188–205.

———. 1890. *Principles of Psychology*. New York: Dover.

Kelso, J. A. Scott. 1995. *Dynamic Patterns*. Cambridge, Mass.: The MIT Press.

Kim, Jaegwon. 1993. *Supervenience and Mind*. Cambridge: Cambridge University Press.

———. 2000. *Mind in a Physical World*. Cambridge, Mass.: The MIT Press.

Kinsbourne, M. 1988. "Integrated Field Theory of Consciousness." In *Consciousness in Contemporary Science*, ed. A. Marcel and E. Bisiach. Oxford: Oxford University Press.

Kronfeld, A. 2001. "Why You Still Cannot Talk to Your Computer." Paper presented at the International Computer Science Institute at Berkeley. Available at http://www.ami-k.com/publications.htm.

Kuhn, T. 1962. *The Structure of Scientific Revolutions*. Chicago: University of Chicago Press.

Lakoff, G. 1987. *Women, Fire, and Dangerous Things*. Chicago: University of Chicago Press.

LeDoux, Joseph. 1996. *The Emotional Brain*. New York: Simon and Schuster.

Letvin, J. Y., H. R. Maturana, W. S. McCulloch, and W. H. Pitts. 1965. "What the Frog's Eye Tells the Frog's Brain." Pp. 230–254 in *Embodiments of Mind*, by W. S. McCulloch. Cambridge, Mass.: The MIT Press.

Lycan, W. G. 1987. *Consciousness*. Cambridge, Mass.: The MIT Press.

MacKay, W. A. 1980. "The Motor Program: Back to the Computer." *Trends in Neurosciences* (April 1980):97–100.

Melzack, R. 1992. "Phantom Limbs." *Scientific American* (April). See http://www.sciam.com/explorations/0492melzak.html#author.

———. 1993. "Pain: Past, Present, and Future." *Canadian Journal of Experimental Psychology*, 47, no. 4:615–629.

Mill, J. S. 1851. *A System of Logic, Rationcinative and Inductive*, vol. 1. London: John W. Parker.

Millikan, Ruth. 1984. *Language, Thought, and Other Biological Categories*. Cambridge, Mass.: The MIT Press.

———. 1993. *White Queen Psychology and Other Essays for Alice*. Cambridge, Mass.: The MIT Press.

———. 1998. "A Common Structure for Concepts of Individuals, Stuffs, and Real Kinds." *Behavior and Brain Sciences* (February), target article with commentary: 55–65.

———. Unpublished. "Different Ways to Think." See www.california.com/~mcmf.

Nagel, Ernst. 1961. *The Structure of Science*. New York: Harcourt Brace and World.

Newton, Natika. 1986. "Churchland on Direct Introspection of Brain States." *Analysis*, 46:97–102.

Pert, Candace. 1987. "Neuropeptides, the Emotions and BodyMind." Pp. 82–87 in *Consciousness and Survival*, ed. J. S. Spong. Sausalito, Cal.: IONS.

———. 1997. *Molecules of Emotion*. New York: Simon and Schuster.

Pert, Candace, and F. O. Schmitt. 1985. "Neuropeptides and Their Receptors: A Psychosomatic Network." *Journal of Immunology*, 135:820–826.

Place, U. T. 1970. "Is Consciousness a Brain Process?" Pp. 48–57 in *The Mind–Brain Identity Theory*, ed. C. V. Borst. New York: St. Martin's Press.

Place, U. T., and J. J. Gibson. 1999. "The Gibson–Place Correspondence." See www.california.com/~mcmf.

Polanyi, M. 1966. *The Tacit Dimension*. Garden City, N.Y.: Doubleday/Anchor.

Polger, T. W. 2001. "Zombies Explained." In *The Definitive Dennett*. Cambridge, Mass.: The MIT Press.

Port, R. F., and T. Van Gelder, eds. 1995. *Mind as Motion: Explorations in the Dynamics of Cognition*. Cambridge, Mass.: The MIT Press.

Putnam, H. L. 1960. "Minds and Machines." In *Dimensions of Mind*, ed. S. Hook. New York: New York University Press.

———. 1975. "The Meaning of 'Meaning.'" In *Minnesota Studies in the Philosophy of Science*, vol. 8, ed. Keith Gunderson. Minneapolis: University of Minnesota Press.

———. 1978. *Meaning and the Moral Sciences*. London: Routledge and Kegan Paul.

———. 1981. *Reason, Truth, and History*. Cambridge: Cambridge University Press.

———. 1987. *The Many Faces of Realism*. LaSalle, Ill.: Open Court.

———. 1988. *Representation and Reality*. Cambridge, Mass.: The MIT Press.

Rockwell, W. T. 1994a. "Beyond Determinism and Indignity: A Reinterpretation of Operant Conditioning." *Behavior and Philosophy*, 22, no. 1:53–66.

———. 1999b. "On What the Mind Is Identical With." *Philosophical Psychology*, 7, no.3:307–24.

———. 1996. "Awareness, Mental Phenomena, and Consciousness (A Synthesis of Dennett and Rosenthal)." *Journal of Consciousness Studies*, 3, no. 5:463–477.

———. 1998. "A Defense of Emergent Downward Causation" at Cognitive Questions. See www.california.com/~mcmf.

———. 1998. "The Modularity of Dynamic Systems." In *Colloquia Manilana*, vol. 6. Also available at Cognitive Questions, www.california.com/~mcmf.

———. 1999. "The Effects of Atomistic Ontology on the History of Psychology" at Cognitive Questions, www.california.com/~mcmf.

———. 2001. "Experience and Sensation: Sellars and Dewey on the Non-Cognitive Aspects of Mental Life." *Education and Culture*, 17, no. 1:9–28. Also available at Cognitive Questions, www.california.com/~mcmf.

Rorty, R. 1979. *Philosophy and the Mirror of Nature*. Princeton, N.J.: Princeton University Press.

Rosenthal, D., ed. 1971. *Materialism and the Mind–Body Problem*. Englewood Cliffs, N.J.: Prentice-Hall.

Rosenthal, D. 1986. "Two Concepts of Consciousness." *Philosophical Studies*, 49:329–359.

———. 1989. "Thinking That One Thinks." ZIF Report no.11. Research group on Mind and Brain, Perspectives in Theoretical Psychology and the Philosophy of Mind. Zentrum für Interdisziplinäre Forschung. Bielefeld, Germany.

———. 1990. "Judgment, Mind, and Will in Descartes." See http://web.gc.cuny.edu/cogsci/jmw.htm.

———. 1990a. "Why Are Verbally Expressed Thoughts Conscious?" ZIF Report no. 32. Zentrum für Interdisciplinäre Forschung. Bielefeld, Germany.

———. 1990b. "A Theory of Consciousness." ZIF Report no. 40. Zentrum für Interdisciplinäre Forschung. Bielefeld, Germany.

———. 1992. "Time and Consciousness." *Behavioral and Brain Sciences*, 15:220–21.

———. 1993. "Multiple Drafts and Facts of the Matter." Paper delivered at Meeting of the Society for Philosophy and Psychology, Vancouver, June 1993.

Rumelhart, D., and R. McClelland. 1986. *Parallel Distributed Processing: Studies in the Microstructure of Cognition*. Cambridge, Mass.: The MIT Press.

Russell, B. 1913. "On the Notion of Cause." In *Logical and Philosophical Papers, 1909–13*, vol. 6. Ed. John G. Slater and Bernd Frohmann. London New York: Routledge, 1992.

Ryle, G. 1949. *The Concept of Mind*. London: Hutchinson.

Saatkamp, H. 1995. *Rorty and Pragmatism: The Philosopher Responds to His Critics*. Nashville: Vanderbilt University Press.

Sacks, Oliver. 1970. *The Man Who Mistook His Wife for a Hat*. New York: Harper.

Schmitt, F. O. 1984. "Molecular Regulation of Brain Function: A New View." *Neuroscience*, 13:991.

Searle, John. 1990. "Consciousness, Explanatory Inversion, and Cognitive Science." *Behavior and Brain Sciences*, 13, no. 4:585–595.

————. 1992. *The Rediscovery of the Mind*. Cambridge, Mass.: The MIT Press.

————. 1995. *The Construction of Social Reality*. New York: Free Press.

————. 1997. "Consciousness and the Philosophers." *New York Review of Books*, March 6.

Sellars, Wilfrid. 1963. "Empiricism and the Philosophy of Mind." In *Science, Perception, and Reality*. London: Routledge and Kegan Paul.

————. 1975. "The Structure of Knowledge." In *Action, Knowledge, and Reality*, ed. Hector-Neri Castaneda. Indianapolis: Bobbs-Merrill.

————. 1981a. "Mental Events." *Philosophical Studies*, 39:325–345.

Skrbina, D. 2003. "Panpsychism as an Underlying Theme in Western Philosophy." *Journal of Consciousness Studies*, 10, no. 3:4–46.

Smart, J. J. C. 1970a. "Materialism." Pp. 159–170 in *The Mind–Brain Identity Theory*, ed. C. V. Brost. New York: St. Martin's Press, 1970.

————. 1970b. "Sensations and Brain Processes." Pp. 52–66 in *The Mind–Brain Identity Theory*, ed. C. V. Borst. New York: St. Martin's Press, 1970.

Stevens, Leonard. 1971. *Explorers of the Brain*. New York: Alfred Knopf.

Tanner, L. 1997. *Dewey's Laboratory School*. New York: Teacher's College Press.

Taylor, R. C. 1978. "Why Change Gaits? Recruitment of Muscles and Muscle Fibers as a Function of Speed and Gait." *American Zoologist*, 18:153–161.

Thelen, E., and L. Smith. 1994. *A Dynamic Systems Approach to the Development of Cognition and Action*. Cambridge, Mass.: The MIT Press.

Weil, Andrew. 1999. "Healing Ulcers: An Integrative Approach." *Self Healing* (May).

Wilson, R. 1995. *Cartesian Pyschology and Physical Minds*. Cambridge: Cambridge University Press.

————. 2001. "Two Views of Realization." *Philosophical Studies*, 104:1–31.

Wittgenstein, Ludwig. 1922. *Tractates Logico-Philosophicus*. London: Routledge Classics.

Index